"HOW MANY MEN HAVE YOU HERE?"
—*In a Hollow of the Hills*

"ARGONAUT EDITION" OF
THE WORKS OF BRET HARTE

BARKER'S LUCK

IN A HOLLOW OF THE HILLS

BY

BRET HARTE

ILLUSTRATED

P. F. COLLIER & SON
NEW YORK

CONTENTS

BARKER'S LUCK.

A BIRD twittered! The morning sun
shining through the open window was apparently more potent than the cool mountain air, which had only caused the sleeper
to curl a little more tightly in his blankets.
Barker's eyes opened instantly upon the
light and the bird on the window ledge.
Like all healthy young animals he would
have tried to sleep again, but with his momentary consciousness came the recollection
that it was *his* turn to cook the breakfast
that morning, and he regretfully rolled out
of his bunk to the floor. Without stopping
to dress he opened the door and stepped
outside, secure in the knowledge that he was
overlooked only by the Sierras, and plunged
his head and shoulders in the bucket of cold
water that stood by the door. Then he began to clothe himself, partly in the cabin and

partly in the open air, with a lapse between
the putting on of his trousers and coat which
he employed in bringing in wood. Raking
together the few embers on the adobe hearth,
not without a prudent regard to the rattlesnake which had once been detected in
haunting the warm ashes, he began to prepare breakfast. By this time the other
sleepers, his partners Stacy and Demorest,
young men of about his own age, were
awake, alert, and lazily critical of his progress.

" I don't care about my quail on toast
being underdone for breakfast," said Stacy,
with a yawn; "and you need n't serve with
red wine. I'm not feeling very peckish
this morning."

" And I reckon you can knock off the
fried oysters after the Spanish mackerel for
me," said Demorest gravely. " The fact is,
that last bottle of Veuve Clicquot we had
for supper was n't as dry as I am this morning."

Accustomed to these regular Barmecide
suggestions, Barker made no direct reply.
Presently, looking up from the fire, he said,
" There's no more saleratus, so you must n't
blame me if the biscuit is extra heavy. I

told you we had none when you went to the
grocery yesterday."

"And I told you we had n't a red cent to
buy any with," said Stacy, who was also
treasurer. "Put these two negatives together and you make the affirmative —
saleratus. Mix freely and bake in a hot
oven."

Nevertheless, after a toilette as primitive
as Barker's they sat down to what he had
prepared, with the keen appetite begotten
of the mountain air and the regretful fasti-
diousness born of the recollection of better
things. Jerked beef, frizzled with salt pork
in a frying-pan, boiled potatoes, biscuit,
and coffee composed the repast. The biscuits, however, proving remarkably heavy
after the first mouthful, were used as mis-
siles, thrown through the open door at an
empty bottle, which had previously served
as a mark for revolver practice, and a few
moments later pipes were lit to counteract
the effects of the meal and take the taste
out of their mouths. Suddenly they heard
the sound of horses' hoofs, saw the quick
passage of a rider in the open space before
the cabin, and felt the smart impact upon
the table of some small object thrown by

him. It was the regular morning delivery
of the county newspaper!

"He's getting to be a mighty sure shot,"
said Demorest approvingly, looking at his
upset can of coffee as he picked up the
paper, rolled into a cylindrical wad as tightly
as a cartridge, and began to straighten it
out. This was no easy matter, as the sheet
had evidently been rolled while yet damp
from the press; but Demorest eventually
opened it and ensconced himself behind it.

"Nary news?" asked Stacy.

"No. There never is any," said Demorest scornfully. "We ought to stop the
paper."

"You mean the paper man ought to. *We*
don't pay him," said Barker gently.

"Well, that's the same thing, smarty.
No news, no pay. Hallo!" he continued,
his eyes suddenly riveted on the paper.
Then, after the fashion of ordinary humanity, he stopped short and read the interesting item to himself. When he had
finished he brought his fist and the paper,
together, violently down upon the table.
"Now look at this! Talk of luck, will you?
Just think of it. Here are *we* — hard-working men with lots of *sabe*, too — grubbin'

away on this hillside like niggers, glad to
get enough at the end of the day to pay for
our soggy biscuits and horse-bean coffee,
and just look what falls into the lap of some
lazy sneakin' greenhorn who never did a
stroke of work in his life! Here are *we*,
with no foolishness, no airs nor graces, and
yet men who would do credit to twice that
amount of luck — and seem born to it, too
— and we're set aside for some long, lank,
pen-wiping scrub who just knows enough to
sit down on his office stool and hold on to a
bit of paper."

"What's up now?" asked Stacy, with
the carelessness begotten of familiarity with
his partner's extravagance.

"Listen," said Demorest, reading. "Another unprecedented rise has taken place in
the shares of the 'Yellow Hammer First
Extension Mine' since the sinking of the
new shaft. It was quoted yesterday at ten
thousand dollars a foot. When it is remembered that scarcely two years ago the original shares, issued at fifty dollars per share,
had dropped to only fifty cents a share, it
will be seen that those who were able to
hold on have got a good thing."

"What mine did you say?" asked Barker, looking up meditatively from the dishes he was already washing.

"The Yellow Hammer First Extension," returned Demorest shortly.

"I used to have some shares in that, and I think I have them still," said Barker musingly.

"Yes," said Demorest promptly; "the paper speaks of it here. 'We understand,'" he continued, reading aloud, 'that our eminent fellow citizen, George Barker, otherwise known as "Get Left Barker" and "Chucklehead," is one of these fortunate individuals.'"

"No," said Barker, with a slight flush of innocent pleasure, "it can't say that. How could it know?"

Stacy laughed, but Demorest coolly continued: "You didn't hear all. Listen! 'We say *was* one of them; but having already sold his apparently useless certificates to our popular druggist, Jones, for corn plasters, at a reduced rate, he is unable to realize.'"

"You may laugh, boys," said Barker, with simple seriousness; "but I really believe I have got 'em yet. Just wait. I'll see!" He rose and began to drag out

a well-worn valise from under his bunk.
" You see," he continued, " they were given
to me by an old chap in return " —

" For saving his life by delaying the
Stockton boat that afterwards blew up,"
returned Demorest briefly. " We know it
all ! His hair was white, and his hand
trembled slightly as he laid these shares in
yours, saying, and you never forgot the
words, ' Take 'em, young man — and ' " —

" For lending him two thousand dollars,
then," continued Barker with a simple ignoring of the interruption, as he quietly
brought out the valise.

" *Two thousand dollars !* " repeated
Stacy. " When did *you* have two thousand dollars ? "

" When I first left Sacramento — three
years ago," said Barker, unstrapping the
valise.

" How long did you have it ? " said Demorest incredulously.

" At least two days, I think," returned
Barker quietly. " Then I met that man.
He was hard up, and I lent him my pile and
took those shares. He died afterwards."

" Of course he did," said Demorest severely. " They always do. Nothing kills a

man more quickly than an action of that kind." Nevertheless the two partners regarded Barker rummaging among some loose clothes and papers with a kind of paternal toleration. "If you can't find them, bring out your government bonds," suggested Stacy. But the next moment, flushed and triumphant, Barker rose from his knees, and came towards them carrying some papers in his hands. Demorest seized them from him, opened them, spread them on the table, examined hurriedly the date, signatures, and transfers, glanced again quickly at the newspaper paragraph, looked wildly at Stacy and then at Barker, and gasped, —

"By the living hookey! it is *so!*"

"B' gosh! he *has* got 'em!" echoed Stacy.

"Twenty shares," continued Demorest breathlessly, "at ten thousand dollars a share — even if it's only a foot — is two hundred thousand dollars! Jerusalem!"

"Tell me, fair sir," said Stacy, with sparkling eyes, "hast still left in yonder casket any rare jewels, rubies, sarcenet, or links of fine gold? Peradventure a pearl or two may have been overlooked!"

"No — that's all," returned Barker simply.

"You hear him! Rothschild says 'that's all.' Prince Esterhazy says he has n't another red cent — only two hundred thousand dollars."

"What ought I to do, boys?" asked Barker, timidly glancing from one to the other. Yet he remembered with delight all that day, and for many a year afterwards, that he only saw in their faces unselfish joy and affection at that supreme moment.

"Do?" said Demorest promptly. "Stand on your head and yell! No! stop! Come here!" he seized both Barker and Stacy by the hand, and ran out into the open air. Here they danced violently with clasped hands around a small buckeye, in perfect silence, and then returned to the cabin, grave but perspiring.

"Of course," said Barker, wiping his forehead, "we 'll just get some money on these certificates and buy up that next claim which belongs to old Carter — where you know we thought we saw the indication."

"We 'll do nothing of the kind," said Demorest decidedly. "*We* ain't in it. That money is yours, old chap — every cent of it — property acquired before marriage, you know; and the only thing we 'll do is to be d—d before we'll see you drop a dime of it into this God-forsaken hole. No!"

"But we're partners," gasped Barker.

"Not in *this!* The utmost we can do for you, opulent sir, — though it ill becomes us horny-handed sons of toil to rub shoulders with Dives, — is perchance to dine with you, to take a pasty and a glass of Malvoisie, at some restaurant in Sacramento — when you've got things fixed, in honor of your return to affluence. But more would ill become us!"

"But what are *you* going to do?" said Barker, with a half-hysteric, half-frightened smile.

"We have not yet looked through our luggage," said Demorest with invincible gravity, "and there's a secret recess — a double *fond* — to my portmanteau, known only to a trusty page, which has not been disturbed since I left my ancestral home in Faginia. There may be a few First Debentures of Erie or what not still there."

"I felt some strange, disk-like protuberances in my dress suit the other day, but belike they are but poker chips," said Stacy thoughtfully.

An uneasy feeling crept over Barker.

The color which had left his fresh cheek
returned to it quickly, and he turned his
eyes away. Yet he had seen nothing in his
companions' eyes but affection — with even
a certain kind of tender commiseration that
deepened his uneasiness. " I suppose," he
said desperately, after a pause, " I ought to
go over to Boomville and make some inquiries."

" At the bank, old chap; at the bank ! "
said Demorest emphatically. " Take my
advice and don't go *anywhere else*. Don't
breathe a word of your luck to anybody.
And don't, whatever you do, be tempted to
sell just now; you don't know how high that
stock 's going to jump yet."

" I thought," stammered Barker, " that
you boys might like to go over with me."

" We can't afford to take another holi-
day on grub wages, and we 're only two to
work to-day," said Demorest, with a slight
increase of color and the faintest tremor in
his voice. " And it won't do, old chap, for
us to be seen bumming round with you on
the heels of your good fortune. For everybody knows we 're poor, and sooner or later
everybody 'll know you *were* rich even when
you first came to us."

"Nonsense!" said Barker indignantly.

"Gospel, my boy!" said Demorest shortly.

"The frozen truth, old man!" said Stacy.

Barker took up his hat with some stiffness and moved towards the door. Here he stopped irresolutely, an irresolution that seemed to communicate itself to his partners. There was a moment's awkward silence. Then Demorest suddenly seized him by the shoulders with a grip that was half a caress, and walked him rapidly to the door. "And now don't stand foolin' with us, Barker boy; but just trot off like a little man, and get your grip on that fortune; and when you've got your hooks in it hang on like grim death. You'll" — he hesitated for an instant only, possibly to find the laugh that should have accompanied his speech — "you're sure to find *us* here when you get back."

Hurt to the quick, but restraining his feelings, Barker clapped his hat on his head and walked quickly away. The two partners stood watching him in silence until his figure was lost in the underbrush. Then they spoke.

"Like him — was n't it?" said Demorest.

"Just him all over," said Stacy.

" Think of him having that stock stowed away all these years and never even bothering his dear old head about it ! "

" And think of his wanting to put the whole thing into this rotten hillside with us ! "

" And he 'd have done it, by gosh ! and never thought of it again. That 's Barker."

" Dear old man ! "

" Good old chap ! "

" I 've been wondering if one of us ought n't to have gone with him ? He 's just as likely to pour his money into the first lap that opens for it," said Stacy.

" The more reason why we should n't prevent him, or seem to prevent him," said Demorest almost fiercely. " There will be knaves and fools enough who will try and put the idea of our using him into his simple heart without that. No ! Let him do as he likes with it — but let him be himself. I 'd rather have him come back to us even after he 's lost the money — his old self and empty-handed — than try to change the stuff God put into him and make him more like others."

The tone and manner were so different from Demorest's usual levity that Stacy was silent. After a pause he said : " Well! we shall miss him on the hillside — won't we ? "

Demorest did not reply. Reaching out his hand abstractedly, he wrenched off a small slip from a sapling near him, and began slowly to pull the leaves off, one by one, until they were all gone. Then he switched it in the air, struck his bootleg smartly with it, said roughly : " Come, let's get to work ! " and strode away.

Meantime Barker on his way to Boomville was no less singular in his manner. He kept up his slightly affected attitude until he had lost sight of the cabin. But, being of a simple nature, his emotions were less complex. If he had not seen the undoubted look of affection in the eyes of his partners he would have imagined that they were jealous of his good fortune. Yet why had they refused his offer to share it with him? Why had they so strangely assumed that their partnership with him had closed? Why had they declined to go with him? Why had this money — of which he had thought so little, and for which he had cared so little — changed them towards him ? It had not changed *him* — *he* was the same! He remembered how they had often talked

and laughed over a prospective " strike " in
mining and speculated what *they* would do
together with the money! And now that
" luck " had occurred to one of them, indi-
vidually, the effect was only to alienate
them! He could not make it out. He was
hurt, wounded — yet oddly enough he was
conscious now of a certain power within
him to hurt and wound in retribution. He
was rich: he would let them see *he* could
do without them. He was quite free now
to think only of himself and Kitty.

For it must be recorded that, with all
this young gentleman's simplicity and unselfishness, with all his loyal attitude to his
partners, his *first* thought at the moment
he grasped the fact of his wealth was of
a young lady. It was Kitty Carter, the
daughter of the hotel keeper at Boomville,
who owned the claim that the partners had
mutually coveted. That a pretty girl's face
should flash upon him with his conviction
that he was now a rich man meant perhaps
no disloyalty to his partners, whom he would
still have helped. But it occurred to him
now, in his half hurt, half vengeful state,
that they had often joked him about Kitty,
and perhaps further confidence with them

was debarred. And it was only due to his dignity that he should now see Kitty at once.

This was easy enough, for, in the naïve simplicity of Boomville, and the economic arrangements of her father, she occasionally waited upon the hotel table. Half the town was always actively in love with her; the other half *had been*, and was silent, cynical, but hopeless in defeat. For Kitty was one of those singularly pretty girls occasionally met with in Southwestern frontier civilization whose distinct and original refinement of face and figure were so remarkable and original as to cast a doubt on the sagacity and prescience of one parent and the morality of the other, yet no doubt with equal injustice. But the fact remained that she was slight, graceful, and self-contained, and moved beside her stumpy, commonplace father, and her faded, commonplace mother, in the dining-room of the Boomville Hotel like some distinguished alien. The three partners, by virtue, perhaps, of their college education and refined manners, had been exceptionally noticed by Kitty. And for some occult reason — the more serious, perhaps, because it had no obvious or logical presumption to the world generally — Barker was particularly favored.

He quickened his pace, and as the flagstaff of the Boomville Hotel rose before him in the little hollow, he seriously debated whether he had not better go to the bank first, deposit his shares, and get a small advance on them to buy a new necktie or a "boiled shirt" in which to present himself to Miss Kitty; but, remembering that he had partly given his word to Demorest that he would keep his shares intact for the present, he abandoned this project, probably from the fact that his projected confidence with Kitty was already a violation of Demorest's injunctions of secrecy, and his conscience was sufficiently burdened with that breach of faith.

But when he reached the hotel, a strange trepidation overcame him. The dining-room was at its slack water, between the ebb of breakfast and before the flow of the preparation for the midday meal. He could not have his interview with Kitty in that dreary waste of reversed chairs and bare trestle-like tables, and she was possibly engaged in her household duties. But Miss Kitty had already seen him cross the road, and had

lounged into the dining-room with an art-
fully simulated air of casually examining
it. At the unexpected vision of his hopes,
arrayed in the sweetest and freshest of rose-
bud sprigged print, his heart faltered. Then,
partly with the desperation of a timid man,
and partly through the working of a half-
formed resolution, he met her bright smile
with a simple inquiry for her father. Miss
Kitty bit her pretty lip, smiled slightly, and
preceded him with great formality to the
office. Opening the door, without raising
her lashes to either her father or the visitor,
she said, with a mischievous accenting of
the professional manner, " Mr. Barker to
see you on business," and tripped sweetly
away.

And this slight incident precipitated the
crisis. For Barker instantly made up his
mind that he must purchase the next claim
for his partners of this man Carter, and that
he would be obliged to confide to him the
details of his good fortune, and, as a proof
of his sincerity and his ability to pay for it,
he did so bluntly. Carter was a shrewd
business man, and the well-known simplicity
of Barker was a proof of his truthfulness, to
say nothing of the shares that were shown

to him. His selling price for his claim had been two hundred dollars, but here was a rich customer who, from a mere foolish sentiment, would be no doubt willing to pay more. He hesitated with a bland but superior smile. "Ah, that was my price at my last offer, Mr. Barker," he said suavely; "but, you see, things are going up since then."

The keenest duplicity is apt to fail before absolute simplicity. Barker, thoroughly believing him, and already a little frightened at his own presumption — not for the amount of the money involved, but from the possibility of his partners refusing his gift utterly — quickly took advantage of this *locus penitentiæ.* "No matter, then," he said hurriedly; "perhaps I had better consult my partners first; in fact," he added, with a gratuitous truthfulness all his own, "I hardly know whether they will take it of me, so I think I'll wait."

Carter was staggered; this would clearly not do! He recovered himself with an insinuating smile. "You pulled me up too short, Mr. Barker; I'm a business man, but hang it all! what's that among friends? If you reckoned I *gave my word* at two

hundred — why, I 'm there! Say no more
about it — the claim 's yours. I 'll make
you out a bill of sale at once."

"But," hesitated Barker, "you see I
have n't got the money yet, and " —

"Money!" echoed Carter bluntly, "what 's
that among friends? Gimme your note at
thirty days — that 's good enough for *me*.
An' we 'll settle the whole thing now, —
nothing like finishing a job while you' re
about it." And before the bewildered and
doubtful visitor could protest, he had filled
up a promissory note for Barker's signature
and himself signed a bill of sale for the
property. "And I reckon, Mr. Barker,
you 'd like to take your partners by surprise about this little gift of yours," he
added smilingly. "Well, my messenger
is starting for the Gulch in five minutes;
he 's going by your cabin, and he can just
drop this bill o' sale, as a kind o' settled
fact, on 'em afore they can say anything,
see! There 's nothing like actin' on the
spot in these sort of things. And don't
you hurry 'bout them either! You see,
you sorter owe us a friendly call — havin'
always dropped inter the hotel only as a
customer — so ye 'll stop here over luncheon,

and I reckon, as the old woman is busy, why Kitty will try to make the time pass till then by playin' for you on her new pianner."

Delighted, yet bewildered by the unexpected invitation and opportunity, Barker mechanically signed the promissory note, and as mechanically addressed the envelope of the bill of sale to Demorest, which Carter gave to the messenger. Then he followed his host across the hall to the apartment known as " Miss Kitty's parlor." He had often heard of it as a sanctum impervious to the ordinary guest. Whatever functions the young girl assumed at the hotel and among her father's boarders, it was vaguely understood that she dropped them on crossing that sacred threshold, and became " *Miss* Carter." The county judge had been entertained there, and the wife of the bank manager. Barker's admission there was consequently an unprecedented honor.

He cast his eyes timidly round the room, redolent and suggestive in various charming little ways of the young girl's presence. There was the cottage piano which had been brought up in sections on the backs of mules from the foot of the mountain ; there was a

crayon head of Minerva done by the fair
occupant at the age of twelve; there was a
profile of herself done by a traveling artist;
there were pretty little china ornaments and
many flowers, notably a faded but still
scented woodland shrub which Barker had
presented to her two weeks ago, and over
which Miss Kitty had discreetly thrown her
white handkerchief as he entered. A wave
of hope passed over him at the act, but it
was quickly spent as Mr. Carter's roughly
playful voice introduced him : —

"Ye kin give Mr. Barker a tune or two to
pass time afore lunch, Kitty. You kin let
him see what you're doing in that line.
But you'll have to sit up now, for this young
man's come inter some property, and will be
sasheying round in 'Frisco afore long with
a biled shirt and a stove-pipe, and be givin'
the go-by to Boomville. Well! you young
folks will excuse me for a while, as I reckon
I'll just toddle over and get the recorder to
put that bill o' sale on record. Nothin' like
squaring things to onct, Mr. Barker."

As he slipped away, Barker felt his heart
sink. Carter had not only bluntly forestalled
him with the news, and taken away his excuse for a confidential interview, but had

put an ostentatious construction on his visit. What could she think of him now? He stood ashamed and embarrassed before her.

But Miss Kitty, far from noticing his embarrassment in a sudden concern regarding the "horrid" untidiness of the room, which made her cheeks quite pink in one spot, and obliged her to take up and set down in exactly the same place several articles, was exceedingly delighted. In fact, she did not remember ever having been so pleased before in her life! These things were always so unexpected! Just like the weather, for instance. It was quite cool last night — and now it was just stifling. And so dusty! Had Mr. Barker noticed the heat coming from the Gulch? Or perhaps, being a rich man, he — with a dazzling smile — was above walking now. It was so kind of him to come here first and tell her father.

"I really wanted to tell only — *you*, Miss Carter," stammered Barker. "You see" — he hesitated. But Miss Kitty saw perfectly. He wanted to tell *her*, and, seeing her, he asked for *her father!* Not that it made the slightest difference to her, for her father would have been sure to have told her. It was also kind of her father to invite him to luncheon. Otherwise she might not have seen him before he left Boomville.

But this was more than Barker could stand. With the same desperate directness and simplicity with which he had approached her father, he now blurted out his whole heart to her. He told her how he had loved her hopelessly from the first time that they had spoken together at the church picnic. Did she remember it? How he had sat and worshiped her, and nothing else, at church! How her voice in the church choir had sounded like an angel's; how his poverty and his uncertain future had kept him from seeing her often, lest he should be tempted to betray his hopeless passion. How as soon as he realized that he had a position, that his love for her need not make her ridiculous to the world's eyes, he came to tell her *all.* He did not even dare to hope! But she would *hear* him at least, would she not?

Indeed, there was no getting away from his boyish, simple, outspoken declaration. In vain Kitty smiled, frowned, glanced at her pink cheeks in the glass, and stopped to look out of the window. The room was filled with his love — it was encompassing her — and, despite his shy attitude, seemed to be almost embracing her. But she managed at last to turn upon him a face that was now as white and grave as his own was eager and glowing.

" Sit down," she said gently.

He did so obediently, but wonderingly. She then opened the piano and took a seat upon the music stool before it, placed some loose sheets of music in the rack, and ran her fingers lightly over the keys. Thus intrenched, she let her hands fall idly in her lap, and for the first time raised her eyes to his.

" Now listen to me — be good and don't interrupt! There! — not so near ; you can hear what I have to say well enough where you are. That will do."

Barker had halted with the chair he was dragging towards her and sat down.

"Now," said Miss Kitty, withdrawing her eyes and looking straight before her, " I believe everything you say; perhaps I ought n't to — or at least *say* it — but I do. There! But because I do believe you — it seems to me all wrong! For the very reasons that you give for not having spoken to me *before*, if you really felt as you say you did, are the same reasons why you should not speak to me now. You see, all this time you have let nobody but yourself know how you felt towards me. In everybody's eyes *you* and your partners have been only the three stuck-up, exclusive, college-bred men who mined a poor claim in the Gulch, and occasionally came here to this hotel as customers. In everybody's eyes *I* have been only the rich hotel keeper's popular daughter, who sometimes waited upon you — but nothing more. But at least we were then pretty much alike, and as good as each other. And now, as soon as you have become suddenly rich, and, of course, the *superior*, you rush down here to ask me to acknowledge it by accepting you!"

"You know I never meant that, Miss Kitty," burst out Barker vehemently, but his protest was drowned in a rapid *roulade* from the young lady's fingers on the keys. He sank back in his chair.

"Of course you never *meant* it," she said with an odd laugh; but everybody will take it in that way, and you cannot go round to everybody in Boomville and make the pretty declaration you have just made to me. Everybody will say I accepted you for your

money; everybody will say it was a put-up
job of my father's. Everybody will say
that you threw yourself away on me. And
I don't know but that they would be right.
Sit down, please! or I shall play again."

"You see," she went on, without looking
at him; "just now you like to remember
that you fell in love with me first as a pretty
waiter girl, but if I became your wife it's
just what you would like to *forget*. And *I*
should n't, for I should always like to think
of the time when you came here, whenever
you could afford it, and sometimes when
you could n't, just to see me; and how we
used to make excuses to speak with each
other over the dishes. You don't know what
these things mean to a woman who" — she
hesitated a moment, and then added ab-
ruptly, "but what does that matter? You
would not care to be reminded of it. So,"
she said, rising up with a grave smile and
grasping her hands tightly behind her, "it's
a good deal better that you should begin to
forget it now. Be a good boy and take my
advice. Go to San Francisco. You will
meet some girl there in a way you will not
afterwards regret. You are young, and
your riches, to say nothing," she added in a

faltering voice that was somewhat inconsistent with the mischievous smile that played upon her lips, " of your kind and simple heart, will secure that which the world would call unselfish affection from one more equal to you, but would always believe was only *bought* if it came from me."

" I suppose you are right," he said simply.

She glanced quickly at him, and her eyebrows straightened. He had risen, his face white and his gray eyes widely opened. " I suppose you are right," he went on, " because you are saying to me what my partners said to me this morning, when I offered to share my wealth with them, God knows as honestly as I offered to share my heart with you. I suppose that you are both right ; that there must be some curse of pride or selfishness upon the money that I have got ; but *I* have not felt it yet, and the fault does not lie with me."

She gave her shoulders a slight shrug, and turned impatiently towards the window. When she turned back again he was gone. The room around her was empty ; this room, which a moment before had seemed to be pulsating with his boyish passion, was now empty, and empty of *him*. She bit her lips,

rose, and ran eagerly to the window. She
saw his straw hat and brown curls as he
crossed the road. She drew her handkerchief sharply away from the withered shrub
over which she had thrown it, and cast the
once treasured remains in the hearth. Then,
possibly because she had it ready in her
hand, she clapped the handkerchief to her
eyes, and, sinking sideways upon the chair
he had risen from, put her elbows on its
back, and buried her face in her hands.

It is the characteristic and perhaps cruelty
of a simple nature to make no allowance
for complex motives, or to even understand
them! So it seemed to Barker that his
simplicity had been met with equal directness. It was the possession of this wealth
that had in some way hopelessly changed
his relations with the world. He did not
love Kitty any the less; he did not even
think she had wronged him; they, his partners and his sweetheart, were cleverer than
he; there must be some occult quality in
this wealth that he would understand when
he possessed it, and perhaps it might even
make him ashamed of his generosity; not
in the way they had said, but in his tempt-
ing them so audaciously to assume a wrong

position.   It behoved him to take possession
of it at once, and to take also upon himself
alone the knowledge, the trials, and responsibilities it would incur.   His cheeks flushed
again as he thought he had tried to tempt
an innocent girl with it, and he was keenly
hurt that he had not seen in Kitty's eyes
the tenderness that had softened his partners' refusal.   He resolved to wait no longer,
but sell his dreadful stock at once.   He
walked directly to the bank.

The manager, a shrewd but kindly man,
to whom Barker was known already, received him graciously in recognition of his
well-known simple honesty, and respectfully
as a representative of the equally well-known
poor but "superior" partnership of the
Gulch.   He listened with marked attention
to Barker's hesitating but brief story, only
remarking at its close: —

"You mean, of course, the '*Second* Extension' when you say 'First'?"

"No," said Barker; "I mean the 'First'
— and it said First in the Bloomville paper."

"Yes, yes! — I saw it — it was a printer's
error.   The stock of the 'First' was called
in two years ago.   No!   You mean the

'Second,' for, of course, you 've followed the quotations, and are likely to know what stock you 're holding shares of. When you go back, take a look at them, and you 'll see I am right."

" But I brought them with me," said Barker, with a slight flushing as he felt in his pocket, "and I am quite sure they are the 'First.'" He brought them out and laid them on the desk before the manager.

The words "First Extension" were plainly visible. The manager glanced curiously at Barker, and his brow darkened.

" Did anybody put this up on you ? " he said sternly. " Did your partners send you here with this stuff ? "

"No ! no ! " said Barker eagerly. " No one ! It 's all *my* mistake. I see it now. I trusted to the newspaper."

" And you mean to say you never examined the stock or the quotations, nor followed it in any way, since you had it ? "

"Never ! " said Barker. " Never thought about *it at all* till I saw the newspaper. So it 's not worth anything ? " And, to the infinite surprise of the manager, there was a slight smile on his boyish face.

" I am afraid it is not worth the paper it 's written on," said the manager gently.

The smile on Barker's face increased to a
little laugh, in which his wondering companion could not help joining. "Thank you,"
said Barker suddenly, and rushed away.

"He beats everything!" said the manager,
gazing after him. "D—d if he did n't seem
even *pleased.*"

He *was* pleased. The burden of wealth
had fallen from his shoulders; the dreadful
incubus that had weighed him down and
parted his friends from him was gone! And
he had not got rid of it by spending it fool-
ishly. It had not ruined anybody yet; it
had not altered anybody in *his* eyes. It
was gone: and he was a free and happy
man once more. He would go directly back
to his partners; they would laugh at him,
of course, but they could not look at him
now with the same sad, commiserating eyes.
Perhaps even Kitty — but here a sudden
chill struck him. He had forgotten the bill
of sale! He had forgotten the dreadful
promissory note given to her father in the
rash presumption of his wealth! How could
it ever be paid? And more than that, it
had been given in a fraud. He had no
money when he gave it, and no prospect of
any but what he was to get from those

worthless shares. Would anybody believe him that it was only a stupid blunder of his own? Yes, his partners might believe him; but, horrible thought, he had already implicated *them* in his fraud! Even now, while he was standing there hesitatingly in the road, they were entering upon the new claim he had *not paid for — could not pay for —* and in the guise of a benefactor he was dishonoring them. Yet it was Carter he must meet first; he must confess all to him. He must go back to the hotel — that hotel where he had indignantly left her, and tell the father he was a fraud. It was terrible to think of; perhaps it was part of that money curse that he could not get rid of, and was now realizing; but it *must* be done. He was simple, but his very simplicity had that unhesitating directness of conclusion which is the main factor of what men call " pluck."

He turned back to the hotel and entered the office. But Mr. Carter had not yet returned. What was to be done? He could not wait there; there was no time to be lost; there was only one other person who knew his expectations, and to whom he could confide his failure — it was Kitty. It was to

taste the dregs of his humiliation, but it
must be done. He ran up the staircase and
knocked timidly at the sitting-room door.
There was a momentary pause, and a weak
voice said " Come in." Barker opened the
door; saw the vision of a handkerchief
thrown away, of a pair of tearful eyes that
suddenly changed to stony indifference, and
a graceful but stiffening figure. But he was
past all insult now.

" I would not intrude," he said simply,
" but I came only to see your father. I have
made an awful blunder — more than a blunder, I think — a *fraud*. Believing that I
was rich, I purchased your father's claim for
my partners, and gave him my promissory
note. I came here to give him back his
claim — for that note can *never* be paid ! I
have just been to the bank ; I find I have
made a stupid mistake in the name of the
shares upon which I based my belief in my
wealth. The ones I own are worthless — I
am as poor as ever — I am even poorer, for
I owe your father money I can never pay ! "

To his amazement he saw a look of pain
and scorn come into her troubled eyes which
he had never seen before. " This is a feeble
trick," she said bitterly ; " it is unlike you
— it is unworthy of you ! "

" Good God ! You must believe me. Listen ! It was all a mistake — a printer's error. I read in the paper that the stock for the First Extension mine had gone up, when it should have been the Second. I had some old stock of the First, which I had kept for years, and only thought of when I read the announcement in the paper this morning. I swear to you " —

But it was unnecessary. There was no doubting the truth of that voice — that manner. The scorn fled from Miss Kitty's eyes to give place to a stare, and then suddenly changed to two bubbling blue wells of laughter. She went to the window and laughed. She sat down to the piano and laughed. She caught up the handkerchief, and hiding half her rosy face in it, laughed. She finally collapsed into an easy-chair, and, burying her brown head in its cushions, laughed long and confidentially until she brought up suddenly against a sob. And then was still.

Barker was dreadfully alarmed. He had heard of hysterics before. He felt he ought to do something. He moved towards her timidly, and gently drew away her handkerchief. Alas ! the blue wells were running over now. He took her cold hands in his ;

he knelt beside her and passed his arm around her waist. He drew her head upon his shoulders. He was not sure that any of these things were effective until she suddenly lifted her eyes to his with the last ray of mirth in them vanishing in a big tear-drop, put her arms round his neck, and sobbed:

"Oh, George! You blessed innocent!"

An eloquent silence was broken by a remorseful start from Barker.

"But I must go and warn my poor partners, dearest; there yet may be time; perhaps they have not yet taken possession of your father's claim."

"Yes, George dear," said the young girl, with sparkling eyes; "and tell them to do so *at once!*"

"What?" gasped Barker.

"At once — do you hear? — or it may be too late! Go quick."

"But your father — Oh, I see, dearest, you will tell him all yourself, and spare me."

"I shall do nothing so foolish, Georgey. Nor shall you! Don't you see the note is n't due for a month. Stop! Have you told anybody but Paw and me?"

"Only the bank manager."

She ran out of the room and returned in a minute tying the most enchanting of hats by a ribbon under her oval chin. " I 'll run over and fix him," she said.

" Fix him ? " returned Barker, aghast.

" Yes, I 'll say your wicked partners have been playing a practical joke on you, and he must n't give you away. He 'll do anything for me."

" But my partners did n't ! On the contrary " —

" Don't tell me, George," said Miss Kitty severely. " *They* ought never to have let you come here with that stuff. But come ! You must go at once. You must not meet Paw ; you 'll blurt out everything to him ; I know you ! I 'll tell him you could not stay to luncheon. Quick, now ; go. What? Well — there ! "

Whatever it represented, the exclamation was apparently so protracted that Miss Kitty was obliged to push her lover to the front landing before she could disappear by the back stairs. But, once in the street, Barker no longer lingered. It was a good three miles back to the Gulch ; he might still reach it by the time his partners were taking their noonday rest, and he resolved that, although the messenger had preceded him, they would not enter upon the new claim until the afternoon. For Barker, in spite of his mistress's injunction, had no idea of taking what he could n't pay for; he would keep the claim intact until something could be settled. For the rest; he walked on air! Kitty loved him! The accursed wealth no longer stood between them. They were both poor now — everything was possible.

The sun was beginning to send dwarf shadows towards the east when he reached the Gulch. Here a new trepidation seized him. How would his partners receive the news of his utter failure? *He* was happy, for he had gained Kitty through it. But they? For a moment it seemed to him that he had purchased his happiness through their loss. He stopped, took off his hat, and ran his fingers remorsefully through his damp curls.

Another thing troubled him. He had reached the crest of the Gulch, where their old working ground was spread before him like a map. They were not there; neither were they lying under the four pines on the ridge where they were wont to rest at mid-day. He turned with some alarm to the

new claim adjoining theirs, but there was no
sign of them there either. A sudden fear
that they had, after parting from him, given
up the claim in a fit of disgust and depression, and departed, now overcame him. He
clapped his hand on his head and ran in the
direction of the cabin.

He had nearly reached it when the rough
challenge of "Who's there?" from the
bushes halted him, and Demorest suddenly
swung into the trail. But the singular look
of sternness and impatience which he was
wearing vanished as he saw Barker, and
with a loud shout of "All right, it's only
Barker! Hooray!" he ran towards him.
In an instant he was joined by Stacy from
the cabin, and the two men, catching hold
of their returning partner, waltzed him joyfully and breathlessly into the cabin. But
the quick-eyed Demorest suddenly let go his
hold and stared at Barker's face. "Why,
Barker, old boy, what's up?"

"Everything's up," gasped the breathless
Barker. "It's all up about these stocks.
It's all a mistake; all an infernal lie of that
newspaper. I never had the right kind
of shares. The ones I have are worthless
rags;" and the next instant he had blurted

out his whole interview with the bank manager.

The two partners looked at each other,
and then, to Barker's infinite perplexity,
the same extraordinary convulsion that had
seized Miss Kitty fell upon them. They
laughed, holding on each other's shoulders ;
they laughed, clinging to Barker's struggling figure ; they went out and laughed
with their backs against a tree. They
laughed separately and in different corners.
And then they came up to Barker with tears
in their eyes, dropped their heads on his
shoulder, and murmured exhaustedly : —

"You blessed ass ! "

"But," said Stacy suddenly, "how did you
manage to buy the claim ? "

"Ah! that's the most awful thing, boys.
I 've *never paid for it*," groaned Barker.

"But Carter sent us the bill of sale,"
persisted Demorest, "or we should n't have
taken it."

"I gave my promissory note at thirty
days," said Barker desperately, "and
where 's the money to come from now?
But," he added wildly, as the men glanced
at each other — "you said 'taken it.' Good
heavens! you don't mean to say that I 'm

too late — that you 've — you 've touched it ? "

" I reckon that 's pretty much what we *have* been doing," drawled Demorest.

" It looks uncommonly like it," drawled Stacy.

Barker glanced blankly from the one to the other. " Shall we pass our young friend in to see the show ? " said Demorest to Stacy.

" Yes, if he 'll be perfectly quiet and not breathe on the glasses," returned Stacy.

They each gravely took one of Barker's hands and led him to the corner of the cabin. There, on an old flour barrel, stood a large tin prospecting pan, in which the partners also occasionally used to knead their bread. A dirty towel covered it. Demorest whisked it dexterously aside, and disclosed three large fragments of decomposed gold and quartz. Barker started back.

" Heft it ! " said Demorest grimly.

Barker could scarcely lift the pan !

" Four thousand dollars' weight if a penny ! " said Stacy, in short staccato sentences. " In a pocket ! Brought it out the second stroke of the pick ! We 'd been aw-

fully blue after you left. Awfully blue, too,
when that bill of sale came, for we thought
you'd been wasting your money on *us*.
Reckoned we ought n't to take it, but send
it straight back to you. Messenger gone!
Then Demorest reckoned as it was done it
could n't be undone, and we ought to make
just one ' prospect' on the claim, and strike
a single stroke for you. And there it is.
And there's more on the hillside."

"But it is n't *mine!* It is n't *yours!*
It's Carter's. I never had the money to
pay for it — and I have n't got it now."

"But you gave the note — and it is not
due for thirty days."

A recollection flashed upon Barker.
"Yes," he said with thoughtful simplicity,
"that's what Kitty said."

"Oh, Kitty said so," said both partners,
gravely.

"Yes," stammered Barker, turning away
with a heightened color, " and, as I did n't
stay there to luncheon, I think I 'd better
be getting it ready." He picked up the
coffee-pot and turned to the hearth as his
two partners stepped beyond the door.

"Was n't it exactly like him?" said Demorest.

" Him all over," said Stacy.

" And his worry over that note ? " said Demorest.

" And ' what Kitty said,' " said Stacy.

" Look here! I reckon that wasn't *all* that Kitty said."

" Of course not."

" What luck!"

A YELLOW DOG.

I NEVER knew why in the Western States of America a yellow dog should be proverbially considered the acme of canine degradation and incompetency, nor why the possession of one should seriously affect the social standing of its possessor. But the fact being established, I think we accepted it at Rattlers Ridge without question. The matter of ownership was more difficult to settle; and although the dog I have in my mind at the present writing attached himself impartially and equally to every one in camp, no one ventured to exclusively claim him; while, after the perpetration of any canine atrocity, everybody repudiated him with indecent haste.

"Well, I can swear he hasn't been near our shanty for weeks," or the retort, "He was last seen comin' out of *your* cabin," expressed the eagerness with which Rattlers Ridge washed its hands of any responsibility. Yet he was by no means a common dog, nor even an unhandsome dog ; and it was a singular fact that his severest critics vied with each other in narrating instances of his sagacity, insight, and agility which they themselves had witnessed.

He had been seen crossing the " flume " that spanned Grizzly Cañon, at a height of nine hundred feet, on a plank six inches wide. He had tumbled down the " shoot " to the South Fork, a thousand feet below, and was found sitting on the river bank " without a scratch, 'cept that he was lazily givin' himself with his off hind paw." He had been forgotten in a snowdrift on a Sierran shelf, and had come home in the early spring with the conceited complacency of an Alpine traveler and a plumpness alleged to have been the result of an exclusive diet of buried mail bags and their contents. He was generally believed to read the advance election posters, and disappear a day or two before the candidates and the brass band — which he hated — came to the Ridge. He was suspected of having overlooked Colonel Johnson's hand at poker, and of having conveyed to the Colonel's adversary, by a succession of barks, the danger of betting against four kings.

While these statements were supplied by wholly unsupported witnesses, it was a very human weakness of Rattlers Ridge that the responsibility of corroboration was passed to *the dog* himself, and *he* was looked upon as a consummate liar.

" Snoopin' round yere, and *callin'* yourself a poker sharp, are ye! Scoot, you yaller pizin!" was a common adjuration whenever the unfortunate animal intruded upon a card party. "Ef thar was a spark, an *atom* of truth in *that dog*, I'd believe my own eyes that I saw him sittin' up and trying to magnetize a jay bird off a tree. But wot are ye goin' to do with a yaller equivocator like that?"

I have said that he was yellow — or, to use the ordinary expression, "yaller." Indeed, I am inclined to believe that much of the ignominy attached to the epithet lay in this favorite pronunciation. Men who habitually spoke of a " *yellow* bird," a " *yellow* hammer," a " *yellow* leaf," always alluded to him as a " *yaller* dog."

He certainly *was* yellow. After a bath — usually compulsory — he presented a decided gamboge streak down his back, from the top of his forehead to the stump of his tail, fading in his sides and flank to a delicate straw color. His breast, legs, and feet — when not reddened by " slumgullion," in which he was fond of wading — were white. A few attempts at ornamental decoration from the India-ink pot of the storekeeper failed, partly through the yellow's dog's excessive agility, which would never give the paint time to dry on him, and partly through his success in transferring his markings to the trousers and blankets of the camp.

The size and shape of his tail — which had been cut off before his introduction to Rattlers Ridge — were favorite sources of speculation to the miners, both as determining his breed and his moral responsibility in coming into camp in that defective condition. There was a general opinion that he could n't have looked worse with a tail, and its removal was therefore a gratuitous effrontery.

His best feature was his eyes, which were a lustrous Vandyke brown, and sparkling with intelligence ; but here again he suffered from evolution through environment, and their original trustful openness was marred by the experience of watching for flying stones, sods, and passing kicks from the rear, so that the pupils were continually reverting to the outer angle of the eyelid.

Nevertheless, none of these characteristics decided the vexed question of his *breed.* His speed and scent pointed to a "hound," and it is related that on one occasion he was laid on the trail of a wildcat with such success that he followed it apparently out of the State, returning at the end of two weeks, footsore, but blandly contented.

Attaching himself to a prospecting party, he was sent under the same belief "into the brush" to drive off a bear, who was supposed to be haunting the camp fire. He returned in a few minutes *with* the bear, *driving it into* the unarmed circle and scattering the whole party. After this the theory of his being a hunting dog was abandoned. Yet it was said — on the usual uncorroborated evidence — that he had "put up" a quail; and his qualities as a retriever were for a long time accepted, until, during a shooting expedition for wild ducks, it was discovered that the one he had brought back had never been *shot,* and the party were obliged to compound damages with an adjacent settler.

His fondness for paddling in the ditches and "slumgullion" at one time suggested a water spaniel. He could swim, and would occasionally bring out of the river sticks and pieces of bark that had been thrown in; but as *he* always had to be thrown in with them, and was a good-sized dog, his aquatic reputation faded also. He remained simply " a yaller dog." What more could be said? His actual name was " Bones " — given to him, no doubt, through the provincial custom of confounding the occupation of the individual with his quality, for which it was pointed out precedent could be found in some old English family names.

But if Bones generally exhibited no preference for any particular individual in camp, he always made an exception in favor of drunkards. Even an ordinary roystering bacchanalian party brought him out from under a tree or a shed in the keenest satisfaction. He would accompany them through the long straggling street of the settlement, barking his delight at every step or mis-step of the revelers, and exhibiting none of that mistrust of eye which marked his attendance upon the sane and the respectable. He accepted even their uncouth play without a snarl or a yelp, hypocritically pretending even to like it; and I conscientiously believe would have allowed a tin can to be attached to his tail if the hand that tied it on were only unsteady, and the voice that bade him "lie still" were husky with liquor. He would "see" the party cheerfully into a saloon, wait outside the door — his tongue fairly lolling from his mouth in enjoyment — until they reappeared, permit them even to tumble over him with pleasure, and then gambol away before them, heedless of awkwardly projected stones and epithets. He would afterwards accompany them separately home, or lie with them at cross roads until they were assisted to their cabins. Then he would trot rakishly to his own haunt by the saloon stove, with the slightly conscious air of having been a bad dog, yet of having had a good time.

We never could satisfy ourselves whether his enjoyment arose from some merely selfish conviction that he was more *secure* with the physically and mentally incompetent, from some active sympathy with active wickedness, or from a grim sense of his own mental superiority at such moments. But the general belief leant towards his kindred sympathy as a "yaller dog" with all that was disreputable. And this was supported by another very singular canine manifestation — the " sincere flattery " of simulation or imitation.

" Uncle Billy " Riley for a short time enjoyed the position of being the camp drunkard, and at once became an object of Bones' greatest solicitude. He not only accompanied him everywhere, curled at his feet or head according to Uncle Billy's attitude at the moment, but, it was noticed, began presently to undergo a singular alteration in his own habits and appearance. From being an active, tireless scout and forager, a bold and unovertakable marauder, he became lazy and apathetic ; allowed gophers to burrow under him without endeavoring to undermine the settlement in his frantic endeavors to dig them out, permitted squirrels to flash their tails at him a hundred yards away, forgot his usual *caches*, and left his favorite bones unburied and bleaching in the sun. His eyes grew dull, his coat lustreless, in proportion as his companion became bleareyed and ragged ; in running, his usual arrow-like directness began to deviate, and it was not unusual to meet the pair together, zig-zagging up the hill. Indeed, Uncle Billy's condition could be predetermined by Bones' appearance at times when his temporary master was invisible. "The old man must have an awful jag on to-day," was casually remarked when an extra fluffiness and imbecility was noticeable in the passing Bones. At first it was believed that he drank also, but when careful investigation proved this hypothesis untenable, he was freely called a "derned time-servin', yaller hypocrite." Not a few advanced the opinion that if Bones did not actually lead Uncle Billy astray, he at least "slavered him over and coddled him until the old man got conceited in his wickedness." This undoubtedly led to a compulsory divorce between them, and Uncle Billy was happily despatched to a neighboring town and a doctor.

Bones seemed to miss him greatly, ran away for two days, and was supposed to have visited him, to have been shocked at his convalescence, and to have been "cut" by Uncle Billy in his reformed character; and he returned to his old active life again, and buried his past with his forgotten bones. It was said that he was afterwards detected in trying to lead an intoxicated tramp into camp after the methods employed by a blind man's dog, but was discovered in time by the — of course — uncorroborated narrator.

I should be tempted to leave him thus in his original and picturesque sin, but the same veracity which compelled me to transcribe his faults and iniquities obliges me to describe his ultimate and somewhat monotonous reformation, which came from no fault of his own.

It was a joyous day at Rattlers Ridge that was equally the advent of his change of heart and the first stage coach that had been induced to diverge from the high road and stop regularly at our settlement. Flags were flying from the post office and Polka saloon — and Bones was flying before the brass band that he detested, when the sweetest girl in the county — Pinkey Preston — daughter of the county judge and hopelessly beloved by all Rattlers Ridge, stepped from the coach which she had glorified by occupying as an invited guest.

"What makes him run away?" she asked quickly, opening her lovely eyes in a possible innocent wonder that anything could be found to run away from her.

"He don't like the brass band," we explained eagerly.

"How funny," murmured the girl; "is it as out of tune as all that?"

This irresistible witticism alone would have been enough to satisfy us — we did nothing but repeat it to each other all the next day — but we were positively transported when we saw her suddenly gather her dainty skirts in one hand and trip off through the red dust towards Bones, who, with his eyes over his yellow shoulder, had halted in the road, and half turned in mingled disgust and rage at the spectacle of the descending trombone. We held our breath as she approached him. Would Bones evade her as he did us at such moments, or would he save our reputation, and consent, for the moment, to accept her as a new kind of inebriate? She came nearer; he saw her; he began to slowly quiver with excitement — his stump of a tail vibrating with such rapidity that the loss of the missing portion was scarcely noticeable. Suddenly she stopped before him, took his yellow head between her little hands, lifted it, and looked down in his handsome brown eyes with her two lovely blue ones. What passed between them in that magnetic glance no one ever knew. She returned with him; said to him casually: "We 're not afraid of brass bands, are we?" to which he apparently acquiesced, at least stifling his disgust of them, while he was near her — which was nearly all the time.

During the speech-making her gloved hand and his yellow head were always near together, and at the crowning ceremony — her public checking of Yuba Bill's "way-bill," on behalf of the township, with a gold pencil, presented to her by the Stage Company — Bones' joy, far from knowing no bounds, seemed to know nothing but them, and he witnessed it apparently in the air. No one dared to interfere. For the first time a local pride in Bones sprang up in our hearts — and we lied to each other in his praises openly and shamelessly.

Then the time came for parting. We were standing by the door of the coach, hats in hand, as Miss Pinkey was about to step into it; Bones was waiting by her side, confidently looking into the interior, and apparently selecting his own seat on the lap of Judge Preston in the corner, when Miss Pinkey held up the sweetest of admonitory fingers. Then, taking his head between her two hands, she again looked into his brimming eyes, and said, simply, " *Good* dog," with the gentlest of emphasis on the adjective, and popped into the coach.

The six bay horses started as one, the gorgeous green and gold vehicle bounded forward, the red dust rose behind, and the yellow dog danced in and out of it to the very outskirts of the settlement. And then he soberly returned.

A day or two later he was missed — but the fact was afterwards known that he was at Spring Valley, the county town where Miss Preston lived — and he was forgiven. A week afterwards he was missed again, but this time for a longer period, and then a pathetic letter arrived from Sacramento for the storekeeper's wife.

"Would you mind," wrote Miss Pinky Preston, "asking some of your boys to come over here to Sacramento and bring back Bones? I don't mind having the dear dog walk out with me at Spring Valley, where every one knows me; but here he *does* make one so noticeable, on account of *his color.* I've got scarcely a frock that he agrees with. He don't go with my pink muslin, and that lovely buff tint he makes three shades lighter. You know yellow is *so* trying."

A consultation was quickly held by the whole settlement, and a deputation sent to

Sacramento to relieve the unfortunate girl. We were all quite indignant with Bones — but, oddly enough, I think it was greatly tempered with our new pride in him. While he was with us alone, his peculiarities had been scarcely appreciated, but the recurrent phrase, "that yellow dog that they keep at the Rattlers," gave us a mysterious importance along the country side, as if we had secured a "mascot" in some zoölogical curiosity.

This was further indicated by a singular occurrence. A new church had been built at the cross roads, and an eminent divine had come from San Francisco to preach the opening sermon. After a careful examination of the camp's wardrobe, and some felicitous exchange of apparel, a few of us were deputed to represent "Rattlers" at the Sunday service. In our white ducks, straw hats, and flannel blouses, we were sufficiently picturesque and distinctive as "honest miners" to be shown off in one of the front pews.

Seated near the prettiest girls, who offered us their hymn-books — in the cleanly odor of fresh pine shavings, and ironed muslin, and blown over by the spices of our own

woods through the open windows, a deep
sense of the abiding peace of Christian communion settled upon us.   At this supreme
moment some one murmured in an awe-
stricken whisper: —

   " *Will* you look at Bones? "

We looked. Bones had entered the
church and gone up in the gallery through
a pardonable ignorance and modesty; but,
perceiving his mistake, was now calmly
walking along the gallery rail before the
astounded worshipers. Reaching the end,
he paused for a moment, and carelessly
looked down. It was about fifteen feet to
the floor below — the simplest jump in the
world for the mountain-bred Bones. Daintily, gingerly, lazily, and yet with a conceited airiness of manner, as if, humanly
speaking, he had one leg in his pocket and
were doing it on three, he cleared the distance, dropping just in front of the chancel,
without a sound, turned himself around
three times, and then lay comfortably down.

Three deacons were instantly in the aisle
coming up before the eminent divine, who,
we fancied, wore a restrained smile. We
heard the hurried whispers: "Belongs to
them." "Quite a local institution here,

you know." "Don't like to offend sensi-
bilities;" and the minister's prompt "By
no means," as he went on with his service.

A short month ago we would have repudiated Bones; to-day we sat there in slightly
supercilious attitudes, as if to indicate that
any affront offered to Bones would be an
insult to ourselves, and followed by our instantaneous withdrawal in a body.

All went well, however, until the minister, lifting the large Bible from the communion table and holding it in both hands
before him, walked towards a reading-stand
by the altar rails. Bones uttered a distinct
growl. The minister stopped.

We, and we alone, comprehended in a
flash the whole situation. The Bible was
nearly the size and shape of one of those
soft clods of sod which we were in the playful habit of launching at Bones when he lay
half asleep in the sun, in order to see him
cleverly evade it.

We held our breath. What was to be
done? But the opportunity belonged to our
leader, Jeff Briggs — a confoundedly good-
looking fellow, with the golden mustache
of a northern viking and the curls of an
Apollo. Secure in his beauty and bland in

his self-conceit, he rose from the pew, and stepped before the chancel rails.

"I would wait a moment, if I were you, sir," he said, respectfully, "and you will see that he will go out quietly."

"What is wrong?" whispered the minister in some concern.

"He thinks you are going to heave that book at him, sir, without giving him a fair show, as we do."

The minister looked perplexed, but remained motionless, with the book in his hands. Bones arose, walked half way down the aisle, and vanished like a yellow flash!

With this justification of his reputation, Bones disappeared for a week. At the end of that time we received a polite note from Judge Preston, saying that the dog had become quite domiciled in their house, and begged that the camp, without yielding up their valuable *property* in him, would allow him to remain at Spring Valley for an indefinite time; that both the judge and his daughter — with whom Bones was already an old friend — would be glad if the members of the camp would visit their old favorite whenever they desired, to assure themselves that he was well cared for.

I am afraid that the bait thus ingenuously thrown out had a good deal to do with our ultimate yielding. However, the reports of those who visited Bones were wonderful and marvelous. He was residing there in state, lying on rugs in the drawing-room, coiled up under the judicial desk in the judge's study, sleeping regularly on the mat outside Miss Pinkey's bedroom door, or lazily snapping at flies on the judge's lawn.

"He's as yaller as ever," said one of our informants, "but it don't somehow seem to be the same back that we used to break clods over in the old time, just to see him scoot out of the dust."

And now I must record a fact which I am aware all lovers of dogs will indignantly deny, and which will be furiously bayed at by every faithful hound since the days of Ulysses. Bones not only *forgot*, but absolutely *cut us !* Those who called upon the judge in "store clothes" he would perhaps casually notice, but he would sniff at them as if detecting and resenting them under their superficial exterior. The rest he simply paid no attention to. The more familiar term of "Bonesy" — formerly applied to him, as in our rare moments of endearment

— produced no response. This pained, I think, some of the more youthful of us; but, through some strange human weakness, it also increased the camp's respect for him. Nevertheless, we spoke of him familiarly to strangers at the very moment he ignored us. I am afraid that we also took some pains to point out that he was getting fat and unwieldy, and losing his elasticity, implying covertly that his choice was a mistake and his life a failure.

A year after he died, in the odor of sanctity and respectability, being found one morning coiled up and stiff on the mat outside Miss Pinkey's door. When the news was conveyed to us, we asked permission, the camp being in a prosperous condition, to erect a stone over his grave. But when it came to the inscription we could only think of the two words murmured to him by Miss Pinkey, which we always believe effected his conversion: —

" *Good* Dog! "

A MOTHER OF FIVE.

SHE was a mother — and a rather exemplary one — of five children, although her own age was barely nine. Two of these children were twins, and she generally alluded to them as "Mr. Amplach's children," referring to an exceedingly respectable gentleman in the next settlement, who, I have reason to believe, had never set eyes on her or them. The twins were quite naturally alike — having been in a previous state of existence two ninepins — and were still somewhat vague and inchoate below their low shoulders in their long clothes, but were also firm and globular about the head, and there were not wanting those who professed to see in this an unmistakable resemblance to their reputed father. The other children were dolls of different ages, sex, and condition, but the twins may be said to have been distinctly her own conception. Yet such was her admirable and impartial maternity that she never made any difference between them. "The Amplach's children" was a description rather than a distinction.

She was herself the motherless child of Robert Foulkes, a hard-working but somewhat improvident teamster on the Express Route between Big Bend and Reno. His daily avocation, when she was not actually with him in the wagon, led to an occasional dispersion of herself and her progeny along the road and at wayside stations between those places. But the family was generally collected together by rough but kindly hands already familiar with the handling of her children. I have a very vivid recollection of Jim Carter trampling into a saloon, after a five-mile walk through a snowdrift, with an Amplach twin in his pocket. "Suthin' ought to be done," he growled, "to make Meary a little more careful o' them Amplach children; I picked up one outer the snow a mile beyond Big Bend." "God bless my soul!" said a casual passenger, looking up hastily; "I did n't know Mr. Amplach was married." Jim winked diabolically at us over his glass. "No more did I," he responded gloomily, "but you can't tell anything about the ways o' them respectable, psalm - singing jay birds."

Having thus disposed of Amplach's character, later on, when he was alone with Mary,
or "Meary," as she chose to pronounce it,
the rascal worked upon her feelings with an
account of the infant Amplach's sufferings
in the snowdrift and its agonized whisper-
ings for "Meary! Meary!" until real tears
stood in Mary's blue eyes. "Let this be a
lesson to you," he concluded, drawing the
ninepin dexterously from his pocket, "for
it took nigh a quart of the best forty-rod
whiskey to bring that child to." Not only
did Mary firmly believe him, but for weeks
afterwards "Julian Amplach" — this unhappy twin — was kept in a somnolent attitude in the cart, and was believed to have
contracted dissipated habits from the effects
of his heroic treatment.

Her numerous family was achieved in
only two years, and succeeded her first
child, which was brought from Sacramento
at considerable expense by a Mr. William
Dodd, also a teamster, on her seventh birth-
day. This, by one of those rare inventions
known only to a child's vocabulary, she at
once called "Misery"— probably a combination of "Missy," as she herself was formerly termed by strangers, and "Missouri,"

her native State. It was an excessively
large doll at first — Mr. Dodd wishing to
get the worth of his money — but time, and
perhaps an excess of maternal care, reme-
died the defect, and it lost flesh and certain
unemployed parts of its limbs very rapidly.
It was further reduced in bulk by falling
under the wagon and having the whole train
pass over it, but singularly enough its greatest attenuation was in the head and shoulders — the complexion peeling off as a solid
layer, followed by the disappearance of distinct strata of its extraordinary composition.
This continued until the head and shoulders
were much too small for even its reduced
frame, and all the devices of childish milli-
nery — a shawl secured with tacks and well
hammered in, and a hat which tilted backwards and forwards and never appeared at
the same angle — failed to restore symme-
try. Until one dreadful morning, after an
imprudent bath, the whole upper structure
disappeared, leaving two hideous iron prongs
standing erect from the spinal column.
Even an imaginative child like Mary could
not accept this sort of thing as a head.
Later in the day Jack Roper, the black-
smith at the "Crossing," was concerned at

the plaintive appearance, before his forge,
of a little girl, clad in a bright blue pinafore of the same color as her eyes, carrying
her monstrous offspring in her arms. Jack
recognized her and instantly divined the
situation. "You have n't," he suggested
kindly, "got another head at home — suthin'
left over?" Mary shook her head sadly;
even her prolific maternity was not equal to
the creation of children in detail. "Nor
anythin' like a head?" he persisted sympa-
thetically. Mary's loving eyes filled with
tears. "No, nuffen!" "You could n't,"
he continued thoughtfully, "use her the
other side up? — we might get a fine pair
o' legs outer them irons," he added, touching the two prongs with artistic suggestion.
"Now look here" — he was about to tilt the
doll over when a small cry of feminine distress and a swift movement of a matronly
little arm arrested the evident indiscretion.
"I see," he said gravely. "Well, you
come here to-morrow, and we 'll fix up
suthin' to work her." Jack was thoughtful
the rest of the day, more than usually impatient with certain stubborn mules to be
shod, and even knocked off work an hour
earlier to walk to Big Bend and a rival

shop. But the next morning when the
trustful and anxious mother appeared at the
forge she uttered a scream of delight. Jack
had neatly joined a hollow iron globe, taken
from the newel post of some old iron staircase railing, to the two prongs, and covered
it with a coat of red fire-proof paint. It
was true that its complexion was rather
high, that it was inclined to be top-heavy,
and that in the long run the other dolls suffered considerably by enforced association
with this unyielding and implacable head
and shoulders, but this did not diminish
Mary's joy over her restored first-born.
Even its utter absence of features was no
defect in a family where features were as
evanescent as in hers, and the most ordinary
student of evolution could see that the
"Amplach" ninepins were in legitimate
succession to the globular-headed "Misery."
For a time I think that Mary even preferred
her to the others. Howbeit it was a pretty
sight to see her on a summer afternoon sitting upon a wayside stump, her other children dutifully ranged around her, and the
hard, unfeeling head of Misery pressed deep
down into her loving little heart, as she
swayed from side to side, crooning her plain-

tive lullaby. Small wonder that the bees took up the song and droned a slumbrous accompaniment, or that high above her head the enormous pines, stirred through their depths by the soft Sierran air — or Heaven knows what — let slip flickering lights and shadows to play over that cast-iron face, until the child, looking down upon it with the quick, transforming power of love, thought that it smiled?

The two remaining members of the family were less distinctive. "Gloriana" — pronounced as two words: "Glory Anna" — being the work of her father, who also named it, was simply a cylindrical roll of canvas wagon-covering, girt so as to define a neck and waist, with a rudely inked face — altogether a weak, pitiable, man-like invention; and "Johnny Dear," alleged to be the representative of John Doremus, a young storekeeper who occasionally supplied Mary with gratuitous sweets. Mary never admitted this, and, as we were all gentlemen along that road, we were blind to the suggestion. "Johnny Dear" was originally a small plaster phrenological cast of a head and bust, begged from some shop window in the county town, with a body clearly

constructed by Mary herself. It was an
ominous fact that it was always dressed as
a *boy*, and was distinctly the most *human*-
looking of all her progeny. Indeed, in
spite of the faculties that were legibly
printed all over its smooth, white, hairless
head, it was appallingly life-like. Left
sometimes by Mary astride of the branch of
a wayside tree, horsemen had been known
to dismount hurriedly and examine it, returning with a mystified smile, and it was
on record that Yuba Bill had once pulled
up the Pioneer Coach at the request of curious and imploring passengers, and then
grimly installed "Johnny Dear" beside him
on the box seat, publicly delivering him to
Mary at Big Bend, to her wide-eyed confusion and the first blush we had ever seen on
her round, chubby, sunburnt cheeks. It
may seem strange that, with her great popularity and her well-known maternal instincts,
she had not been kept fully supplied with
proper and more conventional dolls; but it
was soon recognized that she did not care
for them — left their waxen faces, rolling
eyes, and abundant hair in ditches, or
stripped them to help clothe the more extravagant creatures of her fancy. So it

came that "Johnny Dear's" strictly classical profile looked out from under a girl's fashionable straw sailor hat, to the utter obliteration of his prominent intellectual faculties; the Amplach twins wore bonnets on their ninepin heads, and even an attempt was made to fit a flaxen scalp on the iron-headed Misery. But her dolls were always a creation of her own — her affection for them increasing with the demand upon her imagination. This may seem somewhat inconsistent with her habit of occasionally abandoning them in the woods or in the ditches. But she had an unbounded confidence in the kindly maternity of Nature, and trusted her children to the breast of the Great Mother as freely as she did herself in her own motherlessness. And this confidence was rarely betrayed. Rats, mice, snails, wild cats, panther and bear never touched her lost waifs. Even the elements were kindly; an Amplach twin buried under a snowdrift in high altitudes reappeared smilingly in the spring in all its wooden and painted integrity. We were all Pantheists then — and believed this implicitly. It was only when exposed to the milder forces of civilization that Mary had anything to fear.

Yet even then, when Patsey O'Connor's domestic goat had once tried to "sample" the lost Misery, he had retreated with the loss of three front teeth, and Thompson's mule came out of an encounter with that iron-headed prodigy with a sprained hind leg and a cut and swollen pastern.

But these were the simple Arcadian days of the road between Big Bend and Reno, and progress and prosperity, alas! brought changes in their wake. It was already whispered that Mary ought to be going to school, and Mr. Amplach — still happily oblivious of the liberties taken with his name — as trustee of the public school at Duckville, had intimated that Mary's Bohemian wanderings were a scandal to the county. She was growing up in ignorance, a dreadful ignorance of everything but the chivalry, the deep tenderness, the delicacy and unselfishness of the rude men around her, and obliviousness of faith in anything but the immeasurable bounty of Nature towards her and her children. Of course there was a fierce discussion between "the boys" of the road and the few married families of the settlement on this point, but, of course, progress and "snivelization" — as

the boys chose to call it — triumphed. The
projection of a railroad settled it; Robert
Foulkes, promoted to a foremanship of a
division of the line, was made to understand
that his daughter must be educated. But
the terrible question of Mary's family remained. No school would open its doors to
that heterogeneous collection, and Mary's
little heart would have broken over the rude
dispersal or heroic burning of her children.
The ingenuity of Jack Roper suggested a
compromise. She was allowed to select one
to take to school with her; the others were
adopted by certain of her friends, and she
was to be permitted to visit them every
Saturday afternoon. The selection was a
cruel trial, so cruel that, knowing her undoubted preference for her first-born, Misery, we would not have interfered for worlds,
but in her unexpected choice of "Johnny
Dear " the most unworldly of us knew that
it was the first glimmering of feminine tact
— her first submission to the world of pro-
priety that she was now entering. "Johnny
Dear " was undoubtedly the most presenta-
ble; even more, there was an educational
suggestion in its prominent, mapped out
phrenological organs. The adopted fathers

were loyal to their trust.   Indeed, for years afterwards the blacksmith kept the iron-headed Misery on a rude shelf, like a shrine, near his bunk; nobody but himself and Meary ever knew the secret, stolen, and thrilling interviews that took place during the first days of their separation.   Certain facts, however, transpired concerning Mary's equal faithfulness to another of her children. It is said that one Saturday afternoon, when the road manager of the new line was seated in his office at Reno in private business discussion with two directors, a gentle tap was heard at the door.   It was opened to an eager little face, a pair of blue eyes, and a blue pinafore.   To the astonishment of the directors, a change came over the face of the manager.   Taking the child gently by the hand, he walked to his desk, on which the papers of the new line were scattered, and drew open a drawer from which he took a large ninepin extraordinarily dressed as doll.   The astonishment of the two gentlemen was increased at the following quaint colloquy between the manager and the child.

"She's doing remarkably well in spite of the trying weather, but I have had to keep her very quiet," said the manager, regarding the ninepin critically.

"Ess," said Mary quickly. "It's just the same with Johnny Dear; his cough is f'ightful at nights. But Misery's all right. I've just been to see her."

"There's a good deal of scarlet fever around," continued the manager with quiet concern, "and we can't be too careful. But I shall take her for a little run down the line to-morrow."

The eyes of Mary sparkled and overflowed like blue water. Then there was a kiss, a little laugh, a shy glance at the two curious strangers, the blue pinafore fluttered away, and the colloquy ended. She was equally attentive in her care of the others, but the rag baby "Gloriana," who had found a home in Jim Carter's cabin at the Ridge, living too far for daily visits, was brought down regularly on Saturday afternoon to Mary's house by Jim, tucked in asleep in his saddle bags or riding gallantly before him on the horn of his saddle. On Sunday there was a dress parade of all the dolls, which kept Mary in heart for the next week's desolation.

But there came one Saturday and Sunday when Mary did not appear, and it was known along the road that she had been

called to San Francisco to meet an aunt who
had just arrived from "the States." It was
a vacant Sunday to "the boys," a very hollow, unsanctified Sunday, somehow, without
that little figure. But the next Sunday,
and the next, were still worse, and then it
was known that the dreadful aunt was making much of Mary, and was sending her to
a grand school — a convent at Santa Clara
— where it was rumored girls were turned
out so accomplished that their own parents
did not know them. But *we* knew that was
impossible to our Mary; and a letter which
came from her at the end of the month, and
before the convent had closed upon the blue
pinafore, satisfied us, and was balm to our
anxious hearts. It was characteristic of
Mary; it was addressed to nobody in particular, and would — but for the prudence
of the aunt — have been entrusted to the
Post Office open and undirected. It was
a single sheet, handed to us without a word
by her father; but, as we passed it from
hand to hand, we understood it as if we had
heard our lost playfellow's voice.

"Ther 's more houses in 'Frisco than you
kin shake a stick at and wimmens till you
kant rest, but mules and jakasses ain't got

no sho, nor blacksmiffs shops, wich is not to be seen no wear. Rapits and Skwirls also bares and panfers is on-noun and unforgotten on account of the streets and Sunday skoles. Jim Roper you orter be very good to Mizzery on a kount of my not bein' here, and not harten your hart to her bekos she is top heavy — which is ontroo and simply an imptient lie — like you allus make. I have a kinary bird wot sings deliteful — but is n't a yellerhamer sutch as I know, as you 'd think. Dear Mister Montgommery, don't keep Gulan Amplak to mutch shet up in office drors; it is n't good for his lungs and chest. And don't you ink his head — nother! youre as bad as the rest. Johnny Dear, you must be very kind to your attopted father, and you, Glory Anna, must lov your kind Jimmy Carter verry mutch for taking you hossback so offen. I has been buggy ridin' with an orficer who has killed injuns real! I am comin' back soon with grate affeckshun, so luke out and mind."

But it was three years before she returned, and this was her last and only letter. The "adopted fathers" of her children were faithful, however, and when the new line was

opened, and it was understood that she was
to be present with her father at the ceremony, they came, with a common understanding, to the station to meet their old
playmate. They were ranged along the platform — poor Jack Roper a little overweighted
with a bundle he was carrying on his left
arm. And then a young girl in the freshness of her teens and the spotless purity of
a muslin frock, that although brief in skirt
was perfect in fit, faultlessly booted and
gloved, tripped from the train, and offered
a delicate hand in turn to each of her old
friends. Nothing could be prettier than
the smile on the cheeks that were no longer
sunburnt; nothing could be clearer than the
blue eyes lifted frankly to theirs. And yet,
as she gracefully turned away with her
father, the faces of the four adopted parents
were found to be as red and embarrassed as
her own on the day that Yuba Bill drove
up publicly with "Johnny Dear" on the
box seat.

"You were n't such a fool," said Jack
Montgomery to Roper, "as to bring 'Misery' here with you?"

"I was," said Roper with a constrained
laugh, — "and you?" He had just caught

sight of the head of a ninepin peeping from the manager's pocket. The man laughed, and then the four turned silently away.

"Mary" had indeed come back to them; but not "The Mother of Five!"

BULGER'S REPUTATION.

WE all remembered very distinctly Bulger's advent in Rattlesnake Camp. It was during the rainy season — a season singularly inducive to settled reflective impressions as we sat and smoked around the stove in Mosby's grocery. Like older and more civilized communities, we had our periodic waves of sentiment and opinion, with the exception that they were more evanescent with us, and, as we had just passed through a fortnight of dissipation and extravagance, owing to a visit from some gamblers and speculators, we were now undergoing a severe moral revulsion, partly induced by reduced finances and partly by the arrival of two families with grown-up daughters on the hill. It was raining, with occasional warm breaths, through the open window, of the southwest trades, redolent of the saturated spices of the woods and springing grasses, which perhaps were slightly inconsistent with the hot stove around which we had congregated. But the stove was only an excuse for our listless, gregarious gathering; warmth and idleness went well together, and it was currently accepted that we had caught from the particular reptile which gave its name to our camp much of its pathetic, life-long search for warmth, and its habit of indolently basking in it.

A few of us still went through the affectation of attempting to dry our damp clothes by the stove, and sizzling our wet boots against it; but as the same individuals calmly permitted the rain to drive in upon them through the open window without moving, and seemed to take infinite delight in the amount of steam they generated, even that pretense dropped. Crotalus himself, with his tail in a muddy ditch, and the sun striking cold fire from his slit eyes as he basked his head on a warm stone beside it, could not have typified us better.

Percy Briggs took his pipe from his mouth at last and said, with reflective severity : —

"Well, gentlemen, if we can't get the wagon road over here, and if we 're going to be left out by the stage-coach company, we can at least straighten up the camp, and

not have it look like a cross between a tenement alley and a broken-down circus. I
declare, I was just sick when these two
Baker girls started to make a short cut
through the camp. Darned if they didn't
turn round and take to the woods and the
rattlers again afore they got half-way.
And that benighted idiot, Tom Rollins,
standin' there in the ditch, spattered all
over with slumgullion 'til he looked like a
spotted tarrypin, wavin' his fins and sashay-
ing backwards and forrards and sayin',
' This way, ladies; this way! ' "

"*I* didn't," returned Tom Rollins, quite
casually, without looking up from his steaming boots; "*I* didn't start in night afore
last to dance ' The Green Corn Dance '
outer ' Hiawatha,' with feathers in my hair
and a red blanket on my shoulders, round
that family's new potato patch, in order
that it might ' increase and multiply.' I
didn't sing ' Sabbath Morning Bells ' with
an anvil accompaniment until twelve o'clock
at night over at the Crossing, so that they
might dream of their Happy Childhood's
Home. It seems to me that it wasn't *me*
did it. I might be mistaken — it was late
— but I have the impression that it wasn't
me."

From the silence that followed, this would seem to have been clearly a recent performance of the previous speaker, who, however, responded quite cheerfully : —

"An evenin' o' simple, childish gayety don't count. We've got to start in again *fair*. What we want here is to clear up and encourage decent immigration, and get rid o' gamblers and blatherskites that are makin' this yer camp their happy hunting-ground. We don't want any more permiskus shootin'. We don't want any more paintin' the town red. We don't want any more swaggerin' galoots ridin' up to this grocery and emptyin' their six-shooters in the air afore they 'light. We want to put a stop to it peacefully ..nd without a row — and we kin. We ain't got no bullies of our own to fight back, and they know it, so they know they won't get no credit bullyin' us ; they 'll leave, if we 're only firm. It 's all along of our cussed fool good-nature ; they see it amuses us, and they 'll keep it up as long as the whiskey 's free. What we want to do is, when the next man comes waltzin' along " —

A distant clatter from the rocky hillside here mingled with the puff of damp air through the window.

"Looks as ef we might hev a show even now," said Tom Rollins, removing his feet from the stove as we all instinctively faced towards the window.

"I reckon you're in with us in this, Mosby?" said Briggs, turning towards the proprietor of the grocery, who had been leaning listlessly against the wall behind his bar.

"Arter the man's had a fair show," said Mosby, cautiously. He deprecated the prevailing condition of things, but it was still an open question whether the families would prove as valuable customers as his present clients. "Everything in moderation, gentlemen."

The sound of galloping hoofs came nearer, now swishing in the soft mud of the highway, until the unseen rider pulled up before the door. There was no shouting, however, nor did he announce himself with the usual salvo of fire-arms. But when, after a singularly heavy tread and the jingle of spurs on the platform, the door flew open to the new-comer, he seemed a realization of our worst expectations. Tall, broad, and muscular, he carried in one hand a shot-gun, while from his hip dangled a heavy navy

revolver. His long hair, unkempt but
oiled, swept a greasy circle around his
shoulders; his enormous moustache, dripping with wet, completely concealed his
mouth. His costume of fringed buckskin
was wild and *outré* even for our frontier
camp. But what was more confirmative of
our suspicions was that he was evidently in
the habit of making an impression, and after
a distinct pause at the doorway, with only
a side glance at us, he strode towards the
bar.

"As there don't seem to be no hotel hereabouts, I reckon I kin put up my mustang
here and have a shakedown somewhere behind that counter," he said. His voice
seemed to have added to its natural depth
the hoarseness of frequent over-straining.

"Ye ain't got no bunk to spare, you
boys, hev ye?" asked Mosby, evasively,
glancing at Percy Briggs, without looking
at the stranger. We all looked at Briggs
also; it was *his* affair after all — *he* had
originated this opposition. To our surprise
he said nothing.

The stranger leaned heavily on the counter.

"I was speaking to *you*," he said, with

his eyes on Mosby, and slightly accenting the pronoun with a tap of his revolver-butt on the bar. "Ye don't seem to catch on."

Mosby smiled feebly, and again cast an imploring glance at Briggs. To our greater astonishment, Briggs said, quietly: "Why don't you answer the stranger, Mosby?"

"Yes, yes," said Mosby, suavely, to the newcomer, while an angry flush crossed his cheek as he recognized the position in which Briggs had placed him. "Of course, you're welcome to what doings *I* hev here, but I reckoned these gentlemen over there," with a vicious glance at Briggs, "might fix ye up suthin' better; they're so pow'ful kind to your sort."

The stranger threw down a gold piece on the counter and said: "Fork out your whiskey, then," waited until his glass was filled, took it in his hand, and then, drawing an empty chair to the stove, sat down beside Briggs. "Seein' as you're that kind," he said, placing his heavy hand on Briggs's knee, "mebbe ye kin tell me ef thar's a shanty or a cabin at Rattlesnake that I kin get for a couple o' weeks. I saw an empty one at the head o' the hill. You see, gennelmen," he added confidentially as he swept the drops of whiskey from his long moustache with his fingers and glanced around our group, "I 've got some business over at Bigwood," our nearest town, "but ez a place to *stay at* it ain't my style."

"What 's the matter with Bigwood?" said Briggs, abruptly.

"It 's too howlin', too festive, too rough; thar 's too much yellin' and shootin' goin' day and night. Thar 's too many card sharps and gay gamboliers cavortin' about the town to please me. Too much permis- kus soakin' at the bar and free jim-jams. What I want is a quiet place what a man kin give his mind and elbow a rest from betwixt grippin' his shootin'-irons and crookin' in his whiskey. A sort o' slow, quiet, easy place *like this.*"

We all stared at him, Percy Briggs as fixedly as any. But there was not the slightest trace of irony, sarcasm, or peculiar significance in his manner. He went on slowly : —

"When I struck this yer camp a minit ago; when I seed that thar ditch meanderin' peaceful like through the street, without a hotel or free saloon or express office on either side; with the smoke just a curlin' over the chimbley of that log shanty, and the bresh just set fire to and a smoulderin' in that potato patch with a kind o' old-time stingin' in your eyes and nose, and a few women's duds just a flutterin' on a line by the fence, I says to myself: ' Bulger — this is peace! This is wot you 're lookin' for, Bulger — this is wot you 're wantin' — this is wot *you 'll hev!* ' "

"You say you 've business over at Big-wood. What business?" said Briggs.

"It 's a peculiar business, young fellow," returned the stranger, gravely. "Thar 's different men ez has different opinions about it. Some allows it 's an easy business, some allows it 's a rough business; some says it 's a sad business, others says it 's gay and fes-tive. Some wonders ez how I 've got into it, and others wonder how I 'll ever get out of it. It 's a payin' business — it 's a peace-ful sort o' business when left to itself. It 's a peculiar business — a business that sort o' b'longs to me, though I ain't got no patent from Washington for it. It 's *my own* busi-ness." He paused, rose, and saying, "Let 's meander over and take a look at that empty cabin, and ef she suits me, why, I 'll plank down a slug for her on the spot, and move in to-morrow," walked towards the door. "I 'll pick up suthin' in the way o' boxes and blankets from the grocery," he added, looking at Mosby, "and ef thar 's a corner whar I kin stand my gun and a nail to hang up my revolver — why, I 'm all thar!"

By this time we were no longer astonished when Briggs rose also, and not only accompanied the sinister-looking stranger to the empty cabin, but assisted him in negotiating with its owner for a fortnight's occupancy. Nevertheless, we eagerly assailed Briggs on his return for some explanation of this singular change in his attitude towards the stranger. He coolly reminded us, however, that while his intention of excluding ruffianly adventurers from the camp remained the same, he had no right to go back on the stranger's sentiments, which were evidently in accord with our own, and although Mr. Bulger's appearance was inconsistent with them, that was only an additional reason why we should substitute a mild firmness for that violence which we all deprecated, but which might attend his abrupt dismissal. We were all satisfied except Mosby, who had not yet recovered from Briggs's change of front, which he was pleased to call "craw-fishing." "Seemed to me his account of his business was extraordinary satisfactory! Sorter filled the bill all round — no mistake thar," — he suggested, with a malicious irony. "I like a man that's outspoken."

"I understood him very well," said Briggs, quietly.

"In course you did. Only when you've settled in *your* mind whether he was describing horse-stealing or tract-distributing, mebbe you'll let *me* know."

It would seem, however, that Briggs did not interrogate the stranger again regarding it, nor did we, who were quite content to leave matters in Briggs's hands. Enough that Mr. Bulger moved into the empty cabin the next day, and, with the aid of a few old boxes from the grocery, which he quickly extemporized into tables and chairs, and the purchase of some necessary cooking-utensils, soon made himself at home. The rest of the camp, now thoroughly aroused, made a point of leaving their work in the ditches, whenever they could, to stroll carelessly around Bulger's tenement in the vague hope of satisfying a curiosity that had become tormenting. But they could not find that

he was doing anything of a suspicious character — except, perhaps, from the fact that
it was not *outwardly* suspicious, which I
grieve to say did not lull them to security.
He seemed to be either fixing up his cabin
or smoking in his doorway. On the second
day he checked this itinerant curiosity by
taking the initiative himself, and quietly
walking from claim to claim and from cabin
to cabin with a pacific but by no means a
satisfying interest. The shadow of his tall
figure carrying his inseparable gun, which
had not yet apparently "stood in the corner," falling upon an excavated bank beside
the delving miners, gave them a sense of
uneasiness they could not explain; a few
characteristic yells of boisterous hilarity
from their noontide gathering under a cotton-
wood somehow ceased when Mr. Bulger
was seen gravely approaching, and his casual stopping before a poker party in the
gulch actually caused one of the most reckless gamblers to weakly recede from "a
bluff" and allow his adversary to sweep the
board. After this it was felt that matters
were becoming serious. There was no subsequent patroling of the camp before the
stranger's cabin. Their curiosity was sin-

gularly abated. A general feeling of repul-
sion, kept within bounds partly by the
absence of any overt act from Bulger, and
partly by an inconsistent over-consciousness
of his shot-gun, took its place. But an unexpected occurrence revived it.

One evening, as the usual social circle
were drawn around Mosby's stove, the lazy
silence was broken by the familiar sounds
of pistol-shots and a series of more familiar
shrieks and yells from the rocky hill road.
The circle quickly recognized the voices of
their old friends the roysterers and gamblers
from Sawyer's Dam; they as quickly recognized the returning shouts here and there
from a few companions who were welcoming
them. I grieve to say that in spite of their
previous attitude of reformation a smile of
gratified expectancy lit up the faces of the
younger members, and even the older ones
glanced dubiously at Briggs. Mosby made
no attempt to conceal a sigh of relief as he
carefully laid out an extra supply of glasses
in his bar. Suddenly the oncoming yells
ceased, the wild gallop of hoofs slackened
into a trot, and finally halted, and even the
responsive shouts of the camp stopped also.
We all looked vacantly at each other; Mosby

leaped over his counter and went to the door; Briggs followed with the rest of us. The night was dark, and it was a few minutes before we could distinguish a straggling, vague, but silent procession moving through the moist, heavy air on the hill. But, to our surprise, it was moving *away* from us — absolutely *leaving* the camp! We were still staring in expectancy when out of the darkness slowly emerged a figure which we recognized at once as Captain Jim, one of the most reckless members of our camp. Pushing us back into the grocery he entered without a word, closed the door behind him, and threw himself vacantly into a chair. We at once pressed around him. He looked up at us dazedly, drew a long breath, and said slowly: —

"It's no use, gentlemen! Suthin's *got* to be done with that Bulger; and mighty quick."

"What's the matter?" we asked eagerly.

"Matter!" he repeated, passing his hand across his forehead. "Matter! Look yere! Ye all of you heard them boys from Sawyer's Dam coming over the hill? Ye heard their music — mebbe ye heard *us* join in the chorus? Well, on they came waltzing

down the hill, like old times, and we waitin'
for 'em. Then, jest as they passed the old
cabin, who do you think they ran right into
— shooting-iron, long hair and mustache,
and all that — standing there plump in the
road? — why, Bulger!"

"Well?"

"Well! — Whatever it was — don't ask
me — but, dern my skin, ef after a word or
two from *him* — them boys just stopped
yellin', turned round like lambs, and rode
away, peaceful-like, along with him. We
ran after them a spell, still yellin', when
that thar Bulger faced around, said to us
that he 'd ' come down here for quiet,' and
ef he could n't hev it he 'd have to leave
with those gentlemen *who wanted it* too !
And I 'm gosh darned ef those *gentlemen* —
you know 'em all — Patsey Carpenter,
Snap-shot Harry, and the others — ever
said a darned word, but kinder nodded ' So
long ' and went away!"

Our astonishment and mystification were
complete; and I regret to say, the indignation of Captain Jim and Mosby equally so.
"If we 're going to be bossed by the first
new-comer," said the former, gloomily, "I
reckon we might as well take our chances

with the Sawyer's Dam boys, whom we know."

"Ef we are going to hev the legitimate trade of Rattlesnake interfered with by the cranks of some hidin' horse-thief or retired road agent," said Mosby, "we might as well invite the hull of Joaquin Murietta's gang here at once! But I suppose this is part o' Bulger's particular ' business,'" he added, with a withering glance at Briggs.

"I understand it all," said Briggs, quietly. "You know I told you that bullies could n't live in the same camp together. That's human nature — and that's how plain men like you and me manage to scud along without getting plugged. You see, Bulger was n't going to hev any of his own kind jumpin' his claim here. And I reckon he was pow'ful enough to back down Sawyer's Dam. Anyhow, the bluff told — and here we are in peace and quietness."

"Until he lets us know what *is* his little game," sneered Mosby.

Nevertheless, such is the force of mysterious power that, although it was exercised against what we firmly believed was the independence of the camp, it extorted a certain respect from us. A few thought it was not a bad thing to have a professional bully, and even took care to relate the discomfiture of the wicked youth of Sawyer's Dam for the benefit of a certain adjacent and powerful camp who had looked down upon us. He, himself, returning the same evening from his self-imposed escort, vouchsafed no other reason than the one he had already given. Preposterous as it seemed, we were obliged to accept it, and the still more preposterous inference that he had sought Rattlesnake Camp solely for the purpose of acquiring and securing its peace and quietness. Certainly he had no other occupation; the little work he did upon the tailings of the abandoned claim which went with his little cabin was scarcely a pretense. He rode over on certain days to Bigwood on account of his business, but no one had ever seen him there, nor could the description of his manner and appearance evoke any information from the Bigwoodians. It remained a mystery.

It had also been feared that the advent of Bulger would intensify that fear and dislike of riotous Rattlesnake which the two families had shown, and which was the origin of Briggs's futile attempt at reformation. But it was discovered that since his arrival the young girls had shown less timidity in entering the camp, and had even exchanged some polite conversation and good-humoured badinage with its younger and more impressible members. Perhaps this tended to make these youths more observant, for a few days later, when the vexed question of Bulger's business was again under discussion, one of them remarked, gloomily: —

"I reckon there ain't no doubt *what* he's here for!"

The youthful prophet was instantly sat upon after the fashion of all elderly critics since Job's. Nevertheless, after a pause he was permitted to explain.

"Only this morning, when Lance Forester and me were chirping with them gals out on the hill, who should we see hanging around in the bush but that cussed Bulger! We allowed at first that it might be only a new style of his interferin', so we took no notice, except to pass a few remarks about listeners and that sort o' thing, and perhaps to bedevil the girls a little more than we'd hev done if we'd been alone. Well, they laughed, and we laughed — and that was the end of it. But this afternoon, as Lance

and me were meandering down by their
cabin, we sorter turned into the woods to
wait till they'd come out. Then all of a
suddent Lance stopped as rigid as a pointer
that's flushed somethin', and says, 'B'gosh!'
And thar, under a big redwood, sat that
slimy hypocrite Bulger, twisting his long
mustaches and smiling like clockwork alongside o' little Meely Baker — you know her,
the pootiest of the two sisters — and she
smilin' back on him. Think of it! — that
unknown, unwashed, long-haired tramp and
bully, who must be forty if a day, and that
innocent gal of sixteen. It was simply dis-
gustin'!"

I need not say that the older cynics and
critics already alluded to at once improved
the occasion. What more could be expected? Women, the world over, were
noted for this sort of thing! This long-
haired, swaggering bully, with his air of
mystery, had captivated them, as he always
had done since the days of Homer. Simple
merit, which sat lowly in bar-rooms, and
conceived projects for the public good
around the humble, unostentatious stove,
was nowhere! Youth could not too soon
learn this bitter lesson. And in this case

youth too, perhaps, was right in its conjec-
tures, for this *was*, no doubt, the little
game of the perfidious Bulger. We recalled
the fact that his unhallowed appearance in
camp was almost coincident with the arrival
of the two families. We glanced at Briggs;
to our amazement, for the first time he
looked seriously concerned. But Mosby in
the mean time leaned his elbows lazily over
the counter and, in a slow voice, added fuel
to the flame.

"I would n't hev spoken of it before," he
said, with a sidelong glance at Briggs, "for
it might be all in the line o' Bulger's ' business,' but suthin' happened the other night
that, for a minit, got me! I was passin'
the Bakers' shanty, and I heard one of them
gals a-singing a camp-meeting hymn. I
don't calkilate to run agin you young fellers
in any sparkin' or canoodlin' that 's goin'
on, but her voice sounded so pow'ful sooth-
in' and pretty thet I jest stood there and
listened. Then the old woman — old Mother Baker — *she* joined in, and I listened
too. And then — dern my skin! — but a
man's voice joined in — jest belching outer
that cabin! — and I sorter lifted myself up
and kem away.

"That voice, gentlemen," said Mosby, lingering artistically as he took up a glass and professionally eyed it before wiping it with his towel, "that voice, cumf'bly fixed thar in thet cabin among them wimen folks, was Bulger's!"

Briggs got up, with his eyes looking the darker for his flushed face. "Gentlemen," he said huskily, "thar's only one thing to be done. A lot of us have got to ride over to Sawyer's Dam to-morrow morning and pick up as many square men as we can muster; there's a big camp-meeting goin' on there, and there won't be no difficulty in that. When we've got a big enough crowd to show we mean business, we must march back here and ride Bulger out of this camp! I don't hanker arter Vigilance Committees, as a rule — it's a rough remedy — it's like drinkin' a quart o' whisky agin rattlesnake poison — but it's got to be done! We don't mind being *sold* ourselves — but when it comes to our standin' by and seein' the only innocent people in Rattlesnake given away — we kick! Bulger's got to be fired outer this camp! And he will be!"

But he was not.

For when, the next morning, a determined

and thoughtful procession of the best and most characteristic citizens of Rattlesnake Camp filed into Sawyer's Dam, they found that their mysterious friends had disappeared, although they met with a fraternal but subdued welcome from the general camp. But any approach to the subject of their visit, however, was received with a chilling disapproval. Did they not know that lawlessness of any kind, even under the rude mantle of frontier justice, was to be deprecated and scouted when a "means of salvation, a power of regeneration," such as was now sweeping over Sawyer's Dam, was at hand? Could they not induce this man who was to be violently deported to accompany them willingly to Sawyer's Dam and subject himself to the powerful influence of the "revival" then in full swing?

The Rattlesnake boys laughed bitterly, and described the man of whom they talked so lightly; but in vain. "It's no use, gentlemen," said a more worldly bystander, in a lower voice, "the camp-meetin's got a strong grip here, and betwixt you and me there ain't no wonder. For the man that runs it — the big preacher — has got new ways and methods that fetches the boys every time. He don't preach no cut-and-dried gospel; he don't carry around no slop-shop robes and clap 'em on you whether they fit or not; but he samples and measures the camp afore he wades into it. He scouts and examines; he ain't no mere Sunday preacher with a comfortable house and once-a-week church, but he gives up his days and nights to it, and makes his family work with him, and even sends 'em forward to explore the field. And he ain't no white-choker shadbelly either, but fits himself, like his gospel, to the men he works among. Ye ought to hear him afore you go. His tent is just out your way. I'll go with you."

Too dejected to offer any opposition, and perhaps a little curious to see this man who had unwittingly frustrated their design of lynching Bulger, they halted at the outer fringe of worshipers who packed the huge inclosure. They had not time to indulge their cynicisms over this swaying mass of emotional, half-thinking, and almost irresponsible beings, nor to detect any similarity between *their* extreme methods and the scheme of redemption they themselves were seeking, for in a few moments, apparently lifted to his feet on a wave of religious exultation, the famous preacher arose. The men of Rattlesnake gasped for breath.

It was Bulger!

But Briggs quickly recovered himself. "By what name," said he, turning passionately towards his guide, "does this man — this impostor — call himself here?"

"Baker."

"Baker?" echoed the Rattlesnake contingent.

"Baker?" repeated Lance Forester, with a ghastly smile.

"Yes," returned their guide. "You oughter know it too! For he sent his wife and daughters over, after his usual style, to sample your camp, a week ago! Come, now, what are you givin' us?"

IN THE TULES.

HE had never seen a steamboat in his
life. Born and reared in one of the Western Territories, far from a navigable river,
he had only known the "dug-out" or canoe
as a means of conveyance across the scant
streams whose fordable waters made even
those scarcely a necessity. The long, narrow, hooded wagon, drawn by swaying oxen,
known familiarly as a "prairie schooner,"
in which he journeyed across the plains to
California in '53, did not help his conception by that nautical figure. And when at
last he dropped upon the land of promise
through one of the Southern mountain passes
he halted all unconsciously upon the low
banks of a great yellow river amidst a tangled brake of strange, reed-like grasses that
were unknown to him. The river, broadening as it debouched through many channels
into a lordly bay, seemed to him the *ultima
thule* of his journeyings. Unyoking his
oxen on the edge of the luxuriant meadows

which blended with scarcely any line of de-
marcation into the great stream itself, he
found the prospect "good" according to his
lights and prairial experiences, and, con-
verting his halted wagon into a temporary
cabin, he resolved to rest here and "settle."

There was little difficulty in so doing.
The cultivated clearings he had passed were
few and far between; the land would be his
by discovery and occupation; his habits of
loneliness and self-reliance made him independent of neighbors. He took his first
meal in his new solitude under a spreading
willow, but so near his natural boundary
that the waters gurgled and oozed in the
reeds but a few feet from him. The sun
sank, deepening the gold of the river until it
might have been the stream of Pactolus itself.
But Martin Morse had no imagination; he
was not even a gold-seeker; he had simply
obeyed the roving instincts of the frontiersman in coming hither. The land was virgin
and unoccupied; it was his; he was alone.
These questions settled, he smoked his pipe
with less concern over his three thousand
miles' transference of habitation than the
man of cities who had moved into a next
street. When the sun sank, he rolled him-

self in his blankets in the wagon bed and went quietly to sleep.

But he was presently awakened by something which at first he could not determine to be a noise or an intangible sensation. It was a deep throbbing through the silence of the night — a pulsation that seemed even to be communicated to the rude bed whereon he lay. As it came nearer it separated itself into a labored, monotonous panting, continuous, but distinct from an equally monotonous but fainter beating of the waters, as if the whole track of the river were being coursed and trodden by a multitude of swiftly-trampling feet. A strange feeling took possession of him — half of fear, half of curious expectation. It was coming nearer. He rose, leaped hurriedly from the wagon, and ran to the bank. The night was dark; at first he saw nothing before him but the steel-black sky pierced with far-spaced, irregularly scattered stars. Then there seemed to be approaching him, from the left, another and more symmetrical constellation — a few red and blue stars high above the river, with three compact lines of larger planetary lights flashing towards him and apparently on his own level.

It was almost upon him; he involuntarily drew back as the strange phenomenon swept abreast of where he stood, and resolved itself into a dark yet airy bulk, whose vagueness, topped by enormous towers, was yet illuminated by those open squares of light that he had taken for stars, but which he saw now were brilliantly-lit windows.

Their vivid rays shot through the reeds and sent broad bands across the meadow, the stationary wagon, and the slumbering oxen. But all this was nothing to the inner life they disclosed through lifted curtains and open blinds, which was the crowning revelation of this strange and wonderful spectacle. Elegantly dressed men and women moved through brilliantly lit and elaborately gilt saloons; in one a banquet seemed to be spread, served by white-jacketed servants; in another were men playing cards around marble-topped tables; in another the light flashed back again from the mirrors and glistening glasses and decanters of a gorgeous refreshment saloon; in smaller openings there was the shy disclosure of dainty white curtains and velvet lounges of more intimate apartments.

Martin Morse stood enthralled and mystified. It was as if some invisible Asmodeus had revealed to this simple frontiersman a world of which he had never dreamed. It was *the* world — a world of which he knew nothing in his simple, rustic habits and profound Western isolation — sweeping by him with the rush of an unknown planet. In another moment it was gone; a shower of sparks shot up from one of the towers and fell all around him, and then vanished, even as he remembered the set piece of "Fourth of July" fireworks had vanished in his own rural town when he was a boy. The darkness fell with it too. But such was his utter absorption and breathless preoccupation that only a cold chill recalled him to himself, and he found he was standing mid-leg deep in the surge cast over the low banks by this passage of the first steamboat he had ever seen!

He waited for it the next night, when it appeared a little later from the opposite direction on its return trip. He watched it the next night and the next. Hereafter he never missed it, coming or going — whatever the hard and weary preoccupations of his new and lonely life. He felt he could not have slept without seeing it go by. Oddly enough, his interest and desire did not go further. Even had he the time and money to spend in a passage on the boat, and thus actively realize the great world of which he had only these rare glimpses, a certain proud, rustic shyness kept him from it. It was not *his* world; he could not affront the snubs that his ignorance and inexperience would have provoked, and he was dimly conscious, as so many of us are in our ignorance, that in mingling with it he would simply lose the easy privileges of alien criticism. For there was much that he did not understand, and some things that grated upon his lonely independence.

One night, a lighter one than those previous, he lingered a little longer in the moonlight to watch the phosphorescent wake of the retreating boat. Suddenly it struck him that there was a certain irregular splashing in the water, quite different from the regular, diagonally crossing surges that the boat swept upon the bank. Looking at it more intently, he saw a black object turning in the water like a porpoise, and then the unmistakable uplifting of a black arm in an unskillful swimmer's overhand stroke. It was a struggling man. But it was quickly evident that the current was too strong and the turbulence of the shallow water too great for his efforts. Without a moment's hesitation, clad as he was in only his shirt and trousers, Morse strode into the reeds, and the next moment, with a call of warning, was swimming towards the now wildly struggling figure. But, from some unknown reason, as Morse approached him nearer the man uttered some incoherent protest and desperately turned away, throwing off Morse's extended arm.

Attributing this only to the vague convulsions of a drowning man, Morse, a skilled swimmer, managed to clutch his shoulder, and propelled him at arm's length, still struggling, apparently with as much reluctance as incapacity, towards the bank. As their feet touched the reeds and slimy bottom the man's resistance ceased, and he lapsed quite listlessly in Morse's arms. Half lifting, half dragging his burden, he succeeded at last in gaining the strip of meadow, and deposited the unconscious man beneath the willow tree. Then he ran to his wagon for whiskey.

But, to his surprise, on his return the man was already sitting up and wringing

the water from his clothes. He then saw
for the first time, by the clear moonlight,
that the stranger was elegantly dressed and
of striking appearance, and was clearly a
part of that bright and fascinating world
which Morse had been contemplating in his
solitude. He eagerly took the proffered tin
cup and drank the whiskey. Then he rose
to his feet, staggered a few steps forward,
and glanced curiously around him at the
still motionless wagon, the few felled trees
and evidence of "clearing," and even at the
rude cabin of logs and canvas just beginning to rise from the ground a few paces
distant, and said, impatiently:—

"Where the devil am I?"

Morse hesitated. He was unable to name
the locality of his dwelling-place. He answered briefly:—

"On the right bank of the Sacramento."

The stranger turned upon him a look of
suspicion not unmingled with resentment.
"Oh!" he said, with ironical gravity, "and
I suppose that this water you picked me out
of was the Sacramento River. Thank you!"

Morse, with slow Western patience, explained that he had only settled there three
weeks ago, and the place had no name.

"What's your nearest town, then?"

"Thar ain't any. Thar's a blacksmith's shop and grocery at the cross-roads, twenty miles further on, but it's got no name as I've heard on."

The stranger's look of suspicion passed. "Well," he said, in an imperative fashion, which, however, seemed as much the result of habit as the occasion, "I want a horse, and mighty quick, too."

"H'aint got any."

"No horse? How did you get to this place?"

Morse pointed to the slumbering oxen.

The stranger again stared curiously at him. After a pause he said, with a half-pitying, half-humorous smile: "Pike — are n't you?"

Whether Morse did or did not know that this current California slang for a denizen of the bucolic West implied a certain contempt, he replied simply: —

"I'm from Pike County, Mizzouri."

"Well," said the stranger, resuming his impatient manner, "you must beg or steal a horse from your neighbors."

"Thar ain't any neighbor nearer than fifteen miles."

"Then send fifteen miles! Stop." He opened his still clinging shirt and drew out a belt pouch, which he threw to Morse. "There! there's two hundred and fifty dollars in that. Now, I want a horse. *Sabe?*"

"Thar ain't any one to send," said Morse, quietly.

"Do you mean to say you are all alone here?"

"Yes."

"And you fished me out — all by yourself?"

"Yes."

The stranger again examined him curiously. Then he suddenly stretched out his hand and grasped his companion's.

"All right; if you can't send, I reckon I can manage to walk over there to - morrow."

"I was goin' on to say," said Morse, simply, "that if you 'll lie by to-night, I 'll start over sun up, after puttin' out the cattle, and fetch you back a horse afore noon."

"That 's enough." He, however, remained looking curiously at Morse. "Did you never hear," he said, with a singular smile, "that it was about the meanest kind of luck that could happen to you to save a drowning man?"

"No," said Morse, simply. "I reckon it orter be the meanest if you *did n't.*"

"That depends upon the man you save," said the stranger, with the same ambiguous smile, "and whether the *saving* him is only putting things off. Look here," he added, with an abrupt return to his imperative style, "can't you give me some dry clothes?"

Morse brought him a pair of overalls and a "hickory shirt," well worn, but smelling strongly of a recent wash with coarse soap. The stranger put them on while his companion busied himself in collecting a pile of sticks and dry leaves.

"What's that for?" said the stranger, suddenly.

"A fire to dry your clothes."

The stranger calmly kicked the pile aside.

"Not any fire to-night if I know it," he said, brusquely. Before Morse could resent his quickly changing moods he continued, in another tone, dropping to an easy reclining position beneath the tree, "Now, tell me all about yourself, and what you are doing here."

Thus commanded, Morse patiently repeated his story from the time he had left his backwoods cabin to his selection of the river bank for a "location." He pointed out the rich quality of this alluvial bottom and its adaptability for the raising of stock, which he hoped soon to acquire. The stranger smiled grimly, raised himself to a sitting position, and, taking a penknife from his damp clothes, began to clean his nails in the bright moonlight — an occupation which made the simple Morse wander vaguely in his narration.

"And you don't know that this hole will give you chills and fever till you'll shake yourself out of your boots?"

Morse had lived before in aguish districts, and had no fear.

"And you never heard that some night the whole river will rise up and walk over you and your cabin and your stock?"

"No. For I reckon to move my shanty farther back."

The man shut up his penknife with a click and rose.

"If you've got to get up at sunrise, we'd better be turning in. I suppose you can give me a pair of blankets?"

Morse pointed to the wagon. "Thar's a

shakedown in the wagon bed; you kin lie there." Nevertheless he hesitated, and, with the inconsequence and abruptness of a shy man, continued the previous conversation.

"I should n't like to move far away, for them steamboats is pow'ful kempany o' nights. I never seed one afore I kem here," and then, with the inconsistency of a reserved man, and without a word of further preliminary, he launched into a confidential disclosure of his late experiences. The stranger listened with a singular interest and a quietly searching eye.

"Then you were watching the boat very closely just now when you saw me. What else did you see? Anything before that — before you saw me in the water?"

"No — the boat had got well off before I saw you at all."

"Ah," said the stranger. "Well, I 'm going to turn in." He walked to the wagon, mounted it, and by the time that Morse had reached it with his wet clothes he was already wrapped in the blankets. A moment later he seemed to be in a profound slumber.

It was only then, when his guest was lying helplessly at his mercy, that he began to realize his strange experiences. The domination of this man had been so complete that Morse, although by nature independent and self-reliant, had not permitted himself to question his right or to resent his rudeness. He had accepted his guest's careless or premeditated silence regarding the particulars of his accident as a matter of course, and had never dreamed of questioning him. That it was a natural accident of that great world so apart from his own experiences he did not doubt, and thought no more about it. The advent of the man himself was greater to him than the causes which brought him there. He was as yet quite unconscious of the complete fascination this mysterious stranger held over him, but he found himself shyly pleased with even the slight interest he had displayed in his affairs, and his hand felt yet warm and tingling from his sudden soft but expressive grasp, as if it had been a woman's. There is a simple intuition of friendship in some lonely, self-abstracted natures that is nearly akin to love at first sight. Even the audacities and insolence of this stranger affected Morse as he might have been touched and captivated by the coquetries or imperious-

ness of some bucolic virgin. And this reserved and shy frontiersman found himself
that night sleepless, and hovering with an
abashed timidity and consciousness around
the wagon that sheltered his guest, as if he
had been a very Corydon watching the
moonlit couch of some slumbering Ama-
ryllis.

He was off by daylight — after having
placed a rude breakfast by the side of the
still sleeping guest — and before mid-day
he had returned with a horse. When he
handed the stranger his pouch, less the
amount he had paid for the horse, the man
said curtly —

"What 's that for? "

"Your change. I paid only fifty dollars
for the horse."

The stranger regarded him with his peculiar smile. Then, replacing the pouch in
his belt, he shook Morse's hand again and
mounted the horse.

"So your name 's Martin Morse! Well
— good-by, Morsey! "

Morse hesitated. A blush rose to his
dark cheek. "You did n't tell me *your*
name," he said. "In case " —

"In case I 'm *wanted?* Well, you can

call me Captain Jack." He smiled, and, nodding his head, put spurs to his mustang and cantered away.

Morse did not do much work that day, falling into abstracted moods and living over his experiences of the previous night, until he fancied he could almost see his strange guest again. The narrow strip of meadow was haunted by him. There was the tree under which he had first placed him, and that was where he had seen him sitting up in his dripping but well-fitting clothes. In the rough garments he had worn and returned lingered a new scent of some delicate soap, overpowering the strong alkali flavor of his own. He was early by the river side, having a vague hope, he knew not why, that he should again see him and recognize him among the passengers. He was wading out among the reeds, in the faint light of the rising moon, recalling the exact spot where he had first seen the stranger, when he was suddenly startled by the rolling over in the water of some black object that had caught against the bank, but had been dislodged by his movements. To his horror it bore a faint resemblance to his first vision of the preceding night. But a second glance at the helplessly floating hair and bloated outline showed him that it was a *dead* man, and of a type and build far different from his former companion. There was a bruise upon his matted forehead and an enormous wound in his throat already washed bloodless, white, and waxen. An inexplicable fear came upon him, not at the sight of the corpse, for he had been in Indian massacres and had rescued bodies mutilated beyond recognition; but from some moral dread that, strangely enough, quickened and deepened with the far-off pant of the advancing steamboat. Scarcely knowing why, he dragged the body hurriedly ashore, concealing it in the reeds, as if he were disposing of the evidence of his own crime. Then, to his preposterous terror, he noticed that the panting of the steamboat and the beat of its paddles were "slowing" as the vague bulk came in sight, until a huge wave from the suddenly arrested wheels sent a surge like an enormous heartbeat pulsating through the sedge that half submerged him. The flashing of three or four lanterns on deck and the motionless line of lights abreast of him dazzled his eyes, but he knew that the low fringe of

willows hid his house and wagon completely
from view. A vague murmur of voices
from the deck was suddenly over-ridden by
a sharp order, and to his relief the slowly
revolving wheels again sent a pulsation
through the water, and the great fabric
moved solemnly away. A sense of relief
came over him, he knew not why, and he
was conscious that for the first time he had
not cared to look at the boat.

When the moon arose he again examined
the body, and took from its clothing a few
articles of identification and some papers of
formality and precision, which he vaguely
conjectured to be some law papers from
their resemblance to the phrasing of sher-
iffs' and electors' notices which he had seen
in the papers. He then buried the corpse
in a shallow trench, which he dug by the
light of the moon. He had no question of
responsibility; his pioneer training had not
included coroners' inquests in its experience;
in giving the body a speedy and secure
burial from predatory animals he did what
one frontiersman would do for another —
what he hoped might be done for *him*. If
his previous unaccountable feelings returned
occasionally, it was not from that; but

rather from some uneasiness in regard to his late guest's possible feelings, and a regret that he had not been here at the finding of the body. That it would in some way have explained his own accident he did not doubt.

The boat did not "slow up" the next night, but passed as usual; yet three or four days elapsed before he could look forward to its coming with his old extravagant and half-exalted curiosity — which was his nearest approach to imagination. He was then able to examine it more closely, for the appearance of the stranger whom he now began to call "his friend" in his verbal communings with himself — but whom he did not seem destined to again discover; until one day, to his astonishment, a couple of fine horses were brought to his clearing by a stock-drover. They had been "ordered" to be left there. In vain Morse expostulated and questioned.

"Your name's Martin Morse, ain't it?" said the drover, with business brusqueness; "and I reckon there ain't no other man o' that name around here?"

"No," said Morse.

"Well, then, they're *yours*."

"But who sent them?" insisted Morse. "What was his name, and where does he live?"

"I did n't know ez I was called upon to give the pedigree o' buyers," said the drover drily; "but the horses is ' Morgan,' you can bet your life." He grinned as he rode away.

That Captain Jack sent them, and that it was a natural prelude to his again visiting him, Morse did not doubt, and for a few days he lived in that dream. But Captain Jack did not come. The animals were of great service to him in "rounding up" the stock he now easily took in for pasturage, and saved him the necessity of having a partner or a hired man. The idea that this superior gentleman in fine clothes might ever appear to him in the former capacity had even flitted through his brain, but he had rejected it with a sigh. But the thought that, with luck and industry, he himself might, in course of time, approximate to Captain Jack's evident station, *did* occur to him, and was an incentive to energy. Yet it was quite distinct from the ordinary working man's ambition of wealth and state. It was only that it might make him more worthy of his friend. The great world was still as it had appeared to him in the passing boat — a thing to wonder at — to be above — and to criticise.

For all that, he prospered in his occupation. But one day he woke with listless limbs and feet that scarcely carried him through his daily labors. At night his listlessness changed to active pain and a feverishness that seemed to impel him towards the fateful river, as if his one aim in life was to drink up its waters and bathe in its yellow stream. But whenever he seemed to attempt it, strange dreams assailed him of dead bodies arising with swollen and distorted lips to touch his own as he strove to drink, or of his mysterious guest battling with him in its current, and driving him ashore. Again, when he essayed to bathe his parched and crackling limbs in its flood, he would be confronted with the dazzling lights of the motionless steamboat and the glare of stony eyes — until he fled in aimless terror. How long this lasted he knew not, until one morning he awoke in his new cabin with a strange man sitting by his bed and a negress in the doorway.

"You 've had a sharp attack of ' tule

fever,' " said the stranger, dropping Morse's listless wrist and answering his questioning eyes, "but you're all right now, and will pull through."

"Who are you?" stammered Morse feebly.

"Dr. Duchesne, of Sacramento."

"How did you come here?"

"I was ordered to come to you and bring a nurse, as you were alone. There she is." He pointed to the smiling negress.

" *Who* ordered you? "

The doctor smiled with professional tolerance. "One of your friends, of course."

"But what was his name?"

"Really, I don't remember. But don't distress yourself. He has settled for everything right royally. You have only to get strong now. My duty is ended, and I can safely leave you with the nurse. Only when you are strong again, I say — and *he* says — keep back farther from the river."

And that was all he knew. For even the nurse who attended him through the first days of his brief convalescence would tell him nothing more. He quickly got rid of her and resumed his work, for a new and strange phase of his simple, childish affec-

tion for his benefactor, partly superinduced
by his illness, was affecting him. He was
beginning to feel the pain of an unequal
friendship; he was dimly conscious that his
mysterious guest was only coldly returning
his hospitality and benefits, while holding
aloof from any association with him — and
indicating the immeasurable distance that
separated their future intercourse. He had
withheld any kind message or sympathetic
greeting; he had kept back even his *name*.
The shy, proud, ignorant heart of the frontiersman swelled beneath the fancied slight,
which left him helpless alike of reproach
or resentment. He could not return the
horses, although in a fit of childish indignation he had resolved not to use them; he
could not reimburse him for the doctor's
bill, although he had sent away the nurse.

He took a foolish satisfaction in not moving back from the river, with a faint hope
that his ignoring of Captain Jack's advice
might mysteriously be conveyed to him.
He even thought of selling out his location
and abandoning it, that he might escape the
cold surveillance of his heartless friend.
All this was undoubtedly childish — but
there is an irrepressible simplicity of youth

in all deep feeling, and the worldly inexperience of the frontiersman left him as innocent as a child. In this phase of his unrequited affection he even went so far as to seek some news of Captain Jack at Sacramento, and, following out his foolish quest, to even take the steamboat from thence to Stockton.

What happened to him then was perhaps the common experience of such natures. Once upon the boat the illusion of the great world it contained for him utterly vanished. He found it noisy, formal, insincere, and — had he ever understood or used the word in his limited vocabulary — *vulgar*. Rather, perhaps, it seemed to him that the prevailing sentiment and action of those who frequented it — and for whom it was built — were of a lower grade than his own. And, strangely enough, this gave him none of his former sense of critical superiority, but only of his own utter and complete isolation. He wandered in his rough frontiersman's clothes from deck to cabin, from airy galleries to long saloons, alone, unchallenged, unrecognized, as if he were again haunting it only in spirit, as he had so often done in his dreams.

His presence on the fringe of some voluble crowd caused no interruption; to him their speech was almost foreign in its allusions to things he did not understand, or, worse, seemed inconsistent with their eagerness and excitement. How different from all this were his old recollections of slowly oncoming teams, uplifted above the level horizon of the plains in his former wanderings; the few sauntering figures that met him as man to man, and exchanged the chronicle of the road; the record of Indian tracks; the finding of a spring; the discovery of pasturage, with the lazy, restful hospitality of the night! And how fierce here this continual struggle for dominance and existence, even in this lull of passage. For above all and through all he was conscious of the feverish haste of speed and exertion.

The boat trembled, vibrated, and shook with every stroke of the ponderous piston. The laughter of the crowd, the exchange of gossip and news, the banquet at the long table, the newspapers and books in the reading-room, even the luxurious couches in the state-rooms, were all dominated, thrilled, and pulsating with the perpetual throb of the demon of hurry and unrest. And when at last a horrible fascination dragged him into the engine-room, and he saw the cruel relentless machinery at work, he seemed to recognize and understand some intelligent but pitiless Moloch, who was dragging this feverish world at its heels.

Later he was seated in a corner of the hurricane deck, whence he could view the monotonous banks of the river; yet, perhaps by certain signs unobservable to others, he knew he was approaching his own locality. He knew that his cabin and clearing would be undiscernible behind the fringe of willows on the bank, but he already distinguished the points where a few cottonwoods struggled into a promontory of lighter foliage beyond them. Here voices fell upon his ear, and he was suddenly aware that two men had lazily crossed over from the other side of the boat, and were standing before him looking upon the bank.

"It was about here, I reckon," said one, listlessly, as if continuing a previous lagging conversation, "that it must have happened. For it was after we were making for the bend we 've just passed that the deputy, goin' to the state-room below us, found the door locked and the window open. But

both men — Jack Despard and Seth Hall,
the sheriff — were n't to be found. Not a
trace of 'em. The boat was searched, but
all for nothing. The idea is that the sheriff,
arter getting his prisoner comf'ble in the
state room, took off Jack's handcuffs and
locked the door; that Jack, who was mighty
desp'rate, bolted through the window into
the river, and the sheriff, who was no slouch,
arter him. Others allow — for the chairs
and things was all tossed about in the state-
room — that the two men clinched *thar*, and
Jack choked Hall and chucked him out, and
then slipped cl'ar into the water himself,
for the state-room window was just ahead of
the paddle-box, and the cap'n allows that
no man or men could fall afore the paddles
and live. Anyhow, that was all they ever
knew of it."

"And there was n't no trace of them
found?" said the second man, after a long
pause.

"No. Cap'n says them paddles would
hev' just snatched 'em and slung 'em round
and round and buried 'em 'way down in the
ooze of the river bed, with all the silt of the
current atop of 'em, and they might n't come
up for ages; or else the wheels might have

waltzed 'em 'way up to Sacramento until there was n't enough left of 'em to float, and dropped 'em when the boat stopped."

"It was a mighty fool risk for a man like Despard to take," resumed the second speaker as he turned away with a slight yawn.

"Bet your life! but he was desp'rate, and the sheriff had got him sure! And they *do* say that he was superstititious, like all them gamblers, and allowed that a man who was fixed to die by a rope or a pistol was n't to be washed out of life by water."

The two figures drifted lazily away, but Morse sat rigid and motionless. Yet, strange to say, only one idea came to him clearly out of this awful revelation — the thought that his friend was still true to him — and that his strange absence and mysterious silence were fully accounted for and explained. And with it came the more thrilling fancy that this man was alive now to *him* alone.

He was the sole custodian of his secret. The morality of the question, while it profoundly disturbed him, was rather in reference to its effect upon the chances of Captain Jack and the power it gave his enemies

than his own conscience.   He would rather
that his friend should have proven the proscribed outlaw who retained an unselfish
interest in him than the superior gentleman
who was coldly wiping out his gratitude.
He thought he understood now the reason
of his visitor's strange and varying moods
— even his bitter superstitious warning in
regard to the probable curse entailed upon
one who should save a drowning man.   Of
this he recked little; enough that he fancied
that Captain Jack's concern in his illness
was heightened by that fear, and this assurance of his protecting friendship thrilled
him with pleasure.

There was no reason now why he should
not at once go back to his farm, where, at
least, Captain Jack would always find him;
and he did so, returning on the same boat.
He was now fully recovered from his illness,
and calmer in mind; he redoubled his labors
to put himself in a position to help the mysterious fugitive when the time should come.
The remote farm should always be a haven
of refuge for him, and in this hope he for-
bore to take any outside help, remaining
solitary and alone, that Captain Jack's retreat should be inviolate.   And so the long,

dry season passed, the hay was gathered,
the pasturing herds sent home, and the first
rains, dimpling like shot the broadening surface of the river, were all that broke his
unending solitude. In this enforced attitude of waiting and expectancy he was exalted and strengthened by a new idea. He
was not a religious man, but, dimly remembering the exhortations of some camp-meeting of his boyhood, he conceived the idea
that he might have been selected to work
out the regeneration of Captain Jack.
What might not come of this meeting and
communing together in this lonely spot?
That anything was due to the memory of
the murdered sheriff, whose bones were rot-
ting in the trench that he daily but uncon-
cernedly passed, did not occur to him.
Perhaps his mind was not large enough for
the double consideration. Friendship and
love — and, for the matter of that, religion
— are eminently one-ideaed.

But one night he awakened with a start.
His hand, which was hanging out of his
bunk, was dabbling idly in water. He had
barely time to spring to his middle in what
seemed to be a slowly filling tank before the
door fell out as from that inward pressure,

and his whole shanty collapsed like a pack
of cards. But it fell outwards, the roof
sliding from over his head like a withdrawn
canopy; and he was swept from his feet
against it, and thence out into what might
have been another world! For the rain had
ceased, and the full moon revealed only one
vast, illimitable expanse of water! It was
not an overflow, but the whole rushing river
magnified and repeated a thousand times,
which, even as he gasped for breath and
clung to the roof, was bearing him away he
knew not whither. But it was bearing him
away upon its centre, for as he cast one
swift glance towards his meadows he saw
they were covered by the same sweeping
torrent, dotted with his sailing hay-ricks
and reaching to the wooded foothills. It
was the great flood of '54. In its awe-
inspiring completeness it might have seemed
to him the primeval Deluge.

As his frail raft swept under a cotton-
wood he caught at one of the overhanging
limbs, and, working his way desperately
along the bough, at last reached a secure
position in the fork of the tree. Here he
was for the moment safe. But the devasta-
tion viewed from this height was only the

more appalling. Every sign of his clearing, all evidence of his past year's industry, had disappeared. He was now conscious for the first time of the lowing of the few cattle he had kept, as, huddled together on a slight eminence, they one by one slipped over struggling into the flood. The shining bodies of his dead horses rolled by him as he gazed. The lower-lying limbs of the sycamore near him were bending with the burden of the lighter articles from his over-turned wagon and cabin which they had caught and retained, and a rake was securely lodged in a bough. The habitual solitude of his locality was now strangely invaded by drifting sheds, agricultural implements and fence rails from unknown and remote neigh-bors, and he could faintly hear the far-off calling of some unhappy farmer adrift upon a spar of his wrecked and shattered house. When day broke he was cold and hungry.

Hours passed in hopeless monotony, with no slackening or diminution of the waters. Even the drifts became less, and a vacant sea at last spread before him on which no-thing moved. An awful silence impressed him. In the afternoon rain again began to fall on this gray, nebulous expanse, until the whole world seemed made of aqueous vapor. He had but one idea now — the coming of the evening boat, and he would reserve his strength to swim to it. He did not know until later that it could no longer follow the old channel of the river, and passed far beyond his sight and hearing. With his disappointment and exposure that night came a return of his old fever. His limbs were alternately racked with pain or benumbed and lifeless. He could scarcely retain his position — at times he scarcely cared to — and speculated upon ending his sufferings by a quick plunge downwards. In other moments of lucid misery he was conscious of having wandered in his mind; of having seen the dead face of the murdered sheriff, washed out of his shallow grave by the flood, staring at him from the water; to this was added the hallucination of noises. He heard voices, his own name called by a voice he knew — Captain Jack's!

Suddenly he started, but in that fatal movement lost his balance and plunged downwards. But before the water closed above his head he had had a cruel glimpse of help near him; of a flashing light — of the black hull of a tug not many yards away

— of moving figures — the sensation of a sudden plunge following his own, the grip of a strong hand upon his collar, and — unconsciousness!

When he came to he was being lifted in a boat from the tug and rowed through the deserted streets of a large city, until he was taken in through the second-story window of a half-submerged hotel and cared for. But all his questions yielded only the information that the tug — a privately procured one, not belonging to the Public Relief Association — had been dispatched for him with special directions, by a man who acted as one of the crew, and who was the one who had plunged in for him at the last moment. The man had left the boat at Stockton. There was nothing more? Yes! — he had left a letter. Morse seized it feverishly. It contained only a few lines : —

"We are quits now. You are all right. I have saved *you* from drowning, and shifted the curse to my own shoulders. Good-by.

' CAPTAIN JACK.' "

The astounded man attempted to rise — to utter an exclamation — but fell back, unconscious.

Weeks passed before he was able to leave

his bed — and then only as an impoverished and physically shattered man. He had no means to re-stock the farm left bare by the subsiding water. A kindly train - packer offered him a situation as muleteer in a pack-train going to the mountains — for he knew tracks and passes and could ride. The mountains gave him back a little of the vigor he had lost in the river valley, but none of its dreams and ambitions. One day, while tracking a lost mule, he stopped to slake his thirst in a water-hole — all that the summer had left of a lonely mountain torrent. Enlarging the hole to give drink to his beast also, he was obliged to dislodge and throw out with the red soil some bits of honeycomb rock, which were so queer-looking and so heavy as to attract his attention. Two of the largest he took back to camp with him. They were gold! From the locality he took out a fortune. Nobody wondered. To the Californian's superstition it was perfectly natural. It was "nigger luck" — the luck of the stupid, the ignorant, the inexperienced, the non-seeker — the irony of the gods!

But the simple, bucolic nature that had sustained itself against temptation with patient industry and lonely self-concentration succumbed to rapidly acquired wealth. So it chanced that one day, with a crowd of excitement-loving spendthrifts and companions, he found himself on the outskirts of a lawless mountain town. An eager, frantic crowd had already assembled there — a desperado was to be lynched! Pushing his way through the crowd for a nearer view of the exciting spectacle, the changed and reckless Morse was stopped by armed men only at the foot of a cart, which upheld a quiet, determined man, who, with a rope around his neck, was scornfully surveying the mob, that held the other end of the rope drawn across the limb of a tree above him. The eyes of the doomed man caught those of Morse — his expression changed — a kindly smile lit his face — he bowed his proud head for the first time, with an easy gesture of farewell.

And then, with a cry, Morse threw himself upon the nearest armed guard, and a fierce struggle began. He had overpowered one adversary and seized another in his hopeless fight towards the cart when the half-astonished crowd felt that something must be done. It was done with a sharp report, the upward curl of smoke and the falling back of the guard as Morse staggered forward *free* — with a bullet in his heart. Yet even then he did not fall until he reached the cart, when he lapsed forward, dead, with his arms outstretched and his head at the doomed man's feet.

There was something so supreme and all-powerful in this hopeless act of devotion that the heart of the multitude thrilled and then recoiled aghast at its work, and a single word or a gesture from the doomed man himself would have set him free. But they say — and it is credibly recorded — that as Captain Jack Despard looked down upon the hopeless sacrifice at his feet his eyes blazed, and he flung upon the crowd a curse so awful and sweeping that, hardened as they were, their blood ran cold, and then leaped furiously to their cheeks.

"And now," he said, coolly tightening the rope around his neck with a jerk of his head — "Go on, and be d—d to you! I'm ready."

They did not hesitate this time. And Martin Morse and Captain Jack Despard were buried in the same grave.

A CONVERT OF THE MISSION.

THE largest tent of the Tasajara camp-
meeting was crowded to its utmost extent.
The excitement of that dense mass was at
its highest pitch. The Reverend Stephen
Masterton, the single erect, passionate figure of that confused medley of kneeling
worshipers, had reached the culminating
pitch of his irresistible exhortatory power.
Sighs and groans were beginning to respond
to his appeals, when the reverend brother
was seen to lurch heavily forward and fall
to the ground.

At first the effect was that of a part of
his performance; the groans redoubled, and
twenty or thirty brethren threw themselves
prostrate in humble imitation of the preacher.
But Sister Deborah Stokes, perhaps through
some special revelation of feminine intuition,
grasped the fallen man, tore loose his black
silk necktie, and dragged him free of the
struggling, frantic crowd whose paroxysms
he had just evoked. Howbeit he was pale

and unconscious, and unable to continue the service. Even the next day, when he had slightly recovered, it was found that any attempt to renew his fervid exhortations produced the same disastrous result.

A council was hurriedly held by the elders. In spite of the energetic protests of Sister Stokes, it was held that the Lord "was wrestlin' with his sperrit," and he was subjected to the same extraordinary treatment from the whole congregation that he himself had applied to *them*. Propped up pale and trembling in the "Mourners' Bench" by two brethren, he was "striven with," exhorted, prayed over, and admonished, until insensibility mercifully succeeded convulsions. Spiritual therapeutics having failed, he was turned over to the weak and carnal nursing of "women folk." But after a month of incapacity he was obliged to yield to "the flesh," and, in the local dialect, "to use a doctor."

It so chanced that the medical practitioner of the district was a man of large experience, of military training, and plain speech. When, therefore, he one day found in his surgery a man of rude Western type, strong-limbed and sun-burned, but trembling, hesitating and neurotic in movement, after listening to his symptoms gravely, he asked, abruptly: "And how much are you drinking now?"

"I am a life-long abstainer," stammered his patient in quivering indignation. But this was followed by another question so frankly appalling to the hearer that he staggered to his feet.

"I 'm Stephen Masterton — known of men as a circuit preacher, of the Northern California district," he thundered — "and an enemy of the flesh in all its forms."

"I beg your pardon," responded Dr. Duchesne, grimly, "but as you are suffering from excessive and repeated excitation of the nervous system, and the depression following prolonged artificial exaltation — it makes little difference whether the cause be spiritual, as long as there is a certain physical effect upon your *body* — which I believe you have brought to me to cure. Now — as to diet? you look all wrong there."

"My food is of the simplest — I have no hankering for flesh-pots," responded the patient.

"I suppose you call saleratus bread and salt pork and flapjacks *simple?*" said the doctor, coolly; "they are *common* enough, and if you were working with your muscles instead of your nerves in that frame of yours they might not hurt you; but you are suffering as much from eating more than you can digest as the veriest gourmand. You must stop all that. Go down to a quiet watering-place for two months." . . .

"*I* go to a watering-place?" interrupted Masterton; "to the haunt of the idle, the frivolous and wanton — never!"

"Well, I'm not particular about a ' watering - place,'" said the doctor, with a shrug, "although a little idleness and frivolity with different food wouldn't hurt you — but you must go somewhere and change your habits and mode of life *completely*. I will find you some sleepy old Spanish town in the southern country where you can rest and diet. If this is distasteful to you," he continued, grimly, "you can always call it ' a trial.'"

Stephen Masterton may have thought it so when, a week later, he found himself issuing from a rocky gorge into a rough, badly paved, hilly street, which seemed to be only a continuation of the mountain road itself. It broadened suddenly into a square or plaza, flanked on each side by an irregular row of yellowing adobe houses, with the inevitable verandahed tienda in each corner, and the solitary, galleried fonda, with a half Moorish archway leading into an inner patio or courtyard in the centre.

The whole street stopped as usual at the very door of the Mission church, a few hundred yards further on, and under the shadow of the two belfry towers at each angle of the façade, as if this were the *ultima thule* of every traveler. But all that the eye rested on was ruined, worn, and crumbling. The adobe houses were cracked by the incessant sunshine of the half-year long summer, or the more intermittent earthquake shock; the paved courtyard of the fonda was so uneven and sunken in the centre that the lumbering wagon and faded diligencia stood on an incline, and the mules with difficulty kept their footing while being unladen; the whitened plaster had fallen from the feet of the two pillars that flanked the Mission doorway, like bandages from a gouty limb, leaving the reddish core of adobe visible; there were apparently as many broken tiles in the streets and alleys as there were on the heavy red

roofs that everywhere asserted themselves
— and even seemed to slide down the crumbling walls to the ground. There were
hopeless gaps in grille and grating of doorways and windows, where the iron bars had
dropped helplessly out, or were bent at different angles. The walls of the peaceful
Mission garden and the warlike presidio
were alike lost in the escalading vines or
leveled by the pushing boughs of gnarled
pear and olive trees that now surmounted
them. The dust lay thick and impalpable
in hollow and gutter, and rose in little va-
pory clouds with a soft detonation at every
stroke of his horse's hoofs. Over all this
dust and ruin, idleness seemed to reign supreme. From the velvet-jacketed figures
lounging motionless in the shadows of the
open doorways — so motionless that only
the lazy drift of cigarette smoke betokened
their breathing — to the reclining peons in
the shade of a catalpa, or the squatting In-
dians in the arroyo — all was sloth and dirt.

The Rev. Stephen Masterton felt his
throat swell with his old exhortative indignation. A gaudy yellow fan waved languidly in front of a black rose-crested head
at a white-curtained window. He knew he

was stifling with righteous wrath, and clapped his spurs to his horse.

Nevertheless, in a few days, by the aid of a letter to the innkeeper, he was installed in a dilapidated adobe house, not unlike those he had seen, but situated in the outskirts, and overlooking the garden and part of the refectory of the old Mission. It had even a small garden of its own — if a strip of hot wall, overburdened with yellow and white roses, a dozen straggling callas, a bank of heliotrope, and an almond tree could be called a garden. It had an open doorway, but so heavily recessed in the thick walls that it preserved seclusion, a sitting-room, and an alcoved bed-room with deep embrasured windows, that, however, excluded the unwinking sunlight and kept an even monotone of shade.

Strange to say, he found it cool, restful, and, in spite of the dust, absolutely clean, and, but for the scent of heliotrope, entirely inodorous. The dry air seemed to dissipate all noxious emanations and decay — the very dust itself in its fine impalpability was volatile with a spice-like piquancy, and left no stain.

A wrinkled Indian woman, brown and

veined like a tobacco leaf, ministered to his
simple wants. But these wants had also
been regulated by Dr. Duchesne. He found
himself, with some grave doubts of his effem-
inacy, breakfasting on a single cup of
chocolate instead of his usual bowl of mo-
lasses-sweetened coffee; crumbling a crisp
tortilla instead of the heavy saleratus bread,
greasy flapjack, or the lard-fried steak,
and, more wonderful still, completing his
repast with purple grapes from the Mission
wall. He could not deny that it was simple
— that it was even refreshing and consistent
with the climate and his surroundings. On
the other hand, it was the frugal diet of the
commonest peasant — and were not those
peons slothful idolators?

At the end of the week — his correspondence being also restricted by his doctor to
a few lines to himself regarding his progress
— he wrote to that adviser: —

"The trembling and unquiet has almost
ceased; I have less nightly turmoil and visions; my carnal appetite seems to be amply
mollified and soothed by these viands, whatever may be their ultimate effect upon the
weakness of our common sinful nature.
But I should not be truthful to you if I did

not warn you that I am viewing with the deepest spiritual concern a decided tendency towards sloth, and a folding of the hands over matters that often, I fear, are spiritual as well as temporal. I would ask you to consider, in a spirit of love, if it be not wise to rouse my apathetic flesh, so as to strive, even with the feeblest exhortations — against this sloth in others — if only to keep one's self from falling into the pit of easy indulgence."

What answer he received is not known, but it is to be presumed that he kept loyal faith with his physician, and gave himself up to simple walks and rides and occasional meditation. His solitude was not broken upon; curiosity was too active a vice, and induced too much exertion for his indolent neighbors, and the Americano's basking seclusion, though unlike the habits of his countrymen, did not affect them. The shopkeeper and innkeeper saluted him always with a profound courtesy which awakened his slight resentment, partly because he was conscious that it was grateful to him, and partly that he felt he ought to have provoked in them a less satisfied condition.

Once, when he had unwittingly passed

the confines of his own garden, through a
gap in the Mission orchard, a lissome,
black-coated shadow slipped past him with
an obeisance so profound and gentle that he
was startled at first into an awkward imitation of it himself, and then into an angry
self-examination. He knew that he loathed
that long-skirted, woman-like garment, that
dangling, ostentatious symbol, that air of
secrecy and mystery, and he inflated his
chest above his loosely tied cravat and un-
buttoned waistcoat with a contrasted sense
of freedom. But he was conscious the next
day of weakly avoiding a recurrence of this
meeting, and in his self-examination put it
down to his self-disciplined observance of
his doctor's orders. But when he was
strong again, and fitted for his Master's
work, how strenuously he should improve
the occasion this gave him of attacking the
Scarlet Woman among her slaves and worshipers!

His afternoon meditations and the perusal
of his only book — the Bible — were regularly broken in upon at about sunset by two
or three strokes from the cracked bell that
hung in the open belfry which reared itself
beyond the gnarled pear trees. He could

not say that it was aggressive or persistent, like his own church bells, nor that it even expressed to him any religious sentiment. Moreover, it was not a "Sabbath" bell, but a *daily* one, and even then seemed to be only a signal to ears easily responsive, rather than a stern reminder. And the hour was always a singularly witching one.

It was when the sun had slipped from the glaring red roofs, and the yellowing adobe of the Mission walls and the tall ranks of wild oats on the hillside were all of the one color of old gold. It was when the quivering heat of the arroyo and dusty expanse of plaza was blending with the soft breath of the sea fog that crept through the clefts of the coast range, until a refreshing balm seemed to fall like a benediction on all nature. It was when the trade-wind-swept and irritated surfaces of the rocky gorge beyond were soothed with clinging vapors; when the pines above no longer rocked monotonously, and the great undulating sea of the wild oat plains had gone down and was at rest. It was at this hour, one afternoon, that, with the released scents of the garden, there came to him a strange and subtle perfume that was new to his senses. He laid aside his book, went into the garden, and, half-unconscious of his trespass, passed through the Mission orchard and thence into the little churchyard beside the church.

Looking at the strange inscriptions in an unfamiliar tongue, he was singularly touched with the few cheap memorials lying upon the graves — like childish toys — and for the moment overlooked the papistic emblems that accompanied them. It struck him vaguely that Death, the common leveler, had made even the symbols of a faith eternal inferior to those simple records of undying memory and affection, and he was for a moment startled into doubt.

He walked to the door of the church: to his surprise it was open. Standing upon the threshold he glanced inside, and stood for a moment utterly bewildered. In a man of refined taste and education that bizarre and highly colored interior would have only provoked a smile or shrug; to Stephen Masterton's highly emotional nature, but artistic inexperience, strangely enough it was profoundly impressive. The heavily timbered, roughly hewn roof, barred with alternate bands of blue and Indian red, the crimson hangings, the gold and

black draperies, affected this religious back-
woodsman exactly as they were designed to
affect the heathen and acolytes for whose
conversion the temple had been reared. He
could scarcely take his eyes from the tinsel-
crowned Mother of Heaven, resplendent in
white and gold and glittering with jewels;
the radiant shield before the Host, illuminated by tall spectral candles in the mysterious obscurity of the altar, dazzled him
like the rayed disk of the setting sun.

A gentle murmur, as of the distant sea,
came from the altar. In his naïve bewil-
derment he had not seen the few kneeling
figures in the shadow of column and aisle;
it was not until a man, whom he recognized
as a muleteer he had seen that afternoon
gambling and drinking in the fonda, slipped
by him like a shadow and sank upon his
knees in the centre of the aisle that he realized the overpowering truth.

He, Stephen Masterton, was looking upon
some rite of Popish idolatry! He was turning quickly away when the keeper of the
tienda — a man of sloth and sin — gently
approached him from the shadow of a column with a mute gesture, which he took to
be one of invitation. A fierce protest of

scorn and indignation swelled to his throat, but died upon his lips. Yet he had strength enough to erect his gaunt emaciated figure, throwing out his long arms and extended palms in the attitude of defiant exorcism, and then rush swiftly from the church. As he did so he thought he saw a faint smile cross the shopkeeper's face, and a whispered exchange of words with a neighboring worshiper of more exalted appearance came to his ears. But it was not intelligible to his comprehension.

The next day he wrote to his doctor in that quaint grandiloquence of written speech with which the half-educated man balances the slips of his colloquial phrasing: —

"Do not let the purgation of my flesh be unduly protracted. What with the sloth and idolatries of Baal and Ashteroth, which I see daily around me, I feel that without a protest not only the flesh but the spirit is mortified. But my bodily strength is mercifully returning, and I found myself yesterday able to take a long ride at that hour which they here keep sacred for an idolatrous rite, under the beautiful name of 'The Angelus.' Thus do they bear false witness to Him! Can you tell me the

meaning of the Spanish words, ' Don Key-
hotter?' I am ignorant of these sensuous
Southern languages, and am aware that this
is not the correct spelling, but I have striven
to give the phonetic equivalent. It was
used, I am inclined to think, in reference
to *myself*, by an idolater.

"P. S. — You need not trouble yourself.
I have just ascertained that the words in
question were simply the title of an idle
novel, and, of course, could not possibly
refer to *me*."

Howbeit it was as "Don Quixote" — that
is, the common Spaniard's conception of the
Knight of La Mancha, merely the simple
fanatic and madman — that Mr. Stephen
Masterton ever after rode all unconsciously
through the streets of the Mission, amid the
half-pitying, half-smiling glances of the
people.

In spite of his meditations, his single
volume, and his habit of retiring early, he
found his evenings were growing lonely and
tedious. He missed the prayer - meeting,
and, above all, the hymns. He had a fine
baritone voice, sympathetic, as may be imagined, but not cultivated. One night, in
the seclusion of his garden, and secure in

his distance from other dwellings, he raised his voice in a familiar camp-meeting hymn with a strong Covenanter's ring in the chorus. Growing bolder as he went on, he at last filled the quiet night with the strenuous sweep of his chant. Surprised at his own fervor, he paused for a moment, listening, half-frightened, half-ashamed of his outbreak. But there was only the trilling of the night wind in the leaves, or the far-off yelp of a coyote.

For a moment he thought he heard the metallic twang of a stringed instrument in the Mission garden beyond his own, and remembered his contiguity to the church with a stir of defiance. But he was relieved, nevertheless. His pent-up emotion had found vent, and without the nervous excitement that had followed his old exaltation. That night he slept better. He had found the Lord again — with Psalmody!

The next evening he chanced upon a softer hymn of the same simplicity, but with a vein of human tenderness in its aspirations, which his more hopeful mood gently rendered. At the conclusion of the first verse he was, however, distinctly conscious of being followed by the same twanging

sound he had heard on the previous night,
and which even his untutored ear could recognize as an attempt to accompany him.
But before he had finished the second verse
the unknown player, after an ingenious but
ineffectual essay to grasp the right chord,
abandoned it with an impatient and almost
pettish flourish, and a loud bang upon the
sounding-board of the unseen instrument.
Masterton finished it alone.

With his curiosity excited, however, he
tried to discover the locality of the hidden
player. The sound evidently came from
the Mission garden; but in his ignorance of
the language he could not even interrogate
his Indian housekeeper. On the third
night, however, his hymn was uninterrupted
by any sound from the former musician.
A sense of disappointment, he knew not
why, came over him. The kindly overture
of the unseen player had been a relief to his
loneliness. Yet he had barely concluded
the hymn when the familiar sound again
struck his ears. But this time the musician
played boldly, confidently, and with a singular skill on the instrument.

The brilliant prelude over, to his entire
surprise and some confusion, a soprano

voice, high, childish, but infinitely quaint
and fascinating, was mischievously uplifted.
But alas! even to his ears, ignorant of the
language, it was very clearly a song of levity and wantonness, of freedom and license,
of coquetry and incitement! Yet such was
its fascination that he fancied it was re-
claimed by the delightful childlike and innocent expression of the singer.

Enough that this tall, gaunt, broad-shoul-
dered man arose, and, overcome by a curiosity almost as childlike, slipped into the
garden and glided with an Indian softness
of tread towards the voice. The moon shone
full upon the ruined Mission wall tipped
with clusters of dark foliage. Half hiding,
half mingling with one of them — an indis-
tinct bulk of light-colored huddled fleeces
like an extravagant bird's nest — hung the
unknown musician. So intent was the performer's preoccupation that Masterton actually reached the base of the wall immediately
below the figure without attracting its attention. But his foot slipped on the crumbling
débris with a snapping of dry twigs. There
was a quick little cry from above. He had
barely time to recover his position before
the singer, impulsively leaning over the

parapet, had lost hers, and fell outwards. But Masterton was tall, alert, and self-possessed, and threw out his long arms. The next moment they were full of soft flounces, a struggling figure was against his breast, and a woman's frightened little hands around his neck. But he had broken her fall, and almost instantly, yet with infinite gentleness, he released her unharmed, with hardly her crisp flounces crumpled, in an upright position against the wall. Even her guitar, still hanging from her shoulder by a yellow ribbon, had bounded elastic and resounding against the wall, but lay intact at her satin-slippered feet. She caught it up with another quick little cry, but this time more of sauciness than fear, and drew her little hand across its strings, half defiantly.

"I hope you are not hurt?" said the circuit preacher, gravely.

She broke into a laugh so silvery that he thought it no extravagance to liken it to the moonbeams that played over her made audible. She was lithe, yet plump; barred with black and yellow and small waisted like a pretty wasp. Her complexion in that light was a sheen of pearl satin that made her eyes blacker and her little mouth redder than any other color could. She was small, but, remembering the fourteen-year-old wife of the shopkeeper, he felt that, for all her childish voice and features, she was a grown woman, and a sudden shyness took hold of him.

But she looked pertly in his face, stood her guitar upright before her, and put her hands behind her back as she leaned saucily against the wall and shrugged her shoulders.

"It was the fault of you," she said, in a broken English that seemed as much infantine as foreign. "What for you not remain to yourself in your own *casa?* So it come. You creep so — in the dark — and shake my wall, and I fall. And she," pointing to the guitar, "is a'most broke! And for all thees I have only make to you a serenade. Ingrate!"

"I beg your pardon," said Masterton quickly, "but I was curious. I thought I might help you, and " —

"Make yourself another cat on the wall, eh? No; one is enough, thank you!"

A frown lowered on Masterton's brow. "You don't understand me," he said, bluntly. "I did not know *who* was here."

"Ah, bueno! Then it is Pepita Ramirez,

you see," she said, tapping her bodice with
one little finger, "all the same; the niece
from Manuel Garcia, who keeps the Mission
garden and lif there. And you?"

"My name is Masterton."

"How mooch?"

"Masterton," he repeated.

She tried to pronounce it once or twice
desperately, and then shook her little head
so violently that a yellow rose fastened over
her ear fell to the ground. But she did not
heed it, nor the fact that Masterton had
picked it up.

"Ah, I cannot!" she said, poutingly.
"It is as deefeecult to make go as my guitar
with your serenade."

"Can you not say ' Stephen Masterton '?"
he asked, more gently, with a returning and
forgiving sense of her childishness.

"Es-stefen? Ah, *Esteban!* Yes; Don
Esteban! Bueno! Then, Don Esteban,
what for you sink so melank-olly one night,
and one night so fierce? The melank-olly,
he ees not so bad; but the fierce — ah! he
is weeked! Ess it how the Americano make
always his serenade?"

Masterton's brow again darkened. And
his hymn of exultation had been mistaken

by these people — by this — this wanton child!

"It was no serenade," he replied, curtly; "it was in praise of the Lord!"

"Of how mooch?"

"Of the Lord of Hosts — of the Almighty in Heaven." He lifted his long arms reverently on high.

"Oh!" she said, with a frightened look, slightly edging away from the wall. At a secure distance she stopped. "Then you are a soldier, Don Esteban?"

"No!"

"Then what for you sink ' I am a soldier of the Lord,' and you will make die ' in His army?' Oh, yes; you have said." She gathered up her guitar tightly under her arm, shook her small finger at him gravely, and said, "You are a hoombog, Don Esteban; good a' night," and began to glide away.

"One moment, Miss — Miss Ramirez," called Masterton. "I — that is you — you have — forgotten your rose," he added, feebly, holding up the flower. She halted.

"Ah, yes; he have drop, you have pick him up, he is yours. *I* have drop, you have pick *me* up, but I am *not* yours. Good a' night, *Comandante* Don Esteban!"

With a light laugh she ran along beside the wall for a little distance, suddenly leaped up and disappeared in one of the largest gaps in its ruined and helpless structure. Stephen Masterton gazed after her stupidly, still holding the rose in his hand. Then he threw it away and re-entered his home.

Lighting his candle, he undressed himself, prayed fervently — so fervently that all remembrance of the idle, foolish incident was wiped from his mind, and went to bed. He slept well and dreamlessly. The next morning, when his thoughts recurred to the previous night, this seemed to him a token that he had not deviated from his spiritual integrity; it did not occur to him that the thought itself was a tacit suspicion.

So his feet quite easily sought the garden again in the early sunshine, even to the wall where she had stood. But he had not taken into account the vivifying freshness of the morning, the renewed promise of life and resurrection in the pulsing air and potent sunlight, and as he stood there he seemed to see the figure of the young girl again leaning against the wall in all the charm of her irrepressible and innocent youth. More than that, he found the whole scene re-enact-

ing itself before him; the nebulous drapery
half hidden in the foliage, the cry and the
fall; the momentary soft contact of the
girl's figure against his own, the clinging
arms around his neck, the brush and fra-
grance of her flounces — all this came back
to him with a strength he had *not* felt when
it occurred.

He was turning hurriedly away when his
eyes fell upon the yellow rose still lying in
the débris where he had thrown it — but
still pure, fresh, and unfaded. He picked
it up again, with a singular fancy that it
was the girl herself, and carried it into the
house.

As he placed it half shyly in a glass on
his table a wonderful thought occurred to
him. Was not the episode of last night a
special providence? Was not that young
girl, wayward and childlike, a mere neo-
phyte in her idolatrous religion, as yet un-
steeped in sloth and ignorance, presented
to him as a brand to be snatched from the
burning? Was not this the opportunity of
conversion he had longed for; — this the
chance of exercising his gifts of exhortation,
that he had been hiding in the napkin of
solitude and seclusion? Nay, was not all

this *predestined?* His illness, his conse-
quent exile to this land of false gods — this
contiguity to the Mission — was not all this
part of a supremely ordered plan for the
girl's salvation — and was *he* not elected
and ordained for that service? Nay, more,
was not the girl herself a mere unconscious
instrument in the hands of a higher power;
was not her voluntary attempt to accompany
him in his devotional exercise a vague stirring of that predestined force within her?
Was not even that wantonness and frivolity
contrasted with her childishness — which he
had at first misunderstood — the stirrings of
the flesh and the spirit, and was he to abandon her in that struggle of good and evil?

He lifted his bowed head, that had been
resting on his arm before the little flower
on the table — as if it were a shrine — with
a flash of resolve in his blue eyes. The
wrinkled Concepcion coming to her duties
in the morning scarcely recognized her
gloomily abstracted master in this transfig-
ured man. He looked ten years younger.

She met his greeting, and the few direct
inquiries that his new resolve enabled him
to make more freely, with some information — which a later talk with the shop-

keeper, who had a fuller English vocabulary, confirmed in detail.

"Yes! truly this was a niece of the Mission gardener, who lived with her uncle in the ruined wing of the presidio. She had taken her first communion four years ago. Ah, yes, she was a great musician, and could play on the organ. And the guitar, ah, yes — of a certainty. She was gay, and flirted with the caballeros, young and old, but she cared not for any."

Whatever satisfaction this latter statement gave Masterton, he believed it was because the absence of any disturbing worldly affection would make her an easier convert.

But how continue this chance acquaintance and effect her conversion? For the first time Masterton realized the value of expediency; while his whole nature impelled him to frankly and publicly seek her society and openly exhort her, he knew that this was impossible; still more, he remembered her unmistakable fright at his first expression of faith; he must "be wise as the serpent and harmless as the dove." He must work upon her soul alone, and secretly. He, who would have shrunk from any clandestine association with a girl from mere

human affection, saw no wrong in a covert
intimacy for the purpose of religious salvation. Ignorant as he was of the ways of
the world, and inexperienced in the usages
of society, he began to plan methods of
secretly meeting her with all the intrigue of
a gallant. The perspicacity as well as the
intuition of a true lover had descended upon
him in this effort of mere spiritual conquest.

Armed with his information and a few
Spanish words, he took the yellow Concepcion aside and gravely suborned her to carry
a note to be delivered secretly to Miss Ramirez. To his great relief and some surprise the old woman grinned with intelligence, and her withered hand closed with a
certain familiar dexterity over the epistle
and the accompanying gratuity. To a man
less naïvely one-ideaed it might have awakened some suspicion; but to the more sanguine hopefulness of Masterton it only suggested the fancy that Concepcion herself
might prove to be open to conversion, and
that he should in due season attempt *her*
salvation also. But that would be later.
For Concepcion was always with him and
accessible; the girl was not.

The note, which had cost him some labor

of composition, simple and almost business-like as was the result, ran as follows: —

"I wish to see you upon some matter of grave concern to yourself. Will you oblige me by coming again to the wall of the Mission to-night at early candle-light? It would avert worldly suspicion if you brought also your guitar."

The afternoon dragged slowly on; Concepcion returned; she had, with great difficulty, managed to see the Señorita, but not alone; she had, however, slipped the note into her hand, not daring to wait for an answer.

In his first hopefulness Masterton did not doubt what the answer would be, but as evening approached he grew concerned as to the girl's opportunities of coming, and regretted that he had not given her a choice of time.

Before his evening meal was finished he began to fear for her willingness, and doubt the potency of his note. He was accustomed to exhort *orally* — perhaps he ought to have waited for the chance of *speaking* to her directly without writing.

When the moon rose he was already in the garden. Lingering at first in the shadow

of an olive tree, he waited until the moonbeams fell on the wall and its crests of foliage. But nothing moved among that ebony
tracery; his ear was strained for the familiar tinkle of the guitar — all was silent.
As the moon rose higher he at last boldly
walked to the wall, and listened for any
movement on the other side of it. But
nothing stirred. She was evidently *not*
coming — his note had failed.

He was turning away sadly, but as he
faced his home again he heard a light laugh
beside him. He stopped. A black shadow
stepped out from beneath his own almond
tree. He started, when, with a gesture
that seemed familiar to him, the upper part
of the shadow seemed to fall away with a
long black mantilla and the face of the
young girl was revealed.

He could see now that she was clad in
black lace from head to foot. She looked
taller, older, and he fancied even prettier
than before. A sudden doubt of his ability
to impress her, a swift realization of all the
difficulties of the attempt, and, for the
first time, perhaps, a dim perception of the
incongruity of the situation came over
him.

"I was looking for you on the wall," he stammered.

"Madre de Dios !" she retorted, with a laugh and her old audacity, "you would that I shall *always* hang there, and drop upon you like a pear when you shake the tree? No!"

"You have n't brought your guitar," he continued, still more awkwardly, as he noticed that she held only a long black fan in her hand.

"For why? You would that I *play* it, and when my uncle say ' Where go Pepita? She is loss,' some one shall say, ' Oh! I have hear her tink-a-tink in the garden of the Americano, who lif alone.' And then — it ess finish!"

Masterton began to feel exceedingly uncomfortable. There was something in this situation that he had not dreamed of. But with the persistency of an awkward man he went on.

"But you played on the wall the other night, and tried to accompany me."

"But that was lass night and on the wall. I had not speak to you, you had not speak to me. You had not sent me the leetle note by your peon." She stopped, and suddenly opening her fan before her face, so that only her mischievous eyes were visible, added: "You had not asked me then to come to hear you make lof to me, Don Esteban. That is the difference."

The circuit preacher felt the blood rush to his face. Anger, shame, mortification, remorse, and fear alternately strove with him, but above all and through all he was conscious of a sharp, exquisite pleasure — that frightened him still more. Yet he managed to exclaim: —

"No! no! You cannot think me capable of such a cowardly trick?"

The girl started, more at the unmistakable sincerity of his utterance than at the words, whose full meaning she may have only imperfectly caught.

"A treek? A treek?" she slowly and wonderingly repeated. Then suddenly, as if comprehending him, she turned her round black eyes full upon him and dropped her fan from her face.

"And *what* for you ask me to come here then?"

"I wanted to talk with you," he began, "on far more serious matters. I wished to" — but he stopped. He could not address this quaint child-woman, staring at him in black-eyed wonder, in either the measured or the impetuous terms with which he would have exhorted a maturer responsible being. He made a step towards her; she drew back, striking at his extended hand half impatiently, half mischievously with her fan.

He flushed — and then burst out bluntly, "I want to talk with you about your soul."

"My what?"

"Your immortal soul, unhappy girl."

"What have you to make with that? Are you a devil?" Her eyes grew rounder, though she faced him boldly.

"I am a Minister of the Gospel," he said, in hurried entreaty. "You must hear me for a moment. I would save your soul."

"My immortal soul lif with the Padre at the Mission — you moost seek her there! My mortal *body*," she added, with a mischievous smile, "say to you, ' good a' night, Don Esteban.' " She dropped him a little courtesy and — ran away.

"One moment, Miss Ramirez," said Masterton, eagerly; but she had already slipped beyond his reach. He saw her little black figure passing swiftly beside the moonlit wall, saw it suddenly slide into a shadowy fissure, and vanish.

In his blank disappointment he could not bear to reënter the house he had left so sanguinely a few moments before, but walked moodily in the garden. His discomfiture was the more complete since he felt that his defeat was owing to some mistake in his methods, and not the incorrigibility of his subject.

Was it not a spiritual weakness in him to have resented so sharply the girl's imputation that he wished to make love to her? He should have borne it as Christians had even before now borne slander and false testimony for their faith! He might even have *accepted* it, and let the triumph of her conversion in the end prove his innocence. Or was his purpose incompatible with that sisterly affection he had so often preached to the women of his flock? He might have taken her hand, and called her "Sister Pepita," even as he had called Deborah "Sister." He recalled the fact that he had for an instant held her struggling in his arms: he remembered the thrill that the recollection had caused him, and somehow it now sent a burning blush across his face. He hurried back into the house.

The next day a thousand wild ideas took the place of his former settled resolution. He would seek the Padre, this custodian of the young girl's soul; he would convince *him* of his error, or beseech him to give him an equal access to her spirit! He would seek the uncle of the girl, and work upon his feelings.

Then for three or four days he resolved to put the young girl from his mind, trusting after the fashion of his kind for some special revelation from a supreme source as an indication for his conduct. This revelation presently occurred, as it is apt to occur when wanted.

One evening his heart leaped at the familiar sound of Pepita's guitar in the distance. Whatever his ultimate intention now, he hurriedly ran into the garden. The sound came from the former direction, but as he unhesitatingly approached the Mission wall, he could see that she was not upon it, and as the notes of her guitar were struck again, he knew that they came from the other side. But the chords were a prelude to one of his own hymns, and he stood entranced as her sweet, child-like voice rose with the very words that he had sung. The few defects

were those of purely oral imitation, the
accents, even the slight reiteration of the
"s," were Pepita's own : —

> Cheeldren oof the Heavenly King,
> As ye journey essweetly ssing ;
> Essing your great Redeemer's praise,
> Glorioos in Hees works and ways.

He was astounded. Her recollection of
the air and words was the more wonderful,
for he remembered now that he had only
sung that particular hymn once. But to
his still greater delight and surprise, her
voice rose again in the second verse, with
a touch of plaintiveness that swelled his
throat : —

> We are traveling home to God,
> In the way our farzers trod,
> They are happy now, and we
> Soon their happiness shall see.

The simple, almost childish words — so
childish that they might have been the fitting creation of her own childish lips — here
died away with a sweep and crash of the
whole strings. Breathless silence followed,
in which Stephen Masterton could feel the
beatings of his own heart.

"Miss Ramirez," he called, in a voice
that scarcely seemed his own. There was

no reply. "Pepita!" he repeated; it was strangely like the accent of a lover, but he no longer cared. Still the singer's voice was silent.

Then he ran swiftly beside the wall, as he had seen her run, until he came to the fissure. It was overgrown with vines and brambles almost as impenetrable as an abattis, but if she had pierced it in her delicate crape dress, so could he! He brushed roughly through, and found himself in a glimmering aisle of pear trees close by the white wall of the Mission church.

For a moment in that intricate tracing of ebony and ivory made by the rising moon, he was dazzled, but evidently his irruption into the orchard had not been as lithe and silent as her own, for a figure in a particolored dress suddenly started into activity, and running from the wall, began to course through the trees until it became apparently a part of that involved pattern. Nothing daunted, however, Stephen Masterton pursued, his speed increased as he recognized the flounces of Pepita's barred dress, but the young girl had the advantage of knowing the locality, and could evade her pursuer by unsuspected turns and doubles.

For some moments this fanciful sylvan chase was kept up in perfect silence; it might have been a woodland nymph pursued by a wandering shepherd. Masterton presently saw that she was making towards a tiled roof that was now visible as projecting over the presidio wall, and was evidently her goal of refuge. He redoubled his speed; with skillful audacity and sheer strength of his broad shoulders he broke through a dense ceanothus hedge which Pepita was swiftly skirting, and suddenly appeared between her and her house.

With her first cry, the young girl turned and tried to bury herself in the hedge; but in another stride the circuit preacher was at her side, and caught her panting figure in his arms.

While he had been running he had swiftly formulated what he should do and what he should say to her. To his simple appeal for her companionship and willing ear he would add a brotherly tenderness, that should invite her trustfulness in him; he would confess his wrong and ask her forgiveness of his abrupt solicitations; he would propose to teach her more hymns, they would practise psalmody together;

even this priest, the custodian of her soul, could not object to that; but chiefly he would thank her: he would tell her how she had pleased him, and this would lead to more serious and thoughtful converse. All this was in his mind while he ran, was upon his lips as he caught her and for an instant she lapsed, exhausted, in his arms. But, alas! even in that moment he suddenly drew her towards him, and kissed her as only a lover could!

. . . .

The wire grass was already yellowing on the Tasajara plains with the dusty decay of the long, dry summer, when Dr. Duchesne returned to Tasajara. He came to see the wife of Deacon Sanderson, who, having for the twelfth time added to the population of the settlement, was not "doing as well" as everybody — except, possibly, Dr. Duchesne — expected. After he had made this hollow-eyed, over-burdened, under-nourished woman as comfortable as he could in her rude, neglected surroundings, to change the dreary chronicle of suffering, he turned to the husband, and said, "And what has become of Mr. Masterton, who used to be in your — vocation?" A long groan came from the deacon.

"Hallo! I hope he has not had a relapse," said the Doctor, earnestly. "I thought I'd knocked all that nonsense out of him — I beg your pardon — I mean," he added, hurriedly, "he wrote to me only a few weeks ago that he was picking up his strength again and doing well!"

"In his weak, gross, sinful flesh — yes, no doubt," returned the Deacon, scornfully, "and, perhaps, even in a worldly sense, for those who value the vanities of life; but he is lost to us, for all time, and lost to eternal life forever. Not," he continued in sanctimonious vindictiveness, "but that I often had my doubts of Brother Masterton's steadfastness. He was too much given to imagery and song."

"But what has he done?" persisted Doctor Duchesne.

"Done! He has embraced the Scarlet Woman!"

"Dear me!" said the Doctor, "so soon? Is it anybody you knew here? — not anybody's wife? Eh?"

"He has entered the Church of Rome," said the Deacon, indignantly, "he has forsaken the God of his fathers for the tents of the idolaters; he is the consort of Papists and the slave of the Pope!"

"But are you *sure?*" said Doctor Duchesne, with perhaps less concern than before.

"Sure," returned the Deacon angrily, "didn't Brother Bulkley, on account of warning reports made by a God-fearing and soul-seeking teamster, make a special pilgrimage to this land of Sodom to inquire and spy out its wickedness? Didn't he find Stephen Masterton steeped in the iniquity of practising on an organ — he that scorned even a violin or harmonium in the tents of the Lord — in an idolatrous chapel, with a foreign female Papist for a teacher? Didn't he find him a guest at the board of a Jesuit priest, visiting the schools of the Mission where this young Jezebel of a singer teaches the children to chant in unknown tongues? Didn't he find him living with a wrinkled Indian witch who called him ' Padrone,' — and speaking her gibberish? Didn't they find him, who left here a man mortified in flesh and spirit and pale with striving with sinners, fat and rosy from native wines and flesh pots, and even vain and gaudy in colored apparel? And last of all, didn't Brother Bulkley hear that a rumor was spread far and wide that this miserable backslider was to take to himself a wife — in one of these strange women — that very Jezebel who seduced him? What do you call that?"

"It looks a good deal like human nature," said the Doctor, musingly, "but *I* call it a cure!"

THE INDISCRETION OF ELSBETH.

THE American paused. He had evidently lost his way. For the last half-hour he had been wandering in a mediæval town, in a profound mediæval dream. Only a few days had elapsed since he had left the steamship that carried him hither; and the accents of his own tongue, the idioms of his own people and the sympathetic community of New World tastes and expressions still filled his mind until he woke up, or rather, as it seemed to him, was falling asleep in the past of this Old World town which had once held his ancestors. Although a republican, he had liked to think of them in quaint distinctive garb, representing State and importance — perhaps even aristocratic preëminence — content to let the responsibility of such "bad eminence" rest with them entirely, but a habit of conscientiousness and love for historic truth eventually led him also to regard an honest bauer standing beside his cattle in the quaint market-place, or a kindly-faced black-eyed dienstmädchen in a doorway, with a timid, respectful interest, as a possible type of his progenitors. For, unlike some of his traveling countrymen in Europe, he was not a snob, and it struck him — as an American — that it was, perhaps, better to think of his race as having improved than as having degenerated. In these ingenuous meditations he had passed the long rows of quaint, high houses, whose sagging roofs and unpatched dilapidations were yet far removed from squalor, until he had reached the road bordered by poplars, all so unlike his own country's waysides — and knew that he had wandered far from his hotel.

He did not care, however, to retrace his steps and return by the way he had come. There was, he reasoned, some other street or turning that would eventually bring him to the market-place and his hotel, and yet extend his experience of the town. He turned at right angles into a narrow grass lane, which was, however, as neatly kept and apparently as public as the highway. A few moments' walking convinced him that it was not a thoroughfare and that it led to the open gates of a park. This had something of a public look, which suggested that his intrusion might be, at least, a pardonable trespass, and he relied, like most strangers, on the exonerating quality of a stranger's ignorance. The park lay in the direction he wished to go, and yet it struck him as singular that a park of such extent should be allowed to still occupy such valuable urban space. Indeed, its length seemed to be illimitable as he wandered on, until he became conscious that he must have again lost his way, and he diverged toward the only boundary, a high, thick-set hedge to the right, whose line he had been following.

As he neared it he heard the sound of voices on the other side, speaking in German, with which he was unfamiliar. Having, as yet, met no one, and being now impressed with the fact that for a public place the park was singularly deserted, he was conscious that his position was getting serious, and he determined to take this only chance of inquiring his way. The hedge was thinner in some places than in others, and at times he could see not only the light through it but even the moving figures of the speakers, and the occasional white flash of a summer gown. At last he determined to penetrate it, and with little difficulty emerged on the other side. But here he paused motionless. He found himself behind a somewhat formal and symmetrical group of figures with their backs toward him, but all stiffened into attitudes as motionless as his own, and all gazing with a monotonous intensity in the direction of a handsome building, which had been invisible above the hedge, but which now seemed to arise suddenly before him. Some of the figures were in uniform. Immediately before him, but so slightly separated from the others that he was enabled to see the house between her and her companions, he was confronted by the pretty back, shoulders and blonde braids of a young girl of twenty. Convinced that he had unwittingly intruded upon some august ceremonial, he instantly slipped back into the hedge, but so silently that his momentary presence was evidently undetected. When he regained the park side he glanced back through the interstices; there was no movement of the figures nor break in the silence to indicate that his intrusion had been observed. With a long breath of relief he hurried from the park.

It was late when he finally got back to

his hotel. But his little modern adventure had, I fear, quite outrun his previous medi- æval reflections, and almost his first inquiry of the silver-chained porter in the courtyard was in regard to the park. There was no public park in Alstadt! The Herr possibly alluded to the Hof Gardens — the Schloss, which was in the direction he indicated. The Schloss was the residency of the hered- itary Grand Duke. *Ja wohl!* He was stopping there with several Hoheiten. There was naturally a party there — a fam- ily reunion. But it was a private inclosure. At times, when the Grand Duke was not "in residence," it was open to the public. In point of fact, at such times tickets of admission were to be had at the hotel for fifty pfennige each. There was not, of truth, much to see except a model farm and dairy — the pretty toy of a previous Grand Duchess.

But he seemed destined to come into closer collision with the modern life of Al- stadt. On entering the hotel, wearied by his long walk, he passed the landlord and a man in half-military uniform on the landing near his room. As he entered his apart- ment he had a vague impression, without exactly knowing why, that the landlord and the military stranger had just left it. This feeling was deepened by the evident disarrangement of certain articles in his unlocked portmanteau and the disorganization of his writing-case. A wave of indignation passed over him. It was followed by a knock at the door, and the landlord blandly appeared with the stranger.

"A thousand pardons," said the former, smilingly, "but Herr Sanderman, the Ober-Inspector of Police, wishes to speak with you. I hope we are not intruding?"

"Not *now*," said the American, dryly.

The two exchanged a vacant and deprecating smile.

"I have to ask only a few formal questions," said the Ober-Inspector in excellent but somewhat precise English, "to supplement the report which, as a stranger, you may not know is required by the police from the landlord in regard to the names and quality of his guests who are foreign to the town. You have a passport?"

"I have," said the American still more drily. "But I do not keep it in an unlocked portmanteau or an open writing-case."

"An admirable precaution," said Sanderman, with unmoved politeness. "May I see it? Thanks," he added, glancing over the document which the American produced from his pocket. "I see that you are a born American citizen — and an earlier knowledge of that fact would have prevented this little *contretemps*. You are aware, Mr. Hoffman, that your name is German?"

"It was borne by my ancestors, who came from this country two centuries ago," said Hoffman, curtly.

"We are indeed honored by your return to it," returned Sanderman suavely, "but it was the circumstance of your name being a local one, and the possibility of your still being a German citizen liable to unperformed military duty, which has caused the trouble." His manner was clearly civil and courteous, but Hoffman felt that all the time his own face and features were undergoing a profound scrutiny from the speaker.

"And you are making sure that you will know me again?" said Hoffman, with a smile.

"I trust, indeed, both," returned Sanderman, with a bow, "although you will permit me to say that your description here," pointing to the passport, "scarcely does you jus-

tice. *Ach Gott!* it is the same in all coun-
tries; the official eye is not that of the
young *Damen.*"

Hoffman, though not conceited, had not
lived twenty years without knowing that he
was very good-looking, yet there was something in the remark that caused him to color
with a new uneasiness. The Ober-Inspector
rose with another bow, and moved toward
the door. "I hope you will let me make
amends for this intrusion by doing anything
I can to render your visit here a pleasant
one. Perhaps," he added, "it is not for
long."

But Hoffman evaded the evident question
as he resented what he imagined was a possible sneer.

"I have not yet determined my movements," he said.

The Ober-Inspector brought his heels together in a somewhat stiffer military salute
and departed.

Nothing, however, could have exceeded
the later almost servile urbanity of the landlord, who seemed to have been proud of the
official visit to his guest. He was profuse
in his attentions, and even introduced him
to a singularly artistic-looking man of mid-

dle age, wearing an order in his buttonhole, whom he met casually in the hall.

"Our Court photographer," explained the landlord with some fervor, "at whose studio, only a few houses distant, most of the Hoheiten and Prinzessinen of Germany have sat for their likenesses."

"I should feel honored if the distinguished American Herr would give me a visit," said the stranger gravely, as he gazed at Hoffman with an intensity which recalled the previous scrutiny of the Police-Inspector, "and I would be charmed if he would avail himself of my poor skill to transmit his picturesque features to my unique collection."

Hoffman returned a polite evasion to this invitation, although he was conscious of being struck with this second examination of his face, and the allusion to his personality.

The next morning the porter met him with a mysterious air. The Herr would still like to see the Schloss? Hoffman, who had quite forgotten his adventure in the park, looked vacant. *Ja wohl* — the Hof authorities had no doubt heard of his visit and had intimated to the hotel proprietor that he might have permission to visit the model farm and dairy. As the American still looked indifferent the porter pointed out with some importance that it was a Ducal courtesy not to be lightly treated; that few, indeed, of the burghers themselves had ever been admitted to this eccentric whim of the late Grand Duchess. He would, of course, be silent about it; the Court would not like it known that they had made an exception to their rules in favor of a foreigner; he would enter quickly and boldly alone. There would be a housekeeper or a dairymaid to show him over the place.

More amused at this important mystery over what he, as an American, was inclined to classify as a "free pass" to a somewhat heavy "side show," he gravely accepted the permission, and the next morning after breakfast set out to visit the model farm and dairy. Dismissing his driver, as he had been instructed, Hoffman entered the gateway with a mingling of expectancy and a certain amusement over the "boldness" which the porter had suggested should characterize his entrance. Before him was a beautifully-kept lane bordered by arbored and trellised roses, which seemed to sink into the distance. He was instinctively following it when he became aware that he was mysteriously accompanied by a man in the livery of a *chasseur*, who was walking among the trees almost abreast of him, keeping pace with his step, and after the first introductory military salute preserving a ceremonious silence. There was something so ludicrous in this solemn procession toward a peaceful, rural industry that by the time they had reached the bottom of the lane the American had quite recovered his good humor. But here a new astonishment awaited him. Nestling before him in a green amphitheatre lay a little wooden farmyard and outbuildings, which irresistibly suggested that it had been recently unpacked and set up from a box of Nuremberg toys. The symmetrical trees, the galleried houses with preternaturally glazed windows, even the spotty, disproportionately sized cows in the white-fenced barnyards were all unreal, wooden and toylike.

Crossing a miniature bridge over a little stream, from which he was quite prepared to hook metallic fish with a magnet their own size, he looked about him for some real being to dispel the illusion. The mysterious chasseur had disappeared. But under the arch of an arbor, which seemed to be composed of silk ribbons, green glass and pink tissue paper, stood a quaint but delightful figure.

At first it seemed as if he had only dispelled one illusion for another. For the figure before him might have been made of Dresden china — so daintily delicate and unique it was in color and arrangement. It was that of a young girl dressed in some forgotten mediæval peasant garb of velvet braids, silver stay-laced corsage, lace sleeves and helmeted metallic comb. But, after the Dresden method, the pale yellow of her hair was repeated in her bodice, the pink of her cheeks was in the roses of her chintz overskirt. The blue of her eyes was the blue of her petticoat; the dazzling whiteness of her neck shone again in the sleeves and stockings. Nevertheless she was real and human, for the pink deepened in her cheeks as Hoffman's hat flew from his head, and she recognized the civility with a grave little courtesy.

"You have come to see the dairy," she said in quaintly accurate English; "I will show you the way."

"If you please," said Hoffman, gaily, "but" —

"But what?" she said, facing him suddenly with absolutely astonished eyes.

Hoffman looked into them so long that their frank wonder presently contracted into an ominous mingling of restraint and resentment. Nothing daunted, however, he went on: —

"Could n't we shake all that?"

The look of wonder returned. "Shake all that?" she repeated. "I do not understand."

"Well! I 'm not positively aching to see cows, and you must be sick of showing them. I think, too, I 've about sized the whole show. Would n't it be better if we sat down in that arbor — supposing it won't fall down — and you told me all about the lot? It would save you a heap of trouble and keep your pretty frock cleaner than trapesing round. Of course," he said, with a quick transition to the gentlest courtesy, "if you 're conscientious about this thing we 'll go on and not spare a cow. Consider me in it with you for the whole morning."

She looked at him again, and then sud·

denly broke into a charming laugh. It revealed a set of strong white teeth, as well as a certain barbaric trace in its cadence which civilized restraint had not entirely overlaid.

"I suppose she really is a peasant, in spite of that pretty frock," he said to himself as he laughed too.

But her face presently took a shade of reserve, and with a gentle but singular significance she said: —

"I think you must see the dairy."

Hoffman's hat was in his hand with a vivacity that tumbled the brown curls on his forehead. "By all means," he said instantly, and began walking by her side in modest but easy silence. Now that he thought her a conscientious peasant he was quiet and respectful.

Presently she lifted her eyes, which, despite her gravity, had not entirely lost their previous mirthfulness, and said: —

"But you Americans — in your rich and prosperous country, with your large lands and your great harvests — you must know all about farming."

"Never was in a dairy in my life," said Hoffman gravely. "I'm from the city of

New York, where the cows give swill milk, and are kept in cellars."

Her eyebrows contracted prettily in an effort to understand. Then she apparently gave it up, and said with a slanting glint of mischief in her eyes:—

"Then you come here like the other Americans in hope to see the Grand Duke and Duchess and the Princesses?"

"No. The fact is I almost tumbled into a lot of 'em—standing like wax figures—the other side of the park lodge, the other day—and got away as soon as I could. I think I prefer the cows."

Her head was slightly turned away. He had to content himself with looking down upon the strong feet in their serviceable but smartly-buckled shoes that uplifted her upright figure as she moved beside him.

"Of course," he added with boyish but unmistakable courtesy, "if it's part of your show to trot out the family, why I'm in that, too. I dare say you could make them interesting."

"But why," she said with her head still slightly turned away toward a figure—a sturdy-looking woman, which, for the first time, Hoffman perceived was walking in a

line with them as the chasseur had done —
"why did you come here at all?"

"The first time was a fool accident," he
returned frankly. "I was making a short
cut through what I thought was a public
park. The second time was because I had
been rude to a Police-Inspector whom I
found going through my things, but who
apologized — as I suppose — by getting me
an invitation from the Grand Duke to come
here, and I thought it only the square thing
to both of 'em to accept it. But I'm
mighty glad I came; I would n't have missed
you for a thousand dollars. You see I
have n't struck any one I cared to talk to
since." Here he suddenly remarked that
she had n't looked at him, and that the delicate whiteness of her neck was quite suffused
with pink, and stopped instantly. Presently
he said quite easily: —

"Who's the chorus?"

"The lady?"

"Yes. She's watching us as if she did n't
quite approve, you know — just as if she
did n't catch on."

"She's the head housekeeper of the farm.
Perhaps you would prefer to have her show
you the dairy; shall I call her?"

The figure in question was very short and stout, with voluminous petticoats.

"Please don't; I'll stay without your setting that paper-weight on me. But here's the dairy. Don't let her come inside among those pans of fresh milk with that smile, or there'll be trouble."

The young girl paused too, made a slight gesture with her hand, and the figure passed on as they entered the dairy. It was beautifully clean and fresh. With a persistence that he quickly recognized as mischievous and ironical, and with his characteristic adaptability accepted with even greater gravity and assumption of interest, she showed him all the details. From thence they passed to the farmyard, where he hung with breathless attention over the names of the cows and made her repeat them. Although she was evidently familiar with the subject he could see that her zeal was fitful and impatient.

"Suppose we sit down," he said, pointing to an ostentatious rustic seat in the centre of the green.

"Sit down?" she repeated wonderingly. "What for?"

"To talk. We'll knock off and call it half a day."

"But if you are not looking at the farm you are, of course, going," she said quickly.

"Am I? I don't think these particulars were in my invitation."

She again broke into a fit of laughter, and, at the same time, cast a bright eye around the field.

"Come," he said gently, "there are no other sightseers waiting, and your conscience is clear," and he moved toward the rustic seat.

"Certainly not — there," she added in a low voice.

They moved on slowly together to a copse of willows which overhung the miniature stream.

"You are not staying long in Alstadt?" she said.

"No; I only came to see the old town that my ancestors came from."

They were walking so close together that her skirt brushed his trousers, but she suddenly drew away from him, and looking him fixedly in the eye said: —

"Ah, you have relations here?"

"Yes, but they are dead two hundred years."

She laughed again with a slight expression of relief. They had entered the copse and were walking in dense shadow when she suddenly stopped and sat down upon a rustic bench. To his surprise he found that they were quite alone.

"Tell me about these relatives," she said, slightly drawing aside her skirt to make room for him on the seat.

He did not require a second invitation. He not only told her all about his ancestral progenitors, but, I fear, even about those more recent and more nearly related to him; about his own life, his vocation — he was a clever newspaper correspondent with a roving commission — his ambitions, his beliefs and his romance.

"And then, perhaps, of this visit — you will also make ' copy ' ? "

He smiled at her quick adaptation of his professional slang, but shook his head.

"No," he said gravely. "No — this is *you.* The ' Chicago Interviewer ' is big pay and is rich, but it has n't capital enough to buy you from me."

He gently slid his hand toward hers and slipped his fingers softly around it. She made a slight movement of withdrawal, but even then — as if in forgetfulness or indifference — permitted her hand to rest unresponsively in his. It was scarcely an encouragement to gallantry, neither was it a rejection of an unconscious familiarity.

"But you have n't told me about yourself," he said.

"Oh, I" — she returned, with her first approach to coquetry in a laugh and a sidelong glance, "of what importance is that to you? It is the Grand Duchess and Her Highness the Princess that you Americans seek to know. I am — what I am — as you see."

"You bet," said Hoffman with charming decision.

"I *what?*"

"You *are*, you know, and that 's good enough for me, but I don't even know your name."

She laughed again, and after a pause, said: "Elsbeth."

"But I could n't call you by your first name on our first meeting, you know."

"Then you Americans are really so very formal — eh?" she said slily, looking at her imprisoned hand.

"Well, yes," returned Hoffman, disengaging it. "I suppose we are respectful, or mean to be. But whom am I to inquire for? To write to?"

"You are neither to write nor inquire."

"What?" She had moved in her seat so as to half face him with eyes in which curiosity, mischief and a certain seriousness alternated, but for the first time seemed conscious of his hand, and accented her words with a slight pressure.

"You are to return to your hotel presently, and say to your landlord: ' Pack up my luggage. I have finished with this old town and my ancestors, and the Grand Duke whom I do not care to see, and I shall leave Alstadt to-morrow!' "

"Thank you! I don't catch on."

"Of what necessity should you? I have said it. That should be enough for a chivalrous American like you." She again significantly looked down at her hand.

"If you mean that you know the extent of the favor you ask of me, I can say no more," he said seriously; "but give me some reason for it."

"Ah so!" she said, with a slight shrug of her shoulders. "Then I must tell you. You say you do not know the Grand Duke and Duchess. Well! *they know you.* The day before yesterday you were wandering in the park, as you admit. You say, also, you got through the hedge and interrupted some ceremony. That ceremony was not a Court function, Mr. Hoffman, but something equally sacred — the photographing of the Ducal family before the Schloss. You say that you instantly withdrew. But after the photograph was taken the plate revealed a stranger standing actually by the side of the Princess Alexandrine, and even taking the *pas* of the Grand Duke himself. That stranger was you!"

"And the picture was spoiled," said the American, with a quiet laugh.

"I should not say that," returned the lady, with a demure glance at her companion's handsome face, "and I do not believe that the Princess — who first saw the photograph — thought so either. But she is very young and willful, and has the reputation of being very indiscreet, and unfortunately she begged the photographer not to destroy the plate, but to give it to her, and to say nothing about it, except that the plate was defective, and to take another. Still it would have ended there if her curiosity had not led her to confide a description of the stranger to the Police-Inspector, with the result you know."

"Then I am expected to leave town because I accidentally stumbled into a family group that was being photographed?"

"Because a certain Princess was indiscreet enough to show her curiosity about you," corrected the fair stranger.

"But look here! I'll apologize to the Princess, and offer to pay for the plate."

"Then you do want to see the Princess?" said the young girl smiling; "you are like the others."

"Bother the Princess! I want to see *you*. And I don't see how they can prevent it if I choose to remain."

"Very easily. You will find that there is something wrong with your passport, and you will be sent on to Pumpernickel for examination. You will unwittingly transgress some of the laws of the town and be ordered to leave it. You will be shadowed by the police until you quarrel with them — like a free American — and you are conducted to the frontier. Perhaps you will strike an officer who has insulted you, and then you are finished on the spot."

The American's crest rose palpably until it cocked his straw hat over his curls.

"Suppose I am content to risk it — having first laid the whole matter and its trivial cause before the American Minister, so that he could make it hot for this whole caboodle of a country if they happened to ' down me.' By Jove! I should n't mind being the martyr of an international episode if they 'd spare me long enough to let me get the first ' copy ' over to the other side." His eyes sparkled.

"You could expose them, but they would then deny the whole story, and you have no evidence. They would demand to know your informant, and I should be disgraced, and the Princess, who is already talked about, made a subject of scandal. But no matter! It is right that an American's independence shall not be interfered with."

She raised the hem of her handkerchief to her blue eyes and slightly turned her head aside. Hoffman gently drew the handkerchief away, and in so doing possessed himself of her other hand.

"Look here, Miss — Miss — Elsbeth. You know I would n't give you away, whatever happened. But could n't I get hold of that photographer — I saw him, he wanted me to sit to him — and make him tell me?"

"He wanted you to sit to him," she said hurriedly, "and did you?"

"No," he replied. "He was a little too fresh and previous, though I thought he fancied some resemblance in me to somebody else."

"Ah!" She said something to herself in German which he did not understand, and then added aloud:—

"You did well; he is a bad man, this photographer. Promise me you shall not sit for him."

"How can I if I'm fired out of the place like this?" He added ruefully, "But I'd like to make him give himself away to me somehow."

"He will not, and if he did he would deny it afterward. Do not go near him nor see him. Be careful that he does not photograph you with his instantaneous instrument when you are passing. Now you must go. I must see the Princess."

"Let me go, too. I will explain it to her," said Hoffman.

She stopped, looked at him keenly, and attempted to withdraw her hands. "Ah, then it *is* so. It is the Princess you wish to see. You are curious — you, too; you wish to see this lady who is interested in you. I ought to have known it. You are all alike."

He met her gaze with laughing frankness, accepting her outburst as a charming feminine weakness, half jealousy, half coquetry — but retained her hands.

"Nonsense," he said. "I wish to see her that I may have the right to see you — that you shall not lose your place here through me; that I may come again."

"You must never come here again."

"Then you must come where I am. We will meet somewhere when you have an afternoon off. You shall show me the town — the houses of my ancestors — their tombs; possibly — if the Grand Duke rampages — the probable site of my own."

She looked into his laughing eyes with her clear, steadfast, gravely - questioning blue ones. "Do not you Americans know that it is not the fashion here, in Germany, for the young men and the young women to walk together — unless they are *verlobt?*"

" *Ver* — which? "

"Engaged." She nodded her head thrice: viciously, decidedly, mischievously.

"So much the better."

"Ach Gott!" She made a gesture of hopelessness at his incorrigibility, and again attempted to withdraw her hands.

"I must go now."

"Well then, good-by."

It was easy to draw her closer by simply lowering her still captive hands. Then he suddenly kissed her coldly-startled lips, and instantly released her. She as instantly vanished.

"Elsbeth," he called quickly. "Elsbeth!"

Her now really frightened face reappeared with a heightened color from the dense foliage — quite to his astonishment.

"Hush," she said, with her finger on her lips. "Are you mad?"

"I only wanted to remind you to square me with the Princess," he laughed, as her head disappeared.

He strolled back toward the gate. Scarcely had he quitted the shrubbery before the same chasseur made his appearance with precisely the same salute; and, keeping exactly the same distance, accompanied him to the gate. At the corner of the street he hailed a drosky and was driven to his hotel.

The landlord came up smiling. He

trusted that the Herr had greatly enjoyed himself at the Schloss. It was a distinguished honor — in fact, quite unprecedented. Hoffman, while he determined not to commit himself, nor his late fair companion, was, nevertheless, anxious to learn something more of her relations to the Schloss. So pretty, so characteristic, and marked a figure must be well known to sightseers. Indeed, once or twice the idea had crossed his mind with a slightly jealous twinge that left him more conscious of the impression she had made on him than he had deemed possible. He asked if the model farm and dairy were always shown by the same attendants.

"Ach Gott! no doubt, yes; His Royal Highness had quite a retinue when he was in residence."

"And were these attendants in costume?"

"There was undoubtedly a livery for the servants."

Hoffman felt a slight republican irritation at the epithet — he knew not why. But this costume was rather an historical one; surely it was not intrusted to every-day menials — and he briefly described it.

His host's blank curiosity suddenly

changed to a look of mysterious and arch intelligence.

"Ach Gott! yes!" He remembered now (with his finger on his nose) that when there was a fest at the Schloss the farm and dairy were filled with shepherdesses, in quaint costume worn by the ladies of the Grand Duke's own theatrical company, who assumed the characters with great vivacity. Surely it was the same, and the Grand Duke had treated the Herr to this special courtesy. Yes — there was one pretty, blonde young lady—the Fräulein Wimpfenbuttel, a most popular soubrette, who would play it to the life! And the description fitted her to a hair! Ah, there was no doubt of it; many persons, indeed, had been so deceived.

But happily, now that he had given him the wink, the Herr could corroborate it himself by going to the theatre to-night. Ah, it would be a great joke—quite colossal! if he took a front seat where she could see him. And the good man rubbed his hands in gleeful anticipation.

Hoffman had listened to him with a slow repugnance that was only equal to his gradual conviction that the explanation was a true one, and that he himself had been ridiculously deceived. The mystery of his fair companion's costume, which he had accepted as part of the "show;" the inconsistency of her manner and her evident occupation; her undeniable wish to terminate the whole episode with that single interview; her mingling of worldly aplomb and rustic innocence; her perfect self-control and experienced acceptance of his gallantry under the simulated attitude of simplicity — all now struck him as perfectly comprehensible. He recalled the actress' inimitable touch in certain picturesque realistic details in the dairy — which she had not spared him; he recognized it now even in their bowered confidences (how like a pretty ballet scene their whole interview on the rustic bench was!), and it breathed through their entire conversation — to their theatrical parting at the close! And the whole story of the photograph was, no doubt, as pure a dramatic invention as the rest! The Princess' romantic interest in him — that Princess who had never appeared (why had he not detected the old, well-worn, sentimental situation here?) — was all a part of it. The dark, mysterious hint of his persecution by the police was a necessary culmination to the little farce. Thank Heaven! he had not "risen" at the Princess, even if he had given himself away to the clever actress in her own humble rôle. Then the humor of the whole situation predominated and he laughed until the tears came to his eyes, and his forgotten ancestors might have turned over in their graves without his heeding them. And with this humanizing influence upon him he went to the theatre.

It was capacious even for the town, and although the performance was a special one he had no difficulty in getting a whole box to himself. He tried to avoid this public isolation by sitting close to the next box, where there was a solitary occupant — an officer — apparently as lonely as himself. He had made up his mind that when his fair deceiver appeared he would let her see by his significant applause that he recognized her, but bore no malice for the trick she had played on him. After all, he had kissed her — he had no right to complain. If she should recognize him, and this recognition led to a withdrawal of her prohibition, and their better acquaintance, he would be a fool to cavil at her pleasant artifice.

Her vocation was certainly a more independent and original one than that he had supposed; for its social quality and inequality he cared nothing. He found himself longing for the glance of her calm blue eyes, for the pleasant smile that broke the seriousness of her sweetly-restrained lips. There was no doubt that he should know her even as the heroine of "Der Czar und der Zimmermann" on the bill before him. He was becoming impatient. And the performance evidently was waiting. A stir in the outer gallery, the clatter of sabres, the filing of uniforms into the royal box, and a triumphant burst from the orchestra showed the cause. As a few ladies and gentlemen in full evening dress emerged from the background of uniforms and took their places in the front of the box, Hoffman looked with some interest for the romantic Princess. Suddenly he saw a face and shoulders in a glitter of diamonds that startled him, and then a glance that transfixed him.

He leaned over to his neighbor. "Who is the young lady in the box?"

"The Princess Alexandrine."

"I mean the young lady in blue with blonde hair and blue eyes."

"It is the Princess Alexandrine Elsbeth Marie Stephanie, the daughter of the Grand Duke — there is none other there."

"Thank you."

He sat silently looking at the rising curtain and the stage. Then he rose quietly, gathered his hat and coat and left the box. When he reached the gallery he turned instinctively and looked back at the royal box. Her eyes had followed him, and as he remained a moment motionless in the doorway her lips parted in a grateful smile, and she waved her fan with a faint but unmistakable gesture of farewell.

The next morning he left Alstadt. There was some little delay at the Zoll on the frontier, and when Hoffman received back his trunk it was accompanied by a little sealed packet which was handed to him by the Custom-house Inspector. Hoffman did not open it until he was alone.

°　　.　　.　　.　　.　　.　　.　　.　　.

There hangs upon the wall of his modest apartment in New York a narrow, irregular photograph ingeniously framed, of himself standing side by side with a young German girl, who, in the estimation of his compatriots, is by no means stylish and only passably good-looking. When he is joked by his friends about the post of honor given to this production, and questioned as to the lady, he remains silent. The Princess Alexandrine Elsbeth Marie Stephanie von Westphalen-Alstadt, among her other royal qualities, knew whom to trust.

THE DEVOTION OF ENRIQUEZ.

IN another chronicle which dealt with the exploits of " Chu Chu," a Californian mustang, I gave some space to the accomplishments of Enriquez Saltillo, who assisted me in training her, and who was also brother to Consuelo Saltillo, the young lady to whom I had freely given both the mustang and my youthful affections. I consider it a proof of the superiority of masculine friendship that neither the subsequent desertion of the mustang nor the young lady ever made the slightest difference to Enriquez or me in our exalted amity. To a wondering doubt as to what I ever could possibly have seen in his sister to admire he joined a tolerant skepticism of the whole sex. This he was wont to express in that marvelous combination of Spanish precision and California slang for which he was justly famous. " As to thees women and their little game," he would say, " believe me,

my friend, your old Oncle 'Enry is not in
it. No; he will ever take a back seat when
lofe is around. For why? Regard me here!
If she is a horse, you shall say, 'She will
buck-jump,' 'She will ess-shy,' 'She will not
arrive,' or 'She will arrive too quick.' But
if it is thees women, where are you? For
when you shall say, 'She will ess-shy,' look
you, she will walk straight; or she will remain tranquil when you think she buck-
jump; or else she will arrive and, look you,
you will not. You shall get left. It is ever
so. My father and the brother of my father
have both make court to my mother when
she was but a señorita. My father think
she have lofe his brother more. So he say
to her: 'It is enofe; tranquillize yourself.
I will go. I will efface myself. Adios!
Shake hands! Ta-ta! So long! See you
again in the fall.' And what make my
mother? Regard me! She marry my father — on the instant! Of thees women,
believe me, Pancho, you shall know nothing.
Not even if they shall make you the son of
your father or his nephew."

I have recalled this characteristic speech
to show the general tendency of Enriquez's
convictions at the opening of this little

story. It is only fair to say, however, that his usual attitude toward the sex he so cheerfully maligned exhibited little apprehension or caution in dealing with them. Among the frivolous and light-minded intermixture of his race he moved with great freedom and popularity. He danced well; when we went to fandangos together his agility and the audacity of his figures always procured him the prettiest partners, his professed sentiments, I presume, shielding him from subsequent jealousies, heart-burnings, or envy. I have a vivid recollection of him in the mysteries of the *semicuacua*, a somewhat corybantic dance which left much to the invention of the performers, and very little to the imagination of the spectator. In one of the figures a gaudy handkerchief, waved more or less gracefully by dancer and danseuse before the dazzled eyes of each other, acted as love's signal, and was used to express alternate admiration and indifference, shyness and audacity, fear and transport, coyness and coquetry, as the dance proceeded. I need not say that Enriquez's pantomimic illustration of these emotions was peculiarly extravagant; but it was always performed and accepted with a gravity

that was an essential feature of the dance.
At such times sighs would escape him which
were supposed to portray the incipient stages
of passion; snorts of jealousy burst from
him at the suggestion of a rival; he was
overtaken by a sort of St. Vitus's dance
that expressed his timidity in making the
first advances of affection; the scorn of his
lady-love struck him with something like a
dumb ague; and a single gesture of invitation from her produced marked delirium.
All this was very like Enriquez; but on the
particular occasion to which I refer, I think
no one was prepared to see him begin the
figure with the waving of *four* handkerchiefs! Yet this he did, pirouetting, caper-
ing, brandishing his silken signals like a
bellerina's scarf in the languishment or fire
of passion, until, in a final figure, where the
conquered and submitting fair one usually
sinks into the arms of her partner, need it
be said that the ingenious Enriquez was
found in the centre of the floor supporting
four of the dancers! Yet he was by no
means unduly excited either by the plaudits
of the crowd or by his evident success with
the fair. "Ah, believe me, it is nothing,"
he said quietly, rolling a fresh cigarette as

he leaned against the doorway. " Possibly,
I shall have to offer the chocolate or the
wine to thees girls, or make to them a prome-
nade in the moonlight on the verandah. It
is ever so. Unless, my friend," he said,
suddenly turning toward me in an excess
of chivalrous self-abnegation, " unless you
shall yourself take my place. Behold, I
gif them to you! I vamos! I vanish! I
make track! I skedaddle!" I think he
would have carried his extravagance to the
point of summoning his four gypsy witches
of partners, and committing them to my
care, if the crowd had not at that moment
parted before the remaining dancers, and
left one of the on-lookers, a tall, slender girl,
calmly surveying them through gold-rimmed
eye-glasses in complete critical absorption.
I stared in amazement and consternation ;
for I recognized in the fair stranger Miss
Urania Mannersley, the Congregational
minister's niece !

Everybody knew Rainie Mannersley
throughout the length and breadth of the
Encinal. She was at once the envy and
the goad of the daughters of those Southwestern and Eastern immigrants who had
settled in the valley. She was correct, she

was critical, she was faultless and observant.
She was proper, yet independent; she was
highly educated; she was suspected of knowing Latin and Greek; she even spelled cor-
rectly! She could wither the plainest field
nosegay in the hands of other girls by giving the flowers their botanical names. She
never said, " Ain't you? " but " Are n't
you? " She looked upon " Did I which? "
as an incomplete and imperfect form of
" What did I do? " She quoted from
Browning and Tennyson, and was believed
to have read them. She was from Boston.
What could she possibly be doing at a free-
and-easy fandango?

Even if these facts were not already familiar to every one there, her outward appearance would have attracted attention.
Contrasted with the gorgeous red, black,
and yellow skirts of the dancers, her plain,
tightly fitting gown and hat, all of one delicate gray, were sufficiently notable in themselves, even had they not seemed, like the
girl herself, a kind of quiet protest to the
glaring flounces before her. Her small,
straight waist and flat back brought into
greater relief the corsetless, waistless, swaying figures of the Mexican girls, and her

long, slim, well-booted feet, peeping from
the stiff, white edges of her short skirt,
made their broad, low-quartered slippers,
held on by the big toe, appear more preposterous than ever. Suddenly she seemed to
realize that she was standing there alone,
but without fear or embarrassment. She
drew back a little, glancing carelessly behind her as if missing some previous companion, and then her eyes fell upon mine.
She smiled an easy recognition; then a moment later, her glance rested more curiously
upon Enriquez, who was still by my side.
I disengaged myself and instantly joined
her, particularly as I noticed that a few of
the other bystanders were beginning to
stare at her with little reserve.

"Isn't it the most extraordinary thing
you ever saw?" she said quietly. Then,
presently noticing the look of embarrassment on my face, she went on, more by way
of conversation than of explanation: "I just
left uncle making a call on a parishioner
next door, and was going home with Jocasta
(a peon servant of her uncle's), when I
heard the music, and dropped in. I don't
know what has become of her," she added,
glancing round the room again; "she

seemed perfectly wild when she saw that creature over there bounding about with his handkerchiefs. You were speaking to him just now. Do tell me — is he real?"

"I should think there was little doubt of that," I said with a vague laugh.

"You know what I mean," she said simply. "Is he quite sane? Does he do that because he likes it, or is he paid for it?"

This was too much. I pointed out somewhat hurriedly that he was a scion of one of the oldest Castilian families, that the performance was a national gypsy dance which he had joined in as a patriot and a patron, and that he was my dearest friend. At the same time I was conscious that I wished she hadn't seen his last performance.

"You don't mean to say that all that he did was in the dance?" she said. "I don't believe it. It was only like him." As I hesitated over this palpable truth, she went on: "I do wish he'd do it again. Don't you think you could make him?"

"Perhaps he might if *you* asked him," I said a little maliciously.

"Of course I shouldn't do that," she returned quietly. "All the same, I do believe he is really going to do it — or something else. Do look!"

I looked, and to my horror saw that Enriquez, possibly incited by the delicate gold eye-glasses of Miss Mannersley, had divested himself of his coat, and was winding the four handkerchiefs, tied together, picturesquely around his waist, preparatory to some new performance. I tried furtively to give him a warning look, but in vain.

"Isn't he really too absurd for anything?" said Miss Mannersley, yet with a certain comfortable anticipation in her voice. "You know, I never saw anything like this before. I wouldn't have believed such a creature could have existed."

Even had I succeeded in warning him, I doubt if it would have been of any avail. For, seizing a guitar from one of the musicians, he struck a few chords, and suddenly began to zigzag into the centre of the floor, swaying his body languishingly from side to side in time with the music and the pitch of a thin Spanish tenor. It was a gypsy love-song. Possibly Miss Mannersley's lingual accomplishments did not include a knowledge of Castilian, but she could not fail to see that the gestures and illustrative pantomime were addressed to her. Passionately assuring her that she was the most favored

daughter of the Virgin, that her eyes were
like votive tapers, and yet in the same breath
accusing her of being a " brigand " and " as-
sassin " in her attitude toward " his heart,"
he balanced with quivering timidity toward
her, threw an imaginary cloak in front of
her neat boots as a carpet for her to tread
on, and with a final astonishing pirouette
and a languishing twang of his guitar, sank
on one knee, and blew, with a rose, ᵒ kiss at
her feet.

If I had been seriously angry with him
before for his grotesque extravagance, I
could have pitied him now for the young
girl's absolute unconsciousness of anything
but his utter ludicrousness. The applause
of dancers and bystanders was instantaneous
and hearty; her only contribution to it was
a slight parting of her thin red lips in a
half-incredulous smile. In the silence that
followed the applause, as Enriquez walked
pantingly away, I heard her saying, half to
herself, " Certainly a most extraordinary
creature ! " In my indignation I could not
help turning suddenly upon her and looking
straight into her eyes. They were brown,
with that peculiar velvet opacity common
to the pupils of near-sighted persons, and

seemed to defy internal scrutiny. She only repeated carelessly, " Isn't he ? " and added : " Please see if you can find Jocasta. I suppose we ought to be going now ; and I dare say he won't be doing it again. Ah ! there she is. Good gracious, child ! what have you got there ? "

It was Enriquez' rose which Jocasta had picked up, and was timidly holding out toward her mistress.

" Heavens ! I don't want it. Keep it yourself."

I walked with them to the door, as I did not fancy a certain glitter in the black eyes of the Señoritas Manuela and Pepita, who were watching her curiously. But I think she was as oblivious of this as she was of Enriquez' particular attentions. As we reached the street I felt that I ought to say something more.

" You know," I began casually, " that although those poor people meet here in this public way, their gathering is really quite a homely pastoral and a national custom ; and these girls are all honest, hard-working peons or servants enjoying themselves in quite the old idyllic fashion."

" Certainly," said the young girl, half ab-

stractedly. "Of course it's a Moorish
dance, originally brought over, I suppose,
by those old Andalusian immigrants two
hundred years ago. It's quite Arabic in its
suggestions. I have got something like it
in an old *cancionero* I picked up at a book-
stall in Boston. But," she added, with a
gasp of reminiscent satisfaction, "that's not
like *him !* Oh, no ! *he* is decidedly original.
Heavens ! yes."

I turned away in some discomfiture to
join Enriquez, who was calmly awaiting me,
with a cigarette in his mouth, outside the
sala. Yet he looked so unconscious of any
previous absurdity that I hesitated in what
I thought was a necessary warning. He,
however, quickly precipitated it. Glancing
after the retreating figures of the two women, he said, "Thees mees from Boston is
return to her house. You do not accompany
her ? I shall. Behold me — I am there."
But I linked my arm firmly in his. Then I
pointed out, first, that she was already accompanied by a servant ; secondly, that if I,
who knew her, had hesitated to offer myself
as an escort, it was hardly proper for him,
a perfect stranger, to take that liberty ; that
Miss Mannersley was very punctilious of

etiquette, which he, as a Castilian gentleman, ought to appreciate.

" But will she not regard lofe — the admiration excessif ? " he said, twirling his thin little mustache meditatively.

" No; she will not," I returned sharply; "and you ought to understand that she is on a different level from your Manuelas and Carmens."

" Pardon, my friend," he said gravely; " thees women are ever the same. There is a proverb in my language. Listen: ' Whether the sharp blade of the Toledo pierce the satin or the goatskin, it shall find behind it ever the same heart to wound.' I am that Toledo blade — possibly it is you, my friend. Wherefore, let us together pursue this girl of Boston on the instant."

But I kept my grasp on Enriquez' arm, and succeeded in restraining his mercurial impulses for the moment. He halted, and puffed vigorously at his cigarette; but the next instant he started forward again. " Let us, however, follow with discretion in the rear; we shall pass her house; we shall gaze at it; it shall touch her heart."

Ridiculous as was this following of the young girl we had only just parted from, I nevertheless knew that Enriquez was quite capable of attempting it alone, and I thought it better to humor him by consenting to walk with him in that direction ; but I felt it necessary to say :

" I ought to warn you that Miss Mannersley already looks upon your performances at the sala as something *outré* and peculiar, and if I were you I should n't do anything to deepen that impression."

"You are saying she ees shock ? " said Enriquez, gravely.

I felt I could not conscientiously say that she was shocked, and he saw my hesitation. " Then she have jealousy of the Señoritas," he observed, with insufferable complacency. " You observe ! I have already said. It is ever so."

I could stand it no longer. " Look here, Harry," I said, " if you must know it, she looks upon you as an acrobat — a paid performer."

" Ah ! "— his black eyes sparkled — " the torero, the man who fights the bull, he is also an acrobat."

" Yes ; but she thinks you a clown ! — a *gracioso de teatro*, — there ! "

" Then I have make her laugh ? " he said coolly.

I don't think he had ; but I shrugged my shoulders.

"Bueno!" he said cheerfully. "Lofe, he begin with a laugh, he make feenish with a sigh."

I turned to look at him in the moonlight. His face presented its habitual Spanish gravity — a gravity that was almost ironical. His small black eyes had their characteristic irresponsible audacity — the irresponsibility of the vivacious young animal. It could not be possible that he was really touched with the placid frigidities of Miss Mannersley. I remembered his equally elastic gallantries with Miss Pinky Smith, a blonde Western belle, from which both had harmlessly rebounded. As we walked on slowly I continued more persuasively : "Of course this is only your nonsense ; but don't you see, Miss Mannersley thinks it all in earnest and really your nature?" I hesitated, for it suddenly struck me that it *was* really his nature. "And — hang it all ! — you don't want her to believe you a common buffoon, or some intoxicated muchaco."

"Intoxicated ?" repeated Enriquez, with exasperating languishment. "Yes ; that is the word that shall express itself. My friend,

you have made a shot in the centre — you
have ring the bell every time! It is intoxi-
cation — but not of aquardiente. Look! I
have long time an ancestor of whom is a
pretty story. One day in church he have
seen a young girl — a mere peasant girl —
pass to the confessional. He look her in her
eye, he stagger," — here Enriquez wobbled
pantomimically into the road, — " he fall!"
— he would have suited the action to the
word if I had not firmly held him up.
"They have take him home, where he have
remain without his clothes, and have dance
and sing. But it was the drunkenness of
lofe. And, look you, thees village girl was
a nothing, not even pretty. The name of
my ancestor was " —

" Don Quixote de la Mancha," I suggested
maliciously. " I suspected as much. Come
along. That will do."

" My ancestor's name," continued Enriquez, gravely, " was Antonio Hermenegildo
de Salvatierra, which is not the same.
Thees Don Quixote of whom you speak exist
not at all."

" Never mind. Only, for heaven's sake,
as we are nearing the house, don't make a
fool of yourself again."

It was a wonderful moonlight night. The deep redwood porch of the Mannersley parsonage, under the shadow of a great oak, — the largest in the Encinal, — was diapered in black and silver. As the women stepped upon the porch their shadows were silhouetted against the door. Miss Mannersley paused for an instant, and turned to give a last look at the beauty of the night as Jocasta entered. Her glance fell upon us as we passed. She nodded carelessly and unaffectedly to me, but as she recognized Enriquez she looked a little longer at him with her previous cold and invincible curiosity. To my horror Enriquez began instantly to affect a slight tremulousness of gait and a difficulty of breathing; but I gripped his arm savagely, and managed to get him past the house as the door closed finally on the young lady.

" You do not comprehend, friend Pancho," he said gravely, " but those eyes in their glass are as the *espejo ustorio*, the burning mirror. They burn, they consume me here like paper. Let us affix to ourselves thees tree. She will, without doubt, appear at her window. We shall salute her for goodnight."

"We will do nothing of the kind," I said sharply. Finding that I was determined, he permitted me to lead him away. I was delighted to notice, however, that he had indicated the window which I knew was the minister's study, and that as the bedrooms were in the rear of the house, this later incident was probably not overseen by the young lady or the servant. But I did not part from Enriquez until I saw him safely back to the sala, where I left him sipping chocolate, his arm alternating around the waists of his two previous partners in a delightful Arcadian and childlike simplicity, and an apparent utter forgetfulness of Miss Mannersley.

The fandangoes were usually held on Saturday night, and the next day, being Sunday, I missed Enriquez; but as he was a devout Catholic I remembered that he was at mass in the morning, and possibly at the bull-fight at San Antonio in the afternoon. But I was somewhat surprised on the Monday morning following, as I was crossing the plaza, to have my arm taken by the Rev. Mr. Mannersley in the nearest approach to familiarity that was consistent with the reserve of this eminent divine. I looked at him inquiringly. Although scrupulously correct in attire, his features always had a singular resemblance to the national carica-ture known as "Uncle Sam," but with the humorous expression left out. Softly strok-ing his goatee with three fingers, he began condescendingly: "You are, I think, more or less familiar with the characteristics and customs of the Spanish as exhibited by the settlers here." A thrill of apprehension went through me. Had he heard of Enri-quez' proceedings? Had Miss Mannersley cruelly betrayed him to her uncle? "I have not given that attention myself to their lan-guage and social peculiarities," he continued, with a large wave of the hand, "being much occupied with a study of their religious beliefs and superstitions" — it struck me that this was apt to be a common fault of people of the Mannersley type — "but I have re-frained from a personal discussion of them; on the contrary, I have held somewhat broad views on the subject of their remarkable missionary work, and have suggested a scheme of coöperation with them, quite inde-pendent of doctrinal teaching, to my brethren of other Protestant Christian sects. These views I first incorporated in a sermon last Sunday week, which I am told has created considerable attention." He stopped and coughed slightly. "I have not yet heard from any of the Roman clergy, but I am led to believe that my remarks were not ungrateful to Catholics generally."

I was relieved, although still in some wonder why he should address me on this topic. I had a vague remembrance of having heard that he had said something on Sunday which had offended some Puritans of his flock, but nothing more. He continued: "I have just said that I was unacquainted with the characteristics of the Spanish-American race. I presume, however, they have the impulsiveness of their Latin origin. They gesticulate — eh? They express their gratitude, their joy, their affection, their emotions generally, by spasmodic movements? They naturally dance — sing — eh?" A horrible suspicion crossed my mind; I could only stare helplessly at him. "I see," he said graciously; "perhaps it is a somewhat general question. I will explain myself. A rather singular occurrence happened to me the other night. I had returned from visiting a parishioner, and was alone in my study reviewing my sermon for the next day. It must have been quite late before I concluded, for I distinctly remember my niece had returned with her servant fully an hour before. Presently I heard the sounds of a musical instrument in the road, with the accents of some one singing or rehearsing some metrical composition in words that, although couched in a language foreign to me, in expression and modulation gave me the impression of being distinctly adulatory. For some little time, in the greater preoccupation of my task, I paid little attention to the performance; but its persistency at length drew me in no mere idle curiosity to the window. From thence, standing in my dressing-gown, and believing myself unperceived, I noticed under the large oak in the roadside the figure of a young man, who, by the imperfect light, appeared to be of Spanish extraction. But I evidently miscalculated my own invisibility; for he moved rapidly forward as I came to the window, and in a series of the most extraordinary pantomimic gestures saluted me. Beyond my experience of a few Greek plays in earlier days, I confess I am not an adept in the understanding of gesticulation; but it struck me that the various phases of gratitude, fervor, reverence, and exaltation were successively portrayed. He placed his hands upon his head, his heart, and even clasped them together in this manner." To my consternation the reverend gentleman here imitated Enriquez' most extravagant pantomime. "I am willing to confess," he continued, "that I was singularly moved by them, as well as by the highly creditable and Christian interest that evidently produced them. At last I opened the window. Leaning out, I told him that I regretted that the lateness of the hour prevented any further response from me than a grateful though hurried acknowledgment of his praiseworthy emotion, but that I should be glad to see him for a few moments in the vestry before service the next day, or at early candle-light, before the meeting of the Bible class. I told him that as my sole purpose had been the creation of an evangelical brotherhood and the exclusion of merely doctrinal views, nothing could be more gratifying to me than his spontaneous and unsolicited testimony to my motives. He appeared for an instant to be deeply affected, and, indeed, quite overcome with emotion, and then gracefully retired, with some agility and a slight saltatory movement."

He paused. A sudden and overwhelming idea took possession of me, and I looked impulsively into his face. Was it possible that for once Enriquez' ironical extravagance had been understood, met, and vanquished by a master hand? But the Rev. Mr. Mannersley's self-satisfied face betrayed no ambiguity or lurking humor. He was evidently in earnest; he had complacently accepted for himself the abandoned Enriquez' serenade to his niece. I felt an hysterical desire to laugh, but it was checked by my companion's next words.

" I informed my niece of the occurrence in the morning at breakfast. She had not heard anything of the strange performance, but she agreed with me as to its undoubted origin in a grateful recognition of my liberal efforts toward his co-religionists. It was she, in fact, who suggested that your knowledge of these people might corroborate my impressions."

I was dumfounded. Had Miss Mannersley, who must have recognized Enriquez' hand in this, concealed the fact in a desire to shield him? But this was so inconsistent with her utter indifference to him, except as a grotesque study, that she would have been more likely to tell her uncle all about his previous performance. Nor could it be that she wished to conceal her visit to the fandango. She was far too independent for that, and it was even possible that the reverend gentleman, in his desire to know more of Enriquez' compatriots, would not have objected. In my confusion I meekly added my conviction to hers, congratulated him upon his evident success, and slipped away. But I was burning with a desire to see Enriquez and know all. He was imaginative but not untruthful. Unfortunately, I learned that he was just then following one of his erratic impulses, and had gone to a rodeo at his cousin's, in the foothills, where he was alternately exercising his horsemanship in catching and breaking wild cattle, and delighting his relatives with his incomparable grasp of the American language and customs, and of the airs of a young man of fashion. Then my thoughts recurred to Miss Mannersley. Had she really been oblivious that night to Enriquez' serenade? I resolved to find out, if I could, without betraying Enriquez. Indeed, it was possible, after all, that it might not have been he.

Chance favored me. The next evening I

was at a party where Miss Mannersley, by reason of her position and quality, was a distinguished — I had almost written a popular — guest. But, as I have formerly stated, although the youthful fair of the Encinal were flattered by her casual attentions, and secretly admired her superior style and aristocratic calm, they were more or less uneasy under the dominance of her intelligence and education, and were afraid to attempt either confidence or familiarity. They were also singularly jealous of her, for although the average young man was equally afraid of her cleverness and candor, he was not above paying a tremulous and timid court to her for its effect upon her humbler sisters. This evening she was surrounded by her usual satellites, including, of course, the local notables and special guests of distinction. She had been discussing, I think, the existence of glaciers on Mount Shasta with a spectacled geologist, and had participated with charming frankness in a conversation on anatomy with the local doctor and a learned professor, when she was asked to take a seat at the piano. She played with remarkable skill and wonderful precision, but coldly and brilliantly. As she sat there in her subdued but perfectly fitting evening dress, her regular profile and short but slender neck firmly set upon her high shoulders, exhaling an atmosphere of refined puritanism and provocative intelligence, the utter incongruity of Enriquez' extravagant attentions, if ironical, and their equal hopelessness if not, seemed to me plainer than ever. What had this well-poised, coldly observant spinster to do with that quaintly ironic ruffler, that romantic cynic, that rowdy Don Quixote, that impossible Enriquez? Presently she ceased playing. Her slim, narrow slipper, revealing her thin ankle, remained upon the pedal; her delicate fingers were resting idly on the keys; her head was slightly thrown back, and her narrow eyebrows prettily knit toward the ceiling in an effort of memory.

"Something of Chopin's," suggested the geologist, ardently.

"That exquisite sonata!" pleaded the doctor.

"Suthin' of Rubinstein. Heard him once," said a gentleman of Siskiyou. "He just made that pianner get up and howl. Play Rube."

She shook her head with parted lips and a slight touch of girlish coquetry in her manner. Then her fingers suddenly dropped upon the keys with a glassy tinkle; there were a few quick pizzicato chords, down went the low pedal with a monotonous strumming, and she presently began to hum to herself. I started, — as well I might, — for I recognized one of Enriquez' favorite and most extravagant guitar solos. It was audacious; it was barbaric; it was, I fear, vulgar. As I remembered it, — as he sang it, — it recounted the adventures of one Don Francisco, a provincial gallant and roysterer of the most objectionable type. It had one hundred and four verses, which Enriquez never spared me. I shuddered as in a pleasant, quiet voice the correct Miss Mannersley warbled in musical praise of the *pellejo*, or wine-skin, and a eulogy of the dice-box came caressingly from her thin red lips. But the company was far differently affected: the strange, wild air and wilder accompaniment were evidently catching; people moved towards the piano; somebody whistled the air from a distant corner; even the faces of the geologist and doctor brightened.

"A tarantella, I presume?" blandly suggested the doctor.

Miss Mannersley stopped, and rose carelessly from the piano. "It is a Moorish gypsy song of the fifteenth century," she said dryly.

"It seemed sorter familiar, too," hesitated one of the young men, timidly, "like as if — don't you know? — you had without knowing it, don't you know?" — he blushed slightly — "sorter picked it up somewhere."

"I 'picked it up,' as you call it, in the collection of mediæval manuscripts of the Harvard Library, and copied it," returned Miss Mannersley, coldly, as she turned away.

But I was not inclined to let her off so easily. I presently made my way to her side. "Your uncle was complimentary enough to consult me as to the meaning of the appearance of a certain exuberant Spanish visitor at his house the other night." I looked into her brown eyes, but my own slipped off her velvety pupils without retaining anything. Then she reinforced her gaze with a pince-nez, and said carelessly:

"Oh, it's you? How are you? Well, could you give him any information?"

"Only generally," I returned, still looking into her eyes. "These people are impulsive. The Spanish blood is a mixture of gold and quicksilver."

She smiled slightly. " That reminds me of your volatile friend. He was mercurial enough, certainly. Is he still dancing ? "

" And singing sometimes," I responded pointedly. But she only added casually, " A singular creature," without exhibiting the least consciousness, and drifted away, leaving me none the wiser. I felt that Enriquez alone could enlighten me. I must see him.

I did, but not in the way I expected. There was a bull-fight at San Antonio the next Saturday afternoon, the usual Sunday performance being changed in deference to the Sabbatical habits of the Americans. An additional attraction was offered in the shape of a bull and bear fight, also a concession to American taste, which had voted the bull-fight " slow," and had averred that the bull " did not get a fair show." I am glad that I am able to spare the reader the usual realistic horrors, for in the Californian performances there was very little of the brutality that distinguished this function in the mother country. The horses were not miserable, worn-out hacks, but

young and alert mustangs ; and the display
of horsemanship by the picadors was not
only wonderful, but secured an almost absolute safety to horse and rider. I never saw
a horse gored ; although unskillful riders
were sometimes thrown in wheeling quickly
to avoid the bull's charge, they generally
regained their animals without injury.

The Plaza de Toros was reached through
the decayed and tile-strewn outskirts of an
old Spanish village. It was a rudely built,
oval amphitheatre, with crumbling, white-
washed adobe walls, and roofed only over
portions of the gallery reserved for the provincial "notables," but now occupied by a
few shopkeepers and their wives, with a
sprinkling of American travelers and ranch-
men. The impalpable adobe-dust of the
arena was being whirled into the air by the
strong onset of the afternoon trade-winds,
which happily, however, helped also to dissipate a reek of garlic, and the acrid fumes of
cheap tobacco rolled in corn-husk cigarettes.
I was leaning over the second barrier, waiting for the meagre and circus-like procession
to enter with the keys of the bull-pen, when
my attention was attracted to a movement
in the reserved gallery. A lady and gen-

tleman of a quality that was evidently unfamiliar to the rest of the audience were picking their way along the rickety benches to a front seat. I recognized the geologist with some surprise, and the lady he was leading with still greater astonishment. For it was Miss Mannersley, in her precise, well-fitting walking costume — a monotone of sober color among the parti-colored audience.

However, I was perhaps less surprised than the audience, for I was not only becoming as accustomed to the young girl's vagaries as I had been to Enriquez' extravagance, but I was also satisfied that her uncle might have given her permission to come, as a recognition of the Sunday concession of the management, as well as to conciliate his supposed Catholic friends. I watched her sitting there until the first bull had entered, and, after a rather brief play with the picadors and banderilleros, was dispatched. At the moment when the matador approached the bull with his lethal weapon I was not sorry for an excuse to glance at Miss Mannersley. Her hands were in her lap, her head slightly bent forward over her knees. I fancied that she, too, had dropped her eyes before the brutal situation; to my horror I saw that she had a drawing-book in her hand, and was actually sketching it. I turned my eyes in preference to the dying bull.

The second animal led out for this ingenious slaughter was, however, more sullen, uncertain, and discomposing to his butchers. He accepted the irony of a trial with gloomy, suspicious eyes, and he declined the challenge of whirling and insulting picadors. He bristled with banderillas like a hedgehog, but remained with his haunches backed against the barrier, at times almost hidden in the fine dust raised by the monotonous stroke of his sullenly pawing hoof — his one dull, heavy protest. A vague uneasiness had infected his adversaries; the picadors held aloof, the banderilleros skirmished at a safe distance. The audience resented only the indecision of the bull. Galling epithets were flung at him, followed by cries of " Espada ! " and, curving his elbow under his short cloak, the matador, with his flashing blade in hand, advanced and — stopped. The bull remained motionless.

For at that moment a heavier gust of wind than usual swept down upon the arena, lifted a suffocating cloud of dust, and whirled it around the tiers of benches and the balcony, and for a moment seemed to stop the performance. I heard an exclamation from the geologist, who had risen to his feet. I fancied I heard even a faint cry from Miss Mannersley; but the next moment, as the dust was slowly settling, we saw a sheet of paper in the air, that had been caught up in this brief cyclone, dropping, dipping from side to side on uncertain wings, until it slowly descended in the very middle of the arena. It was a leaf from Miss Mannersley's sketch-book, the one on which she had been sketching.

In the pause that followed it seemed to be the one object that at last excited the bull's growing but tardy ire. He glanced at it with murky, distended eyes; he snorted at it with vague yet troubled fury. Whether he detected his own presentment in Miss Mannersley's sketch, or whether he recognized it as an unknown and unfamiliar treachery in his surroundings, I could not conjecture; for the next moment the matador, taking advantage of the bull's concentration, with a complacent leer at the audience, advanced toward the paper. But at that instant a young man cleared the barrier into the arena with a single bound, shoved the

matador to one side, caught up the paper,
turned toward the balcony and Miss Mannersley with a gesture of apology, dropped
gaily before the bull, knelt down before him
with an exaggerated humility, and held up
the drawing as if for his inspection. A roar
of applause broke from the audience, a cry of
warning and exasperation from the attendants, as the goaded bull suddenly charged
the stranger. But he sprang to one side
with great dexterity, made a courteous gesture to the matador as if passing the bull
over to him, and still holding the paper in his
hand, re-leaped the barrier, and rejoined the
audience in safety. I did not wait to see
the deadly, dominant thrust with which the
matador received the charging bull; my eyes
were following the figure now bounding up
the steps to the balcony, where with an exaggerated salutation he laid the drawing in
Miss Mannersley's lap and vanished. There
was no mistaking that thin lithe form, the
narrow black mustache, and gravely dancing
eyes. The audacity of conception, the extravagance of execution, the quaint irony of
the sequel, could belong to no one but
Enriquez.

I hurried up to her as the six yoked mules

dragged the carcass of the bull away. She
was placidly putting up her book, the unmoved focus of a hundred eager and curious
eyes. She smiled slightly as she saw me.
"I was just telling Mr. Briggs what an
extraordinary creature it was, and how you
knew him. He must have had great experience to do that sort of thing so cleverly and
safely. Does he do it often? Of course,
not just that. But does he pick up cigars
and things that I see they throw to the
matador? Does he belong to the management? Mr. Briggs thinks the whole thing
was a feint to distract the bull," she added,
with a wicked glance at the geologist, who,
I fancied, looked disturbed.

"I am afraid," I said dryly, "that his act
was as unpremeditated and genuine as it was
unusual."

"Why afraid?"

It was a matter-of-fact question, but I
instantly saw my mistake. What right had
I to assume that Enriquez' attentions were
any more genuine than her own easy indifference; and if I suspected that they were, was
it fair in me to give my friend away to this
heartless coquette? "You are not very
gallant," she said, with a slight laugh, as I

was hesitating, and turned away with her escort before I could frame a reply. But at least Enriquez was now accessible, and I should gain some information from him. I knew where to find him, unless he were still lounging about the building, intent upon more extravagance; but I waited until I saw Miss Mannersley and Briggs depart without further interruption.

The hacienda of Ramon Saltillo, Enriquez' cousin, was on the outskirts of the village. When I arrived there I found Enriquez' pinto mustang steaming in the corral, and although I was momentarily delayed by the servants at the gateway, I was surprised to find Enriquez himself lying languidly on his back in a hammock in the patio. His arms were hanging down listlessly on each side as if in the greatest prostration, yet I could not resist the impression that the rascal had only just got into the hammock when he heard of my arrival.

" You have arrived, friend Pancho, in time," he said, in accents of exaggerated weakness. " I am absolutely exhaust. I am bursted, caved in, kerflummoxed. I have behold you, my friend, at the barrier. I speak not, I make no sign at the first, because I was on fire; I speak not at the feenish — for I am exhaust."

"I see; the bull made it lively for you."

He instantly bounded up in the hammock. "The bull! Caramba! Not a thousand bulls! And thees one, look you, was a craven. I snap my fingers over his horn; I roll my cigarette under his nose."

"Well, then — what was it?"

He instantly lay down again, pulling up the sides of the hammock. Presently his voice came from its depths, appealing in hollow tones to the sky. "He asks me — thees friend of my soul, thees brother of my life, thees Pancho that I lofe — what it was? He would that I should tell him why I am game in the legs, why I shake in the hand, crack in the voice, and am generally wipe out! And yet he, my pardner — thees Francisco — know that I have seen the mees from Boston! That I have gaze into the eye, touch the hand, and for the instant possess the picture that hand have drawn! It was a sublime picture, Pancho," he said, sitting up again suddenly, "and have kill the bull before our friend Pepe's sword have touch even the bone of hees back and make feenish of him."

" Look here, Enriquez," I said bluntly, " have you been serenading that girl?"

He shrugged his shoulders without the least embarrassment, and said: " Ah, yes. What would you? It is of a necessity."

" Well," I retorted, " then you ought to know that her uncle took it all to himself — thought you some grateful Catholic pleased with his religious tolerance."

He did not even smile. " Bueno," he said gravely. " That make something, too. In thees affair it is well to begin with the duenna. He is the duenna."

" And," I went on relentlessly, " her escort told her just now that your exploit in the bull-ring was only a trick to divert the bull, suggested by the management."

" Bah! her escort is a geologian. Naturally, she is to him as a stone."

I would have continued, but a peon interrupted us at this moment with a sign to Enriquez, who leaped briskly from the hammock, bidding me wait his return from a messenger in the gateway.

Still unsatisfied of mind I waited, and sat down in the hammock that Enriquez had quitted. A scrap of paper was lying in its meshes, which at first appeared to be of the kind from which Enriquez rolled his cigarettes; but as I picked it up to throw it away, I found it was of much firmer and stouter material. Looking at it more closely, I was surprised to recognize it as a piece of the tinted drawing-paper torn off the " block " that Miss Mannersley had used. It had been deeply creased at right angles as if it had been folded; it looked as if it might have been the outer half of a sheet used for a note.

It might have been a trifling circumstance, but it greatly excited my curiosity. I knew that he had returned the sketch to Miss Mannersley, for I had seen it in her hand. Had she given him another? And if so, why had it been folded to the destruction of the drawing? Or was it part of a note which he had destroyed? In the first impulse of discovery I walked quickly with it toward the gateway where Enriquez had disappeared, intending to restore it to him. He was just outside talking with a young girl. I started, for it was Jocasta — Miss Mannersley's maid.

With this added discovery came that sense of uneasiness and indignation with which we illogically are apt to resent the

withholding of a friend's confidence, even in
matters concerning only himself. It was no
use for me to reason that it was no business
of mine, that he was right in keeping a
secret that concerned another — and a lady ;
but I was afraid I was even more meanly
resentful because the discovery quite upset
my theory of his conduct and of Miss Mannersley's attitude toward him. I continued
to walk on to the gateway, where I bade
Enriquez a hurried good-by, alleging the
sudden remembrance of another engagement,
but without appearing to recognize the girl,
who was moving away, when, to my further
discomfiture, the rascal stopped me with an
appealing wink, threw his arms around my
neck, whispered hoarsely in my ear, " Ah !
you see — you comprehend — but you are
the mirror of discretion ! " and returned to
Jocasta. But whether this meant that he
had received a message from Miss Mannersley, or that he was trying to suborn her
maid to carry one, was still uncertain. He
was capable of either.

During the next two or three weeks I saw
him frequently ; but as I had resolved to try
the effect of ignoring Miss Mannersley in
our conversation, I gathered little further of

their relations, and, to my surprise, after one or two characteristic extravagances of allusion, Enriquez dropped the subject, too. Only one afternoon, as we were parting, he said carelessly: "My friend, you are going to the casa of Mannersley to-night. I too have the honor of the invitation. But you will be my Mercury — my Leporello — you will take of me a message to thees Mees Boston, that I am crushed, desolated, prostrate, and flabbergasted — that I cannot arrive, for I have of that night to sit up with the grandaunt of my brother-in-law, who has a quinsy to the death. It is sad."

This was the first indication I had received of Miss Mannersley's advances. I was equally surprised at Enriquez' refusal.

"Nonsense!" I said bluntly. "Nothing keeps you from going."

"My friend," returned Enriquez, with a sudden lapse into languishment that seemed to make him absolutely infirm; "it is everything that shall restrain me. I am not strong. I shall become weak of the knee and tremble under the eye of Mees Boston. I shall precipitate myself to the geologian by the throat. Ask me another conundrum that shall be easy."

He seemed idiotically inflexible, and did not go. But I did. I found Miss Mannersley exquisitely dressed and looking singularly animated and pretty. The lambent glow of her inscrutable eye as she turned towards me might have been flattering but for my uneasiness in regard to Enriquez. I delivered his excuses as naturally as I could. She stiffened for an instant, and seemed an inch higher. " I am so sorry," she said at last in a level voice. " I thought he would have been so amusing. Indeed, I had hoped we might try an old Moorish dance together which I have found and was practising."

" He would have been delighted, I know. It 's a great pity he did n't come with me," I said quickly ; " but," I could not help adding, with emphasis on her words, " he is such an ' extraordinary creature,' you know."

" I see nothing extraordinary in his devotion to an aged relative," returned Miss Mannersley, quietly, as she turned away, "except that it justifies my respect for his character."

I do not know why I did not relate this to him. Possibly I had given up trying to understand them ; perhaps I was beginning to have an idea that he could take care of himself. But I was somewhat surprised a few days later when, after asking me to go with him to a rodeo at his uncle's he added composedly, "You will meet Mees Boston."

I stared, and but for his manner would have thought it part of his extravagance. For the rodeo — a yearly chase of wild cattle for the purpose of lassoing and branding them — was a rather brutal affair, and purely a man's function ; it was also a family affair — a property stock-taking of the great Spanish cattle-owners — and strangers, particularly Americans, found it difficult to gain access to its mysteries and the festa that followed.

" But how did she get an invitation?" I asked. " You did not dare to ask" — I began.

" My friend," said Enriquez, with a singular deliberation, "the great and respectable Boston herself, and her serene, venerable oncle, and other Boston magnificoes, have of a truth done me the inexpressible honor to solicit of my degraded, papistical oncle that she shall come — that she shall of her own superior eye behold the barbaric customs of our race."

His tone and manner were so peculiar

that I stepped quickly before him, laid my
hands on his shoulders, and looked down
into his face. But the actual devil which I
now for the first time saw in his eyes went
out of them suddenly, and he relapsed again
in affected languishment in his chair. " I
shall be there, friend Pancho," he said, with
a preposterous gasp. " I shall nerve my arm
to lasso the bull, and tumble him before her
at her feet. I shall throw the ' buck-jump '
mustang at the same sacred spot. I shall
pluck for her the buried chicken at full
speed from the ground, and present it to
her. You shall see it, friend Pancho. I
shall be there."

He was as good as his word. When Don
Pedro Amador, his uncle, installed Miss
Mannersley, with Spanish courtesy, on a
raised platform in the long valley where the
rodeo took place, the gallant Enriquez selected a bull from the frightened and galloping herd, and, cleverly isolating him from
the band, lassoed his hind legs, and threw
him exactly before the platform where Miss
Mannersley was seated. It was Enriquez
who caught the unbroken mustang, sprang
from his own saddle to the bare back of his
captive, and with only the lasso for a bridle,

halted him on rigid haunches at Miss Mannersley's feet. It was Enriquez who, in the
sports that followed, leaned from his saddle
at full speed, caught up the chicken buried
to its head in the sand without wringing its
neck, and tossed it unharmed and fluttering
toward his mistress. As for her, she wore
the same look of animation that I had seen
in her face at our previous meeting. Although she did not bring her sketch-book
with her, as at the bull-fight, she did not
shrink from the branding of the cattle,
which took place under her very eyes.

Yet I had never seen her and Enriquez
together; they had never, to my actual
knowledge, even exchanged words. And
now, although she was the guest of his
uncle, his duties seemed to keep him in the
field, and apart from her. Nor, as far as I
could detect, did either apparently make
any effort to have it otherwise. The peculiar circumstance seemed to attract no atten-
'tion from any one else. But for what I
alone knew — or thought I knew — of their
actual relations, I should have thought them
strangers.

But I felt certain that the festa which
took place in the broad patio of Don Pedro's

casa would bring them together. And later in the evening, as we were all sitting on the veranda watching the dancing of the Mexican women, whose white-flounced sayas were monotonously rising and falling to the strains of two melancholy harps, Miss Mannersley rejoined us from the house. She seemed to be utterly absorbed and abstracted in the barbaric dances, and scarcely moved as she leaned over the railing with her cheek resting on her hand. Suddenly she arose with a little cry.

"What is it?" asked two or three.

"Nothing — only I have lost my fan." She had risen, and was looking abstractedly on the floor.

Half a dozen men jumped to their feet. "Let me fetch it," they said.

"No, thank you. I think I know where it is, and will go for it myself." She was moving away.

But Don Pedro interposed with Spanish gravity. Such a thing was not to be heard of in his casa. If the señorita would not permit *him* — an old man — to go for it, it must be brought by Enriquez, her cavalier of the day.

But Enriquez was not to be found. I

glanced at Miss Mannersley's somewhat disturbed face, and begged her to let me fetch it. I thought I saw a flush of relief come into her pale cheek as she said, in a lower voice, "On the stone seat in the garden."

I hurried away, leaving Don Pedro still protesting. I knew the gardens, and the stone seat at an angle of the wall, not a dozen yards from the casa. The moon shone full upon it. There, indeed, lay the little gray-feathered fan. But close beside it, also, lay the crumpled, black, gold-embroidered riding gauntlet that Enriquez had worn at the rodeo.

I thrust it hurriedly into my pocket, and ran back. As I passed through the gateway I asked a peon to send Enriquez to me. The man stared. Did I not know that Don Enriquez had ridden away two minutes ago?

When I reached the veranda, I handed the fan to Miss Mannersley without a word. "Bueno," said Don Pedro, gravely; "it is as well. There shall be no bones broken over the getting of it, for Enriquez, I hear, has had to return to the Encinal this very evening."

Miss Mannersley retired early. I did not inform her of my discovery, nor did I seek

in any way to penetrate her secret. There
was no doubt that she and Enriquez had
been together, perhaps not for the first time;
but what was the result of their interview?
From the young girl's demeanor and Enriquez' hurried departure, I could only fear
the worst for him. Had he been tempted
into some further extravagance and been angrily rebuked, or had he avowed a real passion concealed under his exaggerated mask
and been deliberately rejected? I tossed
uneasily half the night, following in my
dreams my poor friend's hurrying hoof-beats,
and ever starting from my sleep at what I
thought was the sound of galloping hoofs.

I rose early, and lounged into the patio;
but others were there before me, and a small
group of Don Pedro's family were excitedly
discussing something, and I fancied they
turned away awkwardly and consciously as
I approached. There was an air of indefinite uneasiness everywhere. A strange fear
came over me with the chill of the early
morning air. Had anything happened to
Enriquez? I had always looked upon his
extravagance as part of his playful humor.
Could it be possible that under the sting of
rejection he had made his grotesque threat

of languishing effacement real? Surely Miss Mannersley would know or suspect something, if it were the case.

I approached one of the Mexican women and asked if the señorita had risen. The woman started, and looked covertly round before she replied. Did not Don Pancho know that Miss Mannersley and her maid had not slept in their beds that night, but had gone, none knew where?

For an instant I felt an appalling sense of my own responsibility in this suddenly serious situation, and hurried after the retreating family group. But as I entered the corridor a vaquero touched me on the shoulder. He had evidently just dismounted, and was covered with the dust of the road. He handed me a note written in pencil on a leaf from Miss Mannersley's sketch-book. It was in Enriquez' hand, and his signature was followed by his most extravagant rubric.

"Friend Pancho: When you read this line you shall of a possibility think I am no more. That is where you shall slip up, my little brother! I am much more — I am two times as much, for I have marry Miss Boston. At the Mission Church, at five of the morning, sharp! No cards shall be left! I kiss the hand of my venerable uncle-in-law. You shall say to him that we fly to the South wilderness as the combined evangelical missionary to the heathen! Miss Boston herself say this. Ta-ta! How are you now?

"Your own ENRIQUEZ."

IN A HOLLOW OF THE HILLS

IN A HOLLOW OF THE HILLS.

CHAPTER I.

IT was very dark, and the wind was increasing. The last gust had been preceded by an ominous roaring down the whole mountain-side, which continued for some time after the trees in the little valley had lapsed into silence. The air was filled with a faint, cool, sodden odor, as of stirred forest depths. In those intervals of silence the darkness seemed to increase in proportion and grow almost palpable. Yet out of this sightless and soundless void now came the tinkle of a spur's rowels, the dry crackling of saddle leathers, and the muffled plunge of a hoof in the thick carpet of dust and desiccated leaves. Then a voice, which in spite of its matter-of-fact reality the obscurity lent a certain mystery to, said: —

"I can't make out anything! Where

the devil have we got to, anyway? It's as black as Tophet, here ahead! "

" Strike a light and make a flare with something," returned a second voice. " Look where you're shoving to — now — keep your horse off, will ye."

There was more muffled plunging, a silence, the rustle of paper, the quick spurt of a match, and then the uplifting of a flickering flame. But it revealed only the heads and shoulders of three horsemen, framed within a nebulous ring of light, that still left their horses and even their lower figures in impenetrable shadow. Then the flame leaped up and died out with a few zigzagging sparks that were falling to the ground, when a third voice, that was low but somewhat pleasant in its cadence, said : —

" Be careful where you throw that. You were careless last time. With this wind and the leaves like tinder, you might send a furnace blast through the woods."

" Then at least we'd see where we were."

Nevertheless, he moved his horse, whose trampling hoofs beat out the last fallen spark. Complete darkness and silence again followed. Presently the first speaker continued : —

" I reckon we 'll have to wait here till the next squall clears away the scud from the sky. Hello! What 's that?"

Out of the obscurity before them appeared a faint light, — a dim but perfectly defined square of radiance, — which, however, did not appear to illuminate anything around it. Suddenly it disappeared.

" That 's a house — it 's a light in a window," said the second voice.

" House be d—d!" retorted the first speaker. " A house with a window on Galloper's Ridge, fifteen miles from anywhere? You 're crazy!"

Nevertheless, from the muffled plunging and tinkling that followed, they seemed to be moving in the direction where the light had appeared. Then there was a pause.

" There 's nothing but a rocky outcrop here, where a house could n't stand, and we 're off the trail again," said the first speaker impatiently.

" Stop! — there it is again!"

The same square of light appeared once more, but the horsemen had evidently diverged in the darkness, for it seemed to be in a different direction. But it was more distinct, and as they gazed a shadow appeared upon its radiant surface — the profile of a human face. Then the light suddenly went out, and the face vanished with it.

" It *is* a window, and there was some one behind it," said the second speaker emphatically.

" It was a woman's face," said the pleasant voice.

" Whoever it is, just hail them, so that we can get our bearings. Sing out ! All together !"

The three voices rose in a prolonged shout, in which, however, the distinguishing quality of the pleasant voice was sustained. But there was no response from the darkness beyond. The shouting was repeated after an interval with the same result : the silence and obscurity remained unchanged.

" Let 's get out of this," said the first speaker angrily ; " house or no house, man or woman, we 're not wanted, and we 'll make nothing waltzing round here !"

" Hush !" said the second voice. " Sh-h ! Listen."

The leaves of the nearest trees were trilling audibly. Then came a sudden gust that swept the fronds of the taller ferns into their faces, and laid the thin, lithe whips of alder over their horses' flanks sharply. It was followed by the distant sea-like roaring of the mountain-side.

"That's a little more like it!" said the first speaker joyfully. "Another blow like that and we're all right. And look! there's a lightenin' up over the trail we came by."

There was indeed a faint glow in that direction, like the first suffusion of dawn, permitting the huge shoulder of the mountain along whose flanks they had been journeying to be distinctly seen. The sodden breath of the stirred forest depths was slightly tainted with an acrid fume.

"That's the match you threw away two hours ago," said the pleasant voice deliberately. "It's caught the dry brush in the trail round the bend."

"Anyhow, it's given us our bearings, boys," said the first speaker, with satisfied accents. "We're all right now; and the wind's lifting the sky ahead there. Forward now, all together, and let's get out of this hell-hole while we can!"

It was so much lighter that the bulk of each horseman could be seen as they moved forward together. But there was no thinning of the obscurity on either side of them. Nevertheless the profile of the horseman with the pleasant voice seemed to be occasionally turned backward, and he suddenly checked his horse.

"There's the window again!" he said. "Look! There — it's gone again."

"Let it go and be d—d!" returned the leader. "Come on."

They spurred forward in silence. It was not long before the wayside trees began to dimly show spaces between them, and the ferns to give way to lower, thick-set shrubs, which in turn yielded to a velvety moss, with long quiet intervals of netted and tangled grasses. The regular fall of the horses' feet became a mere rhythmic throbbing. Then suddenly a single hoof rang out sharply on stone, and the first speaker reined in slightly.

"Thank the Lord we're on the ridge now! and the rest is easy. Tell you what, though, boys, now we're all right, I don't mind saying that I did n't take no stock in that blamed corpse light down there. If there ever was a will-o'-the-wisp on a square up mountain, that was one. It was n't no window! Some of ye thought ye saw a face too — eh ? "

" Yes, and a rather pretty one," said the pleasant voice meditatively.

" That 's the way they 'd build that sort of thing, of course. It 's lucky ye had to satisfy yourself with looking. Gosh ! I feel creepy yet, thinking of it! What are ye looking back for now like Lot's wife ? Blamed if I don't think that face bewitched ye."

" I was only thinking about that fire you started," returned the other quietly. " I don't see it now."

" Well — if you did ? "

" I was wondering whether it could reach that hollow."

" I reckon that hollow could take care of any casual nat'rel fire that came boomin' along, and go two better every time ! Why, I don't believe there was any fire ; it was all a piece of that infernal *ignis fatuus* phantasmagoriana that was played upon us down there ! "

With the laugh that followed they started forward again, relapsing into the silence of tired men at the end of a long journey. Even their few remarks were interjectional, or reminiscent of topics whose freshness had been exhausted with the day. The gaining light which seemed to come from the ground about them rather than from the still, overcast sky above, defined their individuality more distinctly. The man who had first spoken, and who seemed to be their leader, wore the virgin unshaven beard, mustache, and flowing hair of the Californian pioneer, and might have been the eldest; the second speaker was close shaven, thin, and energetic; the third, with the pleasant voice, in height, litheness, and suppleness of figure appeared to be the youngest of the party. The trail had now become a grayish streak along the level table-land they were following, which also had the singular effect of appearing lighter than the surrounding landscape, yet of plunging into utter darkness on either side of its precipitous walls. Nevertheless, at the end of an hour the leader rose in his stirrups with a sigh of satisfaction.

"There's the light in Collinson's Mill! There's nothing gaudy and spectacular about that, boys, eh? No, sir! it's a square, honest beacon that a man can steer by. We'll be there in twenty minutes." He was pointing into the darkness below the already descending trail. Only a pioneer's eye could have detected the few pin-pricks of light in the impenetrable distance, and it was a signal proof of his leadership that the others accepted it without seeing it. "It's just ten o'clock," he continued, holding a huge silver watch to his eye; "we've wasted an hour on those blamed spooks yonder!"

"We weren't off the trail more than ten minutes, Uncle Dick," protested the pleasant voice.

"All right, my son; go down there if you like and fetch out your Witch of Endor, but as for me, I'm going to throw myself the other side of Collinson's lights. They're good enough for me, and a blamed sight more stationary!"

The grade was very steep, but they took it, California fashion, at a gallop, being genuinely good riders, and using their brains as well as their spurs in the understanding of their horses, and of certain natural laws, which the more artificial riders of civilization are apt to overlook. Hence there was no hesitation or indecision communicated to the nervous creatures they bestrode, who swept over crumbling stones and slippery ledges with a momentum that took away half their weight, and made a stumble or false step, or indeed anything but an actual collision, almost impossible. Closing together they avoided the latter, and holding each other well up, became one irresistible wedge-shaped mass. At times they yelled, not from consciousness nor bravado, but from the purely animal instinct of warning and to combat the breathlessness of their descent, until, reaching the level, they charged across the gravelly bed of a vanished river, and pulled up at Collinson's Mill. The mill itself had long since vanished with the river, but the building that had once stood for it was used as a rude hostelry for travelers, which, however, bore no legend or invitatory sign. Those who wanted it, knew it; those who passed it by, gave it no offense.

Collinson himself stood by the door, smoking a contemplative pipe. As they rode up,

he disengaged himself from the doorpost listlessly, walked slowly towards them, said reflectively to the leader, "I've been thinking
with you that a vote for Thompson is a vote
thrown away," and prepared to lead the
horses towards the water tank. He had
parted with them over twelve hours before,
but his air of simply renewing a recently
interrupted conversation was too common a
circumstance to attract their notice. They
knew, and he knew, that no one else had
passed that way since he had last spoken;
that the same sun had swung silently above
him and the unchanged landscape, and there
had been no interruption nor diversion to his
monotonous thought. The wilderness anni-
hilates time and space with the grim pathos
of patience.

Nevertheless he smiled. "Ye don't seem
to have got through coming down yet," he
continued, as a few small boulders, loosened
in their rapid descent, came more deliberately
rolling and plunging after the travelers
along the gravelly bottom. Then he turned
away with the horses, and, after they were
watered, he reëntered the house. His guests
had evidently not waited for his ministration.

They had already taken one or two bottles from the shelves behind a wide bar and helped themselves, and, glasses in hand, were now satisfying the more imminent cravings of hunger with biscuits from a barrel and slices of smoked herring from a box. Their equally singular host, accepting their conduct as not unusual, joined the circle they had comfortably drawn round the fireplace, and meditatively kicking a brand back at the fire, said, without looking at them : —

" Well ? "

" Well ! " returned the leader, leaning back in his chair after carefully unloosing the buckle of his belt, but with his eyes also on the fire, — " well ! we 've prospected every yard of outcrop along the Divide, and there ain't the ghost of a silver indication any-where."

"Not a smell," added the close-shaven guest, without raising his eyes.

They all remained silent, looking at the fire, as if it were the one thing they had taken into their confidence. Collinson also addressed himself to the blaze as he said presently : " It allus seemed to me that thar was something shiny about that ledge just round the shoulder of the spur, over the long cañon."

The leader ejaculated a short laugh. "Shiny, eh? shiny! Ye think *that* a sign? Why, you might as well reckon that because Key's head, over thar, is gray and silvery that he's got *sabe* and experience." As he spoke he looked towards the man with a pleasant voice. The fire shining full upon him revealed the singular fact that while his face was still young, and his mustache quite dark, his hair was perfectly gray. The object of this attention, far from being disconcerted by the comparison, added with a smile : —

"Or that he had any silver in his pocket."

Another lapse of silence followed. The wind tore round the house and rumbled in the short, adobe chimney.

"No, gentlemen," said the leader reflectively, "this sort o' thing is played out. I don't take no more stock in that cock-and-bull story about the lost Mexican mine. I don't catch on to that Sunday-school yarn about the pious, scientific sharp who collected leaves and vegetables all over the Divide, all the while he scientifically knew

that the range was solid silver, only he
would n't soil his fingers with God-forsaken
lucre. I ain't saying anything agin that
fine-spun theory that Key believes in about
volcanic upheavals that set up on end ar-
gentiferous rock, but I simply say that *I*
don't see it — with the naked eye. And I
reckon it 's about time, boys, as the game 's
up, that we handed in our checks, and left
the board."

There was another silence around the fire,
another whirl and turmoil without. There
was no attempt to combat the opinions of
their leader ; possibly the same sense of disappointed hopes was felt by all, only they
preferred to let the man of greater experience voice it. He went on : —

"We 've had our little game, boys, ever
since we left Rawlin's a week ago ; we 've
had our ups and downs ; we 've been starved
and parched, snowed up and half drowned,
shot at by road-agents and horse-thieves,
kicked by mules and played with by grizzlies.
We 've had a heap o' fun, boys, for our
money, but I reckon the picnic is about over.
So we 'll shake hands to-morrow all round
and call it square, and go on our ways
separately."

" And what do you think you 'll do, Uncle Dick ? " said his close-shaven companion list-lessly.

" I 'll make tracks for a square meal, a bed that a man can comfortably take off his boots and die in, and some violet-scented soap. Civilization 's good enough for me ! I even reckon I would n't mind ' the sound of the church-going bell ' ef there was a the-atre handy, as there likely would be. But the wilderness is played out."

" You 'll be back to it again in six months, Uncle Dick," retorted the other quickly.

Uncle Dick did not reply. It was a peculiarity of the party that in their isolated companionship they had already exhausted discussion and argument. A silence fol-lowed, in which they all looked at the fire as if it was its turn to make a suggestion.

" Collinson," said the pleasant voice ab-ruptly, " who lives in the hollow this side of the Divide, about two miles from the first spur above the big cañon ? "

" Nary soul ! "

" Are you sure ? "

" Sartin ! Thar ain't no one but me betwixt Bald Top and Skinner's — twenty-five miles."

" Of course, *you 'd* know if any one had come there lately ? " persisted the pleasant voice.

" I reckon. It ain't a week ago that I tramped the whole distance that you fellers just rode over."

" There ain't," said the leader deliberately, " any enchanted castle or cabin that goes waltzing round the road with revolving windows and fairy princesses looking out of 'em ? "

But Collinson, recognizing this as purely irrelevant humor, with possibly a trap or pitfall in it, moved away from the fireplace without a word, and retired to the adjoining kitchen to prepare supper. Presently he reappeared.

" The pork bar'l 's empty, boys, so I 'll hev to fix ye up with jerked beef, potatoes, and flapjacks. Ye see, thar ain't anybody ben over from Skinner's store for a week."

" All right; only hurry up ! " said Uncle Dick cheerfully, settling himself back in his chair. " I reckon to turn in as soon as I 've rastled with your hash, for I 've got to turn out agin and be off at sun-up."

They were all very quiet again, — so quiet

that they could not help noticing that the sound of Collinson's preparations for their supper had ceased too. Uncle Dick arose softly and walked to the kitchen door. Collinson was sitting before a small kitchen stove, with a fork in his hand, gazing abstractedly before him. At the sound of his guest's footsteps he started, and the noise of preparation recommenced. Uncle Dick returned to his chair by the fire. Leaning towards the chair of the close-shaven man, he said in a lower voice : —

"He was off agin ! "

"What ? "

"Thinkin' of that wife of his."

"What about his wife ? " asked Key, lowering his voice also.

The three men's heads were close together.

"When Collinson fixed up this mill he sent for his wife in the States," said Uncle Dick, in a half whisper, "waited a year for her, hanging round and boarding every emigrant wagon that came through the Pass. She did n't come — only the news that she was dead." He paused and nudged his chair still closer — the heads were almost touching. "They say, over in the Bar" —

his voice had sunk to a complete whisper
— " that it was a lie ! That she ran away
with the man that was fetchin' her out.
Three thousand miles and three weeks with
another man upsets some women. But *he*
knows nothing about it, only he sometimes
kinder goes off looney-like, thinking of her."
He stopped, the heads separated ; Collinson
had appeared at the doorway, his melancholy
patience apparently unchanged.

"Grub's on, gentlemen ; sit by and eat."

The humble meal was dispatched with
zest and silence. A few interjectional remarks about the uncertainties of prospecting
only accented the other pauses. In ten
minutes they were out again by the fireplace
with their lit pipes. As there were only
three chairs, Collinson stood beside the
chimney.

"Collinson," said Uncle Dick, after the
usual pause, taking his pipe from his lips,
" as we've got to get up and get at sun-up,
we might as well tell you now that we're
dead broke. We've been living for the
last few weeks on Preble Key's loose change
— and that's gone. You'll have to let this
little account and damage stand over."

Collinson's brow slightly contracted, without, however, altering his general expression of resigned patience.

" I 'm sorry for you, boys," he said slowly, " and " (diffidently) " kinder sorry for myself, too. You see, I reckoned on goin' over to Skinner's to-morrow, to fill up the pork bar'l and vote for Mesick and the wagon-road. But Skinner can't let me have anything more until I 've paid suthin' on account, as he calls it."

" D' ye mean to say thar 's any mountain man as low flung and mean as that? " said Uncle Dick indignantly.

" But it is n't *his* fault," said Collinson gently ; " you see, they won't send him goods from Sacramento if he don't pay up, and he *can't* if I *don't*. *Sabe ?* "

" Ah ! that 's another thing. They *are* mean — in Sacramento," said Uncle Dick, somewhat mollified.

The other guests murmured an assent to this general proposition. Suddenly Uncle Dick's face brightened.

" Look here ! I know Skinner, and I 'll stop there — No, blank it all ! I can't, for it 's off my route ! Well, then, we 'll fix it this way. Key will go there and tell Skinner that *I* say that *I'll* send the money to that Sacramento hound. That 'll fix it!"

Collinson's brow cleared; the solution of the difficulty seemed to satisfy everybody, and the close-shaven man smiled.

"And I 'll secure it," he said, "and give Collinson a sight draft on myself at San Francisco."

"What 's that for?" said Collinson, with a sudden suffusion on each cheek.

"In case of accident."

"Wot accident?" persisted Collinson, with a dark look of suspicion on his usually placid face.

"In case we should forget it," said the close-shaven man, with a laugh.

"And do you suppose that if you boys went and forgot it that I 'd have anything to do with your d—d paper?" said Collinson, a murky cloud coming into his eyes.

"Why, that 's only business, Colly," interposed Uncle Dick quickly; "that 's all Jim Parker means; he 's a business man, don't you see. Suppose we got killed! You 've that draft to show."

"Show who?" growled Collinson.

"Why, — hang it! — our friends, our
heirs, our relations — to get your money,"
hesitated Uncle Dick.

"And do you kalkilate," said Collinson,
with deeply laboring breath, "that if you
got killed, that I'd be coming on your folks
for the worth of the d—d truck I giv ye?
Go 'way! Lemme git out o' this. You're
makin' me tired." He stalked to the door,
lit his pipe, and began to walk up and down
the gravelly river-bed. Uncle Dick followed
him. From time to time the two other
guests heard the sounds of alternate protest
and explanation as they passed and repassed
the windows. Preble Key smiled, Parker
shrugged his shoulders.

"He'll be thinkin' you've begrudged him
your grub if you don't — that's the way
with these business men," said Uncle Dick's
voice in one of these intervals. Presently
they reëntered the house, Uncle Dick saying casually to Parker, "You can leave that
draft on the bar when you're ready to go
to-morrow;" and the incident was presumed
to have ended. But Collinson did not glance
in the direction of Parker for the rest of the
evening; and, indeed, standing with his back

to the chimney, more than once fell into that
stolid abstraction which was supposed to be
the contemplation of his absent wife.

From this silence, which became infec-
tious, the three guests were suddenly aroused
by a furious clattering down the steep descent of the mountain, along the trail they
had just ridden! It came near, increasing
in sound, until it even seemed to scatter the
fine gravel of the river-bed against the sides
of the house, and then passed in a gust of
wind that shook the roof and roared in the
chimney. With one common impulse the
three travelers rose and went to the door.
They opened it to a blackness that seemed
to stand as another and an iron door before
them, but to nothing else.

"Somebody went by then," said Uncle
Dick, turning to Collinson. "Did n't you
hear it?"

"Nary," said Collinson patiently, without
moving from the chimney.

"What in God's name was it, then?"

"Only some of them boulders you loosed
coming down. It's touch and go with them
for days after. When I first came here I
used to start up and rush out into the road

— like as you would — yellin' and screechin'
after folks that never was there and never
went by. Then it got kinder monotonous,
and I 'd lie still and let 'em slide. Why,
one night I 'd 'a' sworn that some one pulled
up with a yell and shook the door. But I
sort of allowed to myself that whatever it
was, it was n't wantin' to eat, drink, sleep,
or it would come in, and I had n't any
call to interfere. And in the mornin' I
found a rock as big as that box, lying chock-
a-block agin the door. Then I knowed I
was right."

Preble Key remained looking from the
door.

"There 's a glow in the sky over Big
Cañon," he said, with a meaning glance at
Uncle Dick.

"Saw it an hour ago," said Collinson.
"It must be the woods afire just round the
bend above the cañon. Whoever goes to
Skinner's had better give it a wide berth."

Key turned towards Collinson as if to
speak, but apparently changed his mind, and
presently joined his companions, who were
already rolling themselves in their blankets,
in a series of wooden bunks or berths,

ranged as in a ship's cabin, around the walls
of a resinous, sawdusty apartment that had
been the measuring room of the mill. Collinson disappeared, — no one knew or seemed
to care where, — and, in less than ten minutes from the time that they had returned
from the door, the hush of sleep and rest
seemed to possess the whole house. There
was no light but that of the fire in the front
room, which threw flickering and gigantic
shadows on the walls of the three empty
chairs before it. An hour later it seemed
as if one of the chairs were occupied, and a
grotesque profile of Collinson's slumbering
— or meditating — face and figure was projected grimly on the rafters as though it
were the hovering guardian spirit of the
house. But even that passed presently and
faded out, and the beleaguering darkness
that had encompassed the house all the evening began to slowly creep in through every
chink and cranny of the rambling, ill-jointed
structure, until it at last obliterated even the
faint embers on the hearth. The cool fra-
grance of the woodland depths crept in with
it until the steep of human warmth, the reek
of human clothing, and the lingering odors

of stale human victual were swept away in
that incorruptible and omnipotent breath.
An hour later — and the wilderness had re-
possessed itself of all.

Key, the lightest sleeper, awoke early, —
so early that the dawn announced itself only
in two dim squares of light that seemed to
grow out of the darkness at the end of the
room where the windows looked out upon
the valley. This reminded him of his woodland vision of the night before, and he lay
and watched them until they brightened and
began to outline the figures of his still
sleeping companions. But there were faint
stirrings elsewhere, — the soft brushing of a
squirrel across the shingled roof, the tiny
flutter of invisible wings in the rafters, the
" peep " and " squeak " of baby life below
the floor. And then he fell into a deeper
sleep, and awoke only when it was broad
day.

The sun was shining upon the empty
bunks ; his companions were already up
and gone. They had separated as they
had come together, — with the light-hearted
irresponsibility of animals, — without regret,
and scarcely reminiscence ; bearing, with

cheerful philosophy and the hopefulness of
a future unfettered by their past, the final
disappointment of their quest.   If they ever
met again, they would laugh and remember;
if they did not, they would forget without a
sigh.   He hurriedly dressed himself, and
went outside to dip his face and hands in
the bucket that stood beside the door; but
the clear air, the dazzling sunshine, and the
unexpected prospect half intoxicated him.

The abandoned mill stretched beside him
in all the pathos of its premature decay.
The ribs of the water-wheel appeared amid
a tangle of shrubs and driftwood, and were
twined with long grasses and straggling
vines; mounds of sawdust and heaps of
" brush " had taken upon themselves a velvety moss where the trickling slime of the
vanished river lost itself in sluggish pools,
discolored with the dyes of redwood.   But
on the other side of the rocky ledge dropped
the whole length of the valley, alternately
bathed in sunshine or hidden in drifts of
white and clinging smoke.   The upper end
of the long cañon, and the crests of the
ridge above him, were lost in this fleecy
cloud, which at times seemed to overflow

the summits and fall in slow leaps like lazy
cataracts down the mountain-side. Only the
range before the ledge was clear; there the
green pines seemed to swell onward and upward in long mounting billows, until at last
they broke against the sky.

In the keen stimulus of the hour and the
air Key felt the mountaineer's longing for
action, and scarcely noticed that Collinson
had pathetically brought out his pork barrel
to scrape together a few remnants for his last
meal. It was not until he had finished his
coffee, and Collinson had brought up his
horse, that a slight sense of shame at his own
and his comrades' selfishness embarrassed
his parting with his patient host. He himself was going to Skinner's to plead for him;
he knew that Parker had left the draft, —
he had seen it lying in the bar, — but a new
sense of delicacy kept him from alluding to
it now. It was better to leave Collinson
with his own peculiar ideas of the responsibilities of hospitality unchanged. Key
shook his hand warmly, and galloped up
the rocky slope. But when he had finally
reached the higher level, and fancied he
could even now see the dust raised by his

departing comrades on their two diverging paths, although he knew that they had already gone their different ways, — perhaps never to meet again, — his thoughts and his eyes reverted only to the ruined mill below him and its lonely occupant.

He could see him quite distinctly in that clear air, still standing before his door. And then he appeared to make a parting gesture with his hand, and something like snow fluttered in the air above his head. It was only the torn fragments of Parker's draft, which this homely gentleman of the Sierras, standing beside his empty pork barrel, had scattered to the four winds.

CHAPTER II.

KEY'S attention was presently directed to
something more important to his present
purpose. The keen wind which he had
faced in mounting the grade had changed,
and was now blowing at his back. His experience of forest fires had already taught
him that this was too often only the cold air
rushing in to fill the vacuum made by the
conflagration, and it needed not his sensation of an acrid smarting in his eyes, and
an unaccountable dryness in the air which
he was now facing, to convince him that the
fire was approaching him. It had evidently
traveled faster than he had expected, or
had diverged from its course. He was disappointed, not because it would oblige him
to take another route to Skinner's, as Collinson had suggested, but for a very different reason. Ever since his vision of the
preceding night, he had resolved to revisit
the hollow and discover the mystery. He

had kept his purpose a secret, — partly because he wished to avoid the jesting remarks
of his companions, but particularly because
he wished to go alone, from a very singular
impression that although they had witnessed
the incident he had really seen more than
they did. To this was also added the haunting fear he had felt during the night that
this mysterious habitation and its occupants
were in the track of the conflagration. He
had not dared to dwell upon it openly on
account of Uncle Dick's evident responsibility for the origin of the fire; he appeased
his conscience with the reflection that the
inmates of the dwelling no doubt had ample
warning in time to escape. But still, he
and his companions ought to have stopped
to help them, and then — but here he
paused, conscious of another reason he could
scarcely voice then, or even now. Preble
Key had not passed the age of romance, but
like other romancists he thought he had
evaded it by treating it practically.

Meantime he had reached the fork where
the trail diverged to the right, and he must
take that direction if he wished to make
a détour of the burning woods to reach

Skinner's. His momentary indecision communicated itself to his horse, who halted.
Recalled to himself, he looked down mechanically, when his attention was attracted
by an unfamiliar object lying in the dust of
the trail. It was a small slipper — so small
that at first he thought it must have belonged to some child. He dismounted and
picked it up. It was worn and shaped to
the foot. It could not have lain there long,
for it was not filled nor discolored by the
wind-blown dust of the trail, as all other
adjacent objects were. If it had been
dropped by a passing traveler, that traveler
must have passed Collinson's, going or coming, within the last twelve hours. It was
scarcely possible that the shoe could have
dropped from the foot without the wearer's
knowing it, and it must have been dropped
in an urgent flight, or it would have been
recovered. Thus practically Key treated his
romance. And having done so, he instantly
wheeled his horse and plunged into the road
in the direction of the fire.

But he was surprised after twenty minutes'
riding to find that the course of the fire had
evidently changed. It was growing clearer

before him ; the dry heat seemed to come
more from the right, in the direction of the
détour he should have taken to Skinner's.
This seemed almost providential, and in
keeping with his practical treatment of his
romance, as was also the fact that in all
probability the fire had not yet visited the
little hollow which he intended to explore.
He knew he was nearing it now; the locality had been strongly impressed upon him
even in the darkness of the previous evening. He had passed the rocky ledge ; his
horse's hoofs no longer rang out clearly;
slowly and perceptibly they grew deadened
in the springy mosses, and were finally lost
in the netted grasses and tangled vines that
indicated the vicinity of the densely wooded
hollow. Here were already some of the
wider spaced vanguards of that wood ; but
here, too, a peculiar circumstance struck him.
He was already descending the slight decliv-
ity; but the distance, instead of deepening
in leafy shadow, was actually growing lighter.
Here were the outskirting sentinels of the
wood — but the wood itself was gone ! He
spurred his horse through the tall arch between the opened columns, and pulled up in
amazement.

The wood, indeed, was gone, and the whole hollow filled with the already black and dead stumps of the utterly consumed forest! More than that, from the indications before him, the catastrophe must have almost immediately followed his retreat from the hollow on the preceding night. It was evident that the fire had leaped the intervening shoulder of the spur in one of the unaccountable, but by no means rare, phenomena of this kind of disaster. The circling heights around were yet untouched; only the hollow, and the ledge of rock against which they had blundered with their horses when they were seeking the mysterious window in last evening's darkness, were calcined and destroyed. He dismounted and climbed the ledge, still warm from the spent fire. A large mass of grayish outcrop had evidently been the focus of the furnace blast of heat which must have raged for hours in this spot. He was skirting its crumbling débris when he started suddenly at a discovery which made everything else fade into utter insignificance. Before him, in a slight depression formed by a fault or lapse in the upheaved strata, lay the charred

and incinerated remains of a dwelling-house
leveled to the earth! Originally half hidden by a natural *abattis* of growing myrtle
and ceanothus which covered this counter-
scarp of rock towards the trail, it must
have stood within a hundred feet of them
during their halt!

Even in its utter and complete obliteration by the furious furnace blast that had
swept across it, there was still to be seen an
unmistakable ground plan and outline of a
four-roomed house. While everything that
was combustible had succumbed to that intense heat, there was still enough half-fused
and warped metal, fractured iron plate, and
twisted and broken bars to indicate the
kitchen and tool shed. Very little had, evidently, been taken away; the house and its
contents were consumed where they stood.
With a feeling of horror and desperation
Key at last ventured to disturb two or three
of the blackened heaps that lay before him.
But they were only vestiges of clothing, bed-
ding, and crockery — there was no human
trace that he could detect. Nor was there
any suggestion of the original condition
and quality of the house, except its size:

whether the ordinary unsightly cabin of frontier " partners," or some sylvan cottage — there was nothing left but the usual ignoble and unsavory ruins of burnt-out human habitation.

And yet its very existence was a mystery. It had been unknown at Collinson's, its nearest neighbor, and it was presumable that it was equally unknown at Skinner's. Neither he nor his companions had detected it in their first journey by day through the hollow, and only the tell-tale window at night had been a hint of what was even then so successfully concealed that they could not discover it when they had blundered against its rock foundation. For concealed it certainly was, and intentionally so. But for what purpose?

He gave his romance full play for a few minutes with this question. Some recluse, preferring the absolute simplicity of nature, or perhaps wearied with the artificialities of society, had secluded himself here with the company of his only daughter. Proficient as a pathfinder, he had easily discovered some other way of provisioning his house from the settlements than by the ordinary

trails past Collinson's or Skinner's, which
would have betrayed his vicinity. But re-
cluses are not usually accompanied by young
daughters, whose relations with the world,
not being as antagonistic, would make them
uncertain companions. Why not a wife?
His presumption of the extreme youth of
the face he had seen at the window was
after all only based upon the slipper he had
found. And if a wife, whose absolute acceptance of such confined seclusion might
be equally uncertain, why not somebody
else's wife? Here was a reason for conceal-
ment, and the end of an episode, not unknown even in the wilderness. And here
was the work of the Nemesis who had overtaken them in their guilty contentment!
The story, even to its moral, was complete.
And yet it did not entirely satisfy him, so
superior is the absolutely unknown to the
most elaborate theory.

His attention had been once or twice
drawn towards the crumbling wall of outcrop, which during the conflagration must
have felt the full force of the fiery blast
that had swept through the hollow and spent
its fury upon it. It bore evidence of the

intense heat in cracked fissures and the
crumbling débris that lay at its feet. Key
picked up some of the still warm fragments,
and was not surprised that they easily broke
in a gritty, grayish powder in his hands. In
spite of his preoccupation with the human
interest, the instinct of the prospector was
still strong upon him, and he almost mechanically put some of the pieces in his
pockets. Then after another careful survey
of the locality for any further record of its
vanished tenants, he returned to his horse.
Here he took from his saddle-bags, half listlessly, a precious phial encased in wood, and,
opening it, poured into another thick glass
vessel part of a smoking fluid; he then
crumbled some of the calcined fragments
into the glass, and watched the ebullition
that followed with mechanical gravity.
When it had almost ceased he drained off
the contents into another glass, which he set
down, and then proceeded to pour some
water from his drinking-flask into the ordinary tin cup which formed part of his culi-
nary traveling-kit. Into this he put three
or four pinches of salt from his provision
store. Then dipping his fingers into the

salt and water, he allowed a drop to fall into the glass. A white cloud instantly gathered in the colorless fluid, and then fell in a fine film to the bottom of the glass. Key's eyes concentrated suddenly, the listless look left his face. His fingers trembled lightly as he again let the salt water fall into the solution, with exactly the same result! Again and again he repeated it, until the bottom of the glass was quite gray with the fallen precipitate. And his own face grew as gray.

His hand trembled no longer as he carefully poured off the solution so as not to disturb the precipitate at the bottom. Then he drew out his knife, scooped a little of the gray sediment upon its point, and emptying his tin cup, turned it upside down upon his knee, placed the sediment upon it, and began to spread it over the dull surface of its bottom with his knife. He had intended to rub it briskly with his knife blade. But in the very action of spreading it, the first stroke of his knife left upon the sediment and the cup the luminous streak of burnished silver!

He stood up and drew a long breath to

still the beatings of his heart. Then he
rapidly re-climbed the rock, and passed over
the ruins again, this time plunging hurriedly
through, and kicking aside the charred
heaps without a thought of what they had
contained. Key was not an unfeeling man,
he was not an unrefined one: he was a gentleman by instinct, and had an intuitive
sympathy for others; but in that instant his
whole mind was concentrated upon the calcined outcrop! And his first impulse was
to see if it bore any evidence of previous
examination, prospecting, or working by its
suddenly evicted neighbors and owners.
There was none: they had evidently not
known it. Nor was there any reason to
suppose that they would ever return to their
hidden home, now devastated and laid bare
to the open sunlight and open trail. They
were already far away; their guilty personal secret would keep them from revisit-
ing it. An immense feeling of relief came
over the soul of this moral romancer; a
momentary recognition of the Most High
in this perfect poetical retribution. He ran
back quickly to his saddle-bags, drew out
one or two carefully written, formal notices

of preëmption and claim, which he and his
former companions had carried in their brief
partnership, erased their signatures and left
only his own name, with another grateful
sense of Divine interference, as he thought
of them speeding far away in the distance,
and returned to the ruins. With unconscious irony, he selected a charred post from
the embers, stuck it in the ground a few
feet from the débris of outcrop, and finally
affixed his "Notice." Then, with a conscientiousness born possibly of his new
religious convictions, he dislodged with his
pickaxe enough of the brittle outcrop to
constitute that presumption of "actual
work" upon the claim which was legally
required for its maintenance, and returned
to his horse. In replacing his things in
his saddle-bags he came upon the slipper,
and for an instant so complete was his preoccupation in his later discovery, that he
was about to throw it away as useless im-
pedimenta, until it occurred to him, albeit
vaguely, that it might be of service to him
in its connection with that discovery, in
the way of refuting possible false claimants.
He was not aware of any faithlessness to his

momentary romance, any more than he was conscious of any disloyalty to his old companions, in his gratification that his good fortune had come to him alone. This singular selection was a common experience of prospecting. And there was something about the magnitude of his discovery that seemed to point to an individual achievement. He had made a rough calculation of the richness of the lode from the quantity of precipitate in his rude experiment ; he had estimated its length, breadth, and thickness from his slight knowledge of geology and the theories then ripe ; and the yield would be colossal! Of course, he would require capital to work it, he would have to " let in " others to his scheme and his prosperity ; but the control of it would always be *his own.*

Then he suddenly started as he had never in his life before started at the foot of man ! For there was a footfall in the charred brush ; and not twenty yards from him stood Collinson, who had just dismounted from a mule. The blood rushed to Key's pale face.

" Prospectin' agin ? " said the proprietor of the mill, with his weary smile.

" No," said Key quickly, "only straight-
ening my pack." The blood deepened in
his cheek at his instinctive lie. Had he
carefully thought it out before, he would
have welcomed Collinson, and told him all.
But now a quick, uneasy suspicion flashed
upon him. Perhaps his late host had lied,
and knew of the existence of the hidden
house. Perhaps — he had spoken of some
" silvery rock " the night before — he even
knew something of the lode itself. He turned
upon him with an aggressive face. But Collinson's next words dissipated the thought.

" I 'm glad I found ye, anyhow," he
said. " Ye see, arter you left, I saw ye turn
off the trail and make for the burning woods
instead o' goin' round. I sez to myself, 'That
fellow is making straight for Skinner's.
He 's sorter worried about me and that
empty pork bar'l,' — I had n't oughter spoke
that away afore you boys, anyhow, — 'and
he 's takin' risks to help me.' So I reckoned
I 'd throw my leg over Jenny here, and look
arter ye — and go over to Skinner's myself
— and vote."

" Certainly," said Key with cheerful
alacrity, and the one thought of getting Col-

linson away; " we 'll go together, and we 'll
see that that pork barrel is filled ! " He
glowed quite honestly with this sudden idea
of remembering Collinson through his good
fortune. " Let 's get on quickly, for we
may find the fire between us on the outer
trail." He hastily mounted his horse.

" Then you did n't take this as a short
cut," said Collinson, with dull perseverance
in his idea. " Why not? It looks all clear
ahead."

" Yes," said Key hurriedly, " but it 's
been only a leap of the fire, it 's still raging
round the bend. We must go back to
the cross-trail." His face was still flushing
with his very equivocating, and his anxiety
to get his companion away. Only a few
steps further might bring Collinson before
the ruins and the " Notice," and that discovery must not be made by him until Key's
plans were perfected. A sudden aversion to
the man he had a moment before wished to
reward began to take possession of him.
" Come on," he added almost roughly.

But to his surprise, Collinson yielded with
his usual grim patience, and even a slight
look of sympathy with his friend's annoy-

ance. "I reckon you're right, and mebbee you're in a hurry to get to Skinner's all along o' *my* business. I ought n't hev told you boys what I did." As they rode rapidly away he took occasion to add, when Key had reined in slightly, with a feeling of relief at being out of the hollow, "I was thinkin', too, of what you'd asked about any one livin' here unbeknownst to me."

"Well," said Key, with a new nervousness.

"Well; I only had an idea o' proposin' that you and me just took a look around that holler whar you thought you saw suthin'!" said Collinson tentatively.

"Nonsense," said Key hurriedly. "We really saw nothing — it was all a fancy; and Uncle Dick was joking me because I said I thought I saw a woman's face," he added with a forced laugh.

Collinson glanced at him, half sadly. "Oh! You were only funnin', then. I oughter guessed that. I oughter have knowed it from Uncle Dick's talk!" They rode for some moments in silence; Key preoccupied and feverish, and eager only to reach Skinner's. Skinner was not only

postmaster but "registrar" of the district,
and the new discoverer did not feel entirely
safe until he had put his formal notification
and claims "on record." This was no pub-
lication of his actual secret, nor any indication of success, but was only a record that
would in all probability remain unnoticed
and unchallenged amidst the many other
hopeful dreams of sanguine prospectors.
But he was suddenly startled from his preoccupation.

"Ye said ye war straightenin' up yer
pack just now," said Collinson slowly.

"Yes!" said Key almost angrily, "and I
was."

"Ye did n't stop to straighten it up down
at the forks of the trail, did ye?"

"I may have," said Key nervously. "But
why?"

"Ye won't mind my axin' ye another
question, will ye? Ye ain't carryin' round
with ye no woman's shoe?"

Key felt the blood drop from his cheeks.
"What do you mean?" he stammered,
scarcely daring to lift his conscious eyelids
to his companion's glance. But when he
did so he was amazed to find that Collin-

son's face was almost as much disturbed as his 'own.

"I know it ain't the square thing to ask ye, but this is how it is," said Collinson hesitatingly. "Ye see just down by the fork of the trail where you came I picked up a woman's shoe. It sorter got me! For I sez to myself, 'Thar ain't no one bin by my shanty, comin' or goin', for weeks but you boys, and that shoe, from the looks of it, ain't bin there as many hours.' I knew there was n't any wimin hereabouts. I reckoned it could n't hev bin dropped by Uncle Dick or that other man, for you would have seen it on the road, So I allowed it might have bin *you.* And yer it is." He slowly drew from his pocket — what Key was fully prepared to see — the mate of the slipper Key had in his saddle-bags! The fair fugitive had evidently lost them both.

But Key was better prepared now (perhaps this kind of dissimulation is progressive), and quickly alive to the necessity of throwing Collinson off this unexpected scent. And his companion's own suggestion was right to his hand, and, as it seemed, again quite providential! He laughed, with a quick color, which, however, appeared to help his lie, as he replied half hysterically, " You 're right, old man, I own up, it 's mine ! It 's d—d silly, I know — but then, we 're all fools where women are concerned — and I would n't have lost that slipper for a mint of money."

He held out his hand gayly, but Collinson retained the slipper while he gravely examined it.

" You would n't mind telling me where you mought hev got that? " he said meditatively.

" Of course I should mind," said Key with a well-affected mingling of mirth and indignation. " What are you thinking of, you old rascal? What do you take me for? "

But Collinson did not laugh. " You would n't mind givin' me the size and shape and general heft of her as wore that shoe ? "

" Most decidedly I should do nothing of the kind ! " said Key half impatiently. " Enough, that it was given to me by a very pretty girl. There ! that 's all you will know."

" *Given* to you ? " said Collinson, lifting his eyes.

" Yes," returned Key sharply.

Collinson handed him the slipper gravely.
" I only asked you," he said slowly, but
with a certain quiet dignity which Key had
never before seen in his face, " because thar
was suthin' about the size, and shape, and
fillin' out o' that shoe that kinder reminded
me of some 'un ; but that some 'un — her as
mought hev stood up in that shoe — ain't o'
that kind as would ever stand in the shoes
of her as *you* know at all."   The rebuke, if
such were intended, lay quite as much in the
utter ignoring of Key's airy gallantry and
levity as in any conscious slur upon the fair
fame of his invented Dulcinea.   Yet Key
oddly felt a strong inclination to resent the
aspersion as well as Collinson's gratuitous
morality ; and with a mean recollection of
Uncle Dick's last evening's scandalous gossip, he said sarcastically, " And, of course,
that some one *you* were thinking of was your
lawful wife."

" It war ! " said Collinson gravely.

Perhaps it was something in Collinson's
manner, or his own preoccupation, but he
did not pursue the subject, and the conversation lagged.   They were nearing, too, the

outer edge of the present conflagration, and
the smoke, lying low in the unburnt woods,
or creeping like an actual exhalation of the
soil, blinded them so that at times they lost
the trail completely. At other times, from
the intense heat, it seemed as if they were
momentarily impinging upon the burning
area, or were being caught in a closing circle.
It was remarkable that with his sudden ac-
cession of fortune Key seemed to lose his
usual frank and careless fearlessness, and
impatiently questioned his companion's wood-
craft. There were intervals when he regretted his haste to reach Skinner's by this
shorter cut, and began to bitterly attribute
it to his desire to serve Collinson. Ah, yes!
it would be fine indeed, if just as he were
about to clutch the prize he should be sacri-
ficed through the ignorance and stupidity of
this heavy-handed moralist at his side! But
it was not until, through that moralist's
guidance, they climbed a steep acclivity to a
second ridge, and were comparatively safe,
that he began to feel ashamed of his surly
silence or surlier interruptions. And Collinson, either through his unconquerable
patience, or possibly in a fit of his usual

uxorious abstraction, appeared to take no notice of it.

A sloping table-land of weather-beaten boulders now effectually separated them from the fire on the lower ridge. They presently began to descend on the further side of the crest, and at last dropped upon a wagon-road, and the first track of wheels that Key had seen for a fortnight. Rude as it was, it seemed to him the highway to fortune, for he knew that it passed Skinner's and then joined the great stage-road to Marysville, — now his ultimate destination. A few rods further on they came in view of Skinner's, lying like a dingy forgotten winter snowdrift on the mountain shelf.

It contained a post-office, tavern, black-smith's shop, "general store," and express-office, scarcely a dozen buildings in all, but all differing from Collinson's Mill in some vague suggestion of vitality, as if the daily regular pulse of civilization still beat, albeit languidly, in that remote extremity. There was anticipation and accomplishment twice a day; and as Key and Collinson rode up to the express-office, the express-wagon was standing before the door ready to start to meet the stagecoach at the cross-roads three miles away. This again seemed a special providence to Key. He had a brief official communication with Skinner as registrar, and duly recorded his claim; he had a hasty and confidential aside with Skinner as general storekeeper, and such was the unconscious magnetism developed by this embryo millionaire that Skinner extended the necessary credit to Collinson on Key's word alone. That done, he rejoined Collinson in high spirits with the news, adding cheerfully, "And I dare say, if you want any further advances Skinner will give them to you on Parker's draft."

"You mean that bit o' paper that chap left," said Collinson gravely.

"Yes."

"I tore it up."

"You tore it up?" ejaculated Key.

"You hear me? Yes!" said Collinson.

Key stared at him. Surely it was again providential that he had not intrusted his secret to this utterly ignorant and prejudiced man! The slight twinges of conscience that his lie about the slippers had caused him disappeared at once. He could not have trusted him even in that; it would have been like this stupid fanatic to have prevented Key's preëmption of that claim, until he, Collinson, had satisfied himself of the whereabouts of the missing proprietor. Was he quite sure that Collinson would not revisit the spot when he had gone? But he was ready for the emergency.

He had intended to leave his horse with Skinner as security for Collinson's provisions, but Skinner's liberality had made this unnecessary, and he now offered it to Collinson to use and keep for him until called for. This would enable his companion to "pack" his goods on the mule, and oblige him to return to the mill by the wagon-road and "outside trail," as more commodious for the two animals.

"Ye ain't afeared o' the road agents?" suggested a bystander; "they just swarm on Galloper's Ridge, and they 'held up' the down stage only last week."

"They're not so lively since the deputy-sheriff's got a new idea about them, and has been lying low in the brush near Bald Top," returned Skinner. "Anyhow, they don't stop teams nor 'packs' unless there's

a chance of their getting some fancy horse-
flesh by it; and I reckon thar ain't much to
tempt them thar," he added, with a satirical
side glance at his customer's cattle.   But
Key was already standing in the express-
wagon, giving a farewell shake to his patient companion's hand, and this ingenuous
pleasantry passed unnoticed.   Nevertheless,
as the express-wagon rolled away, his active
fancy began to consider this new danger
that might threaten the hidden wealth of
his claim.   But he reflected that for a time,
at least, only the crude ore would be taken
out and shipped to Marysville in a shape
that offered no profit to the highwaymen.
Had it been a gold mine! — but here again
was the interposition of Providence!

A week later Preble Key returned to
Skinner's with a foreman and ten men, and
an unlimited credit to draw upon at Marysville!   Expeditions of this kind created no
surprise at Skinner's.   Parties had before
this entered the wilderness gayly, none knew
where or what for; the sedate and silent
woods had kept their secret while there; they
had evaporated, none knew when or where
— often, alas! with an unpaid account at

Skinner's. Consequently, there was nothing in Key's party to challenge curiosity. In another week a rambling, one-storied shed of pine logs occupied the site of the mysterious ruins, and contained the party; in two weeks excavations had been made, and the whole face of the outcrop was exposed; in three weeks every vestige of former tenancy which the fire had not consumed was trampled out by the alien feet of these toilers of the "Sylvan Silver Hollow Company." None of Key's former companions would have recognized the hollow in its blackened leveling and rocky foundation; even Collinson would not have remembered this stripped and splintered rock, with its heaps of fresh débris, as the place where he had overtaken Key. And Key himself had forgotten, in his triumph, everything but the chance experiment that had led to his success.

Perhaps it was well, therefore, that one night, when the darkness had mercifully fallen upon this scene of sylvan desolation, and its still more incongruous and unsavory human restoration, and the low murmur of the pines occasionally swelled up from the unscathed mountain-side, a loud shout and the trampling of horses' feet awoke the dwellers in the shanty. Springing to their feet, they hurriedly seized their weapons and rushed out, only to be confronted by a dark, motionless ring of horsemen, two flaming torches of pine knots, and a low but distinct voice of authority. In their excitement, half-awakened suspicion, and confusion, they were affected by its note of calm preparation and conscious power.

" Drop those guns — hold up your hands! We 've got every man of you covered."

Key was no coward; the men, though flustered, were not cravens : but they obeyed.

" Trot out your leader! Let him stand out there, clear, beside that torch ! "

One of the gleaming pine knots disengaged itself from the dark circle and moved to the centre, as Preble Key, cool and confident, stepped beside it.

" That will do," said the immutable voice. " Now, we want Jack Riggs, Sydney Jack, French Pete, and One-eyed Charley."

A vivid reminiscence of the former night scene in the hollow — of his own and his companions' voices raised in the darkness — flashed across Key. With an instinctive premonition that this invasion had something to do with the former tenant, he said calmly : —

" *Who* wants them ? "

" The State of California," said the voice.

" The State of California must look further," returned Key in his old pleasant voice ; " there are no such names among my party."

" Who are you ? "

" The manager of the 'Sylvan Silver Hollow Company,' and these are my workmen."

There was a hurried movement, and the sound of whispering in the hitherto dark and silent circle, and then the voice rose again :

" You have the papers to prove that ? "

" Yes, in the cabin.   And you ? "

" I 've a warrant to the sheriff of Sierra."

There was a pause, and the voice went on less confidently : —

" How long have you been here ? "

" Three weeks.   I came here the day of the fire and took up this claim."

" There was no other house here ? "

" There were ruins, — you can see them still.   It may have been a burnt-up cabin."

The voice disengaged itself from the vague background and came slowly forwards : —

" It was a den of thieves. It was the hiding-place of Jack Riggs and his gang of road agents. I 've been hunting this spot for three weeks. And now the whole thing 's up ! "

There was a laugh from Key's men, but it was checked as the owner of the voice slowly ranged up beside the burning torch and they saw his face. It was dark and set with the defeat of a brave man.

" Won't you come in and take something ? " said Key kindly.

" No. It 's enough fool work for me to have routed ye out already. But I suppose it 's all in my d—d day's work ! Goodnight ! Forward there ! Get ! "

The two torches danced forwards, with the trailing off of vague shadows in dim procession ; there was a clatter over the rocks and they were gone. Then, as Preble Key gazed after them, he felt that with them had passed the only shadow that lay upon his great fortune ; and with the last tenant of the hollow a proscribed outlaw and fugitive, he was henceforth forever safe in his claim and his discovery. And yet, oddly enough, at that moment, as he turned away, for the first time in three weeks there passed before his fancy with a stirring of reproach a vision of the face that he had seen at the window.

CHAPTER III.

OF the great discovery in Sylvan Silver
Hollow it would seem that Collinson as yet
knew nothing. In spite of Key's fears that
he might stray there on his return from
Skinner's, he did not, nor did he afterwards
revisit the locality. Neither the news of the
registry of the claim nor the arrival of Key's
workmen ever reached him. The few travelers who passed his mill came from the valley to cross the Divide on their way to Skinner's, and returned by the longer but easier
détour of the stage - road over Galloper's
Ridge. He had no chance to participate in
the prosperity that flowed from the opening
of the mine, which plentifully besprinkled
Skinner's settlement; he was too far away
to profit even by the chance custom of Key's
Sabbath wandering workmen. His isolation
from civilization (for those who came to
him from the valley were rude Western emigrants like himself) remained undisturbed.

The return of the prospecting party to his humble hospitality that night had been an exceptional case ; in his characteristic simplicity he did not dream that it was because they had nowhere else to go in their penniless condition. It was an incident to be pleasantly remembered, but whose nonrecurrence did not disturb his infinite patience. His pork barrel and flour sack had been replenished for other travelers ; his own wants were few.

It was a day or two after the midnight visit of the sheriff to Silver Hollow that Key galloped down the steep grade to Collinson's. He was amused, albeit, in his new importance, a little aggrieved also, to find that Collinson had as usual confounded his descent with that of the generally detached boulder, and that he was obliged to add his voice to the general uproar. This brought Collinson to his door.

" I 've had your hoss hobbled out among the chickweed and clover in the green pasture back o' the mill, and he 's picked up that much that he 's lookin' fat and sassy," he said quietly, beginning to mechanically unstrap Key's bridle, even while his guest

was in the act of dismounting. " His back's
quite healed up."

Key could not restrain a shrug of impatience. It was three weeks since they had
met, — three weeks crammed with excitement, energy, achievement, and fortune to
Key; and yet this place and this man were
as stupidly unchanged as when he had left
them. A momentary fancy that this was
the reality, that he himself was only awak-
ening from some delusive dream, came over
him. But Collinson's next words were
practical.

" I reckoned that maybe you 'd write
from Marysville to Skinner to send for the
hoss, and forward him to ye, for I never
kalkilated you 'd come back."

It was quite plain from this that Collinson had heard nothing. But it was also
awkward, as Key would now have to tell the
whole story, and reveal the fact that he had
been really experimenting when Collinson
overtook him in the hollow. He evaded this
by post-dating his discovery of the richness
of the ore until he had reached Marysville.
But he found some difficulty in recount-
ing his good fortune: he was naturally no

boaster, he had no desire to impress Collinson with his penetration, nor the undaunted energy he had displayed in getting up his company and opening the mine, so that he was actually embarrassed by his own understatement; and under the grave, patient eyes of his companion, told his story at best lamely. Collinson's face betrayed neither profound interest nor the slightest resentment. When Key had ended his awkward recital, Collinson said slowly: —

" Then Uncle Dick and that other Parker feller ain't got no show in this yer find."

"No," said Key quickly. "Don't you remember we broke up our partnership that morning and went off our own ways. You don't suppose," he added with a forced half-laugh, "that if Uncle Dick or Parker had struck a lead after they left me, they'd have put me in it?"

"Would n't they?" asked Collinson gravely.

"Of course not." He laughed a little more naturally, but presently added, with an uneasy smile, "What makes you think they would?"

"Nuthin'!" said Collinson promptly.

Nevertheless, when they were seated before the fire, with glasses in their hands, Collinson returned patiently to the subject:

"You wuz saying they went their way, and you went yours. But your way was back on the old way that you'd all gone together."

But Key felt himself on firmer ground here, and answered deliberately and truthfully, "Yes, but I only went back to the hollow to satisfy myself if there really was any house there, and if there was, to warn the occupants of the approaching fire."

"And there was a house there," said Collinson thoughtfully.

"Only the ruins." He stopped and flushed quickly, for he remembered that he had denied its existence at their former meeting. "That is," he went on hurriedly, "I found out from the sheriff, you know, that there had been a house there. But," he added, reverting to his stronger position, "my going back there was an accident, and my picking up the outcrop was an accident, and had no more to do with our partnership prospecting than you had. In fact," he said, with a reassuring laugh, "you'd

have had a better right to share in my claim,
coming there as you did at that moment,
than they. Why, if I 'd have known what
the thing was worth, I might have put you
in — only it wanted capital and some experience." He was glad that he had pitched
upon that excuse (it had only just occurred
to him), and glanced affably at Collinson.
But that gentleman said soberly : —

" No, you would n't nuther."

" Why not ?" said Key half angrily.

Collinson paused. After a moment he
said, " 'Cos I would n't hev took anything
outer thet place."

Key felt relieved. From what he knew
of Collinson's vagaries he believed him. He
was wise in not admitting him to his confidences at the beginning ; he might have
thought it his duty to tell others.

" I 'm not so particular," he returned
laughingly, " but the silver in that hole was
never touched, nor I dare say even imagined
by mortal man before. However, there is
something else about the hollow that I want
to tell you. You remember the slipper that
you picked up ?"

" Yes."

" Well, I lied to you about that; I never dropped it. On the contrary, I had picked up the mate of it very near where you found yours, and I wanted to know to whom it belonged. For I don't mind telling you now, Collinson, that I believe there *was* a woman in that house, and the same woman whose face I saw at the window. You remember how the boys joked me about it — well, perhaps I did n't care that you should laugh at me too, but I 've had a sore conscience over my lie, for I remembered that you seemed to have some interest in the matter too, and I thought that maybe I might have thrown you off the scent. It seemed to me that if you had any idea who it was, we might now talk the matter over and compare notes. I think you said — at least, I gathered the idea from a remark of yours," he added hastily, as he remembered that the suggestion was his own, and a satirical one — " that it reminded you of your wife's slipper. Of course, as your wife is dead, that would offer no clue, and can only be a chance resemblance, unless " — He stopped.

" Have you got 'em yet ? "

" Yes, both." He took them from the pocket of his riding-jacket.

As Collinson received them, his face took upon itself an even graver expression. " It 's mighty cur'ous," he said reflectively, " but looking at the two of 'em the likeness is more fetchin'. Ye see, my wife had a *straight* foot, and never wore reg'lar rights and lefts like other women, but kinder changed about; ye see, these shoes is reg'lar rights and lefts, but never was worn as sich ! "

" There may be other women as peculiar," suggested Key.

" There *must* be," said Collinson quietly.

For an instant Key was touched with the manly security of the reply, for, remembering Uncle Dick's scandal, it had occurred to him that the unknown tenant of the robbers' den might be Collinson's wife. He was glad to be relieved on that point, and went on more confidently : —

" So, you see, this woman was undoubtedly in that house on the night of the fire. She escaped, and in a mighty hurry too, for she had not time to change her slippers for shoes; she escaped on horseback, for that is how she lost them. Now what was she doing there with those rascals, for the face I saw looked as innocent as a saint's."

" Seemed to ye sort o' contrairy, jist as I reckoned my wife's foot would have looked in a slipper that you said was *giv* to ye," suggested Collinson pointedly, but with no implication of reproach in his voice.

" Yes," said Key impatiently.

" I 've read yarns afore now about them Eyetalian brigands stealin' women," said Collinson reflectively, " but that ain't California road-agent style. Great Scott! if one even so much as spoke to a woman, they 'd have been wiped outer the State long ago. No! the woman as *was* there came there to *stay !* "

As Key's face did not seem to express either assent or satisfaction at this last statement, Collinson, after a glance at it, went on with a somewhat gentler gravity: " I see wot 's troublin' *you*, Mr. Key; you 've bin thinkin' that mebbee that poor woman might hev bin the better for a bit o' that fortin' that you discovered under the very spot where them slippers of hers had often trod. You 're thinkin' that mebbee it might hev turned her and those men from their evil ways."

Mr. Key had been thinking nothing of

the kind, but for some obscure reason the skeptical jeer that had risen to his lips remained unsaid. He rose impatiently. "Well, there seems to be no chance of discovering anything now ; the house is burnt, the gang dispersed, and she has probably gone with them." He paused, and then laid three or four large gold pieces on the table. "It's for that old bill of our party, Collinson," he said. "I'll settle and collect from each. Some time when you come over to the mine, and I hope you'll give us a call, you can bring the horse. Meanwhile you can use him ; you'll find he's a little quicker than the mule. How is business ?" he added, with a perfunctory glance around the vacant room and dusty bar.

"Thar ain't much passin' this way," said Collinson with equal carelessness, as he gathered up the money, "'cept those boys from the valley, and they're most always strapped when they come here."

Key smiled as he observed that Collinson offered him no receipt, and, moreover, as he remembered that he had only Collinson's word for the destruction of Parker's draft. But he merely glanced at his unconscious

host, and said nothing. After a pause he
returned in a lighter tone: "I suppose you
are rather out of the world here. Indeed, I
had an idea at first of buying out your mill,
Collinson, and putting in steam power to get
out timber for our new buildings, but you
see you are so far away from the wagon-
road, that we could n't haul the timber away.
That was the trouble, or I 'd have made you
a fair offer."

"I don't reckon to ever sell the mill,"
said Collinson simply. Then observing the
look of suspicion in his companion's face, he
added gravely, "You see, I rigged up the
whole thing when I expected my wife out
from the States, and I calkilate to keep it
in memory of her."

Key slightly lifted his brows. "But you
never told us, by the way, *how* you ever
came to put up a mill here with such an uncertain water-supply."

"It was n't onsartin when I came here,
Mr. Key; it was a full-fed stream straight
from them snow peaks. It was the earthquake did it."

"The earthquake!" repeated Key.

"Yes. Ef the earthquake kin heave up

that silver-bearing rock that you told us about the first day you kem here, and that you found t' other day, it could play roots with a mere mill-stream, I reckon."

" But the convulsion I spoke of happened ages on ages ago, when this whole mountain range was being fashioned," said Key with a laugh.

" Well, this yer earthquake was ten years ago, just after I came. I reckon I oughter remember it. It was a queer sort o' day in the fall, dry and hot as if thar might hev bin a fire in the woods, only thar was n't no wind. Not a breath of air anywhar. The leaves of them alders hung straight as a plumb-line. Except for that thar stream and that thar wheel, nuthin' moved. Thar was n't a bird on the wing over that cañon; thar was n't a squirrel skirmishin' in the hull wood; even the lizards in the rocks stiffened like stone Chinese idols. It kept gettin' quieter and quieter, ontil I walked out on that ledge and felt as if I 'd have to give a yell just to hear my own voice. Thar was a thin veil over everything, and betwixt and between everything, and the sun was rooted in the middle of it as if it could n't move neither. Everythin' seemed to be waitin', waitin', waitin'. Then all of a suddin suthin' seemed to give somewhar! Suthin' fetched away with a queer sort of rumblin', as if the peg had slipped outer creation. I looked up and kalkilated to see half a dozen of them boulders come, lickity switch, down the grade. But, darn my skin, if one of 'em stirred! and yet while I was looking, the whole face o' that bluff bowed over softly, as if saying 'Good-by,' and got clean away somewhar before I knowed it. Why, you see that pile agin the side o' the cañon! Well, a thousand feet under that there's trees, three hundred feet high, still upright and standin'. You know how them pines over on that far mountain-side always seem to be climbin' up, up, up, over each other's heads to the very top? Well, Mr. Key, *I saw 'em* climbin'! And when I pulled myself together and got back to the mill, everything was quiet; and, by G—d, so was the mill-wheel, and there was n't two inches of water in the river!"

"And what did you think of it?" said Key, interested in spite of his impatience.

"I thought, Mr. Key— No! I must n't

say I thought, for I knowed it. I knowed
that suthin' had happened to my wife!"

Key did not smile, but even felt a faint
superstitious thrill as he gazed at him.
After a pause Collinson resumed : "I heard
a month after that she had died about that
time o' yaller fever in Texas with the party
she was comin' with. Her folks wrote that
they died like flies, and wuz all buried together, unbeknownst and promiscuous, and
thar was n't no remains. She slipped away
from me like that bluff over that cañon, and
that was the end of it."

"But she might have escaped," said Key
quickly, forgetting himself in his eagerness.

But Collinson only shook his head. "Then
she 'd have been here," he said gravely.

Key moved towards the door still abstractedly, held out his hand, shook that of
his companion warmly, and then, saddling
his horse himself, departed. A sense of
disappointment — in which a vague dissatis-
faction with himself was mingled — was all
that had come of his interview. He took
himself severely to task for following his romantic quest so far. It was unworthy of
the president of the Sylvan Silver Hollow

Company, and he was not quite sure but
that his confidences with Collinson might
have imperiled even the interests of the
company. To atone for this momentary aberration, and correct his dismal fancies, he
resolved to attend to some business at Skinner's before returning, and branched off on
a long détour that would intersect the traveled stage-road. But here a singular incident overtook him. As he wheeled into the
turnpike, he heard the trampling hoof-beats
and jingling harness of the oncoming coach
behind him. He had barely time to draw
up against the bank before the six galloping
horses and swinging vehicle swept heavily
by. He had a quick impression of the heat
and steam of sweating horse-hide, the reek
of varnish and leather, and the momentary
vision of a female face silhouetted against
the glass window of the coach! But even
in that flash of perception he recognized the
profile that he had seen at the window of
the mysterious hut!

He halted for an instant dazed and bewildered in the dust of the departing wheels.
Then, as the bulk of the vehicle reappeared,
already narrowing in the distance, without a

second thought he dashed after it. His disappointment, his self-criticism, his practical resolutions were forgotten. He had but one idea now — the vision was providential! The clue to the mystery was before him — he *must* follow it!

Yet he had sense enough to realize that the coach would not stop to take up a passenger between stations, and that the next station was the one three miles below Skinner's. It would not be difficult to reach this by a cut-off in time, and although the vehicle had appeared to be crowded, he could no doubt obtain a seat on top.

His eager curiosity, however, led him to put spurs to his horse, and range up alongside of the coach as if passing it, while he examined the stranger more closely. Her face was bent listlessly over a book; there was unmistakably the same profile that he had seen, but the full face was different in outline and expression. A strange sense of disappointment that was almost a revulsion of feeling came over him; he lingered, he glanced again; she was certainly a very pretty woman : there was the beautifully rounded chin, the short straight nose, and

delicately curved upper lip, that he had seen
in the profile, — and yet — yet it was not
the same face he had dreamt of. With an
odd, provoking sense of disillusion, he swept
ahead of the coach, and again slackened his
speed to let it pass. This time the fair unknown raised her long lashes and gazed suddenly at this persistent horseman at her side,
and an odd expression, it seemed to him
almost a glance of recognition and expectation, came into her dark, languid eyes. The
pupils concentrated upon him with a singular significance, that was almost, he even
thought, a reply to his glance, and yet it
was as utterly unintelligible. A moment
later, however, it was explained. He had
fallen slightly behind in a new confusion of
hesitation, wonder, and embarrassment, when
from a wooded trail to the right, another
horseman suddenly swept into the road before him. He was a powerfully built man,
mounted on a thoroughbred horse of a quality
far superior to the ordinary roadster. Without looking at Key he easily ranged up beside the coach as if to pass it, but Key, with
a sudden resolution, put spurs to his own
horse and ranged also abreast of him, in

time to see his fair unknown start at the apparition of this second horseman and unmistakably convey some signal to him, — a signal that to Key's fancy now betrayed some warning of himself. He was the more convinced as the stranger, after continuing a few paces ahead of the coach, allowed it to pass him at a curve of the road, and slackened his pace to permit Key to do the same. Instinctively conscious that the stranger's object was to scrutinize or identify him, he determined to take the initiative, and fixed his eyes upon him as they approached. But the stranger, who wore a loose brown linen duster over clothes that appeared to be superior in fashion and material, also had part of his face and head draped by a white silk handkerchief worn under his hat, ostensibly to keep the sun and dust from his head and neck, — and had the advantage of him. He only caught the flash of a pair of steel-gray eyes, as the newcomer, apparently having satisfied himself, gave rein to his spirited steed and easily repassed the coach, disappearing in a cloud of dust before it. But Key had by this time reached the " cut-off," which the stranger, if he intended to follow

the coach, either disdained or was ignorant
of, and he urged his horse to its utmost
speed. Even with the stranger's advantages
it would be a close race to the station.

Nevertheless, as he dashed on, he was by
no means insensible to the somewhat quix-
otic nature of his undertaking. If he was
right in his suspicion that a signal had been
given by the lady to the stranger, it was exceedingly probable that he had discovered
not only the fair inmate of the robbers' den,
but one of the gang itself, or at least a confederate and ally. Yet far from deterring
him, in that ingenious sophistry with which
he was apt to treat his romance, he now
looked upon his adventure as a practical
pursuit in the interests of law and justice.
It was true that it was said that the band of
road agents had been dispersed; it was a
fact that there had been no spoliation of
coach or teams for three weeks; but none of
the depredators had ever been caught, and
their booty, which was considerable, was
known to be still intact. It was to the interest of the mine, his partners, and his
workmen that this clue to a danger which
threatened the locality should be followed to

the end. As to the lady, in spite of the disappointment that still rankled in his breast, he could be magnanimous! She might be the paramour of the strange horseman, she might be only escaping from some hateful companionship by his aid. And yet one thing puzzled him : she was evidently not acquainted with the personality of the active gang, for she had, without doubt, at first mistaken *him* for one of them, and after recognizing her real accomplice had communicated her mistake to him.

It was a great relief to him when the rough and tangled " cut-off " at last broadened and lightened into the turnpike road again, and he beheld, scarcely a quarter of a mile before him, the dust cloud that overhung the coach as it drew up at the lonely wayside station. He was in time, for he knew that the horses were changed there ; but a sudden fear that the fair unknown might alight, or take some other conveyance, made him still spur his jaded steed forward. As he neared the station he glanced eagerly around for the other horseman, but he was nowhere to be seen. He had evidently either abandoned the chase or ridden ahead.

It seemed equally a part of what he believed was a providential intercession, that on arriving at the station he found there was a vacant seat inside the coach. It was diagonally opposite that occupied by the lady, and he was thus enabled to study her face as it was bent over her book, whose pages, however, she scarcely turned. After her first casual glance of curiosity at the new passenger, she seemed to take no more notice of him, and Key began to wonder if he had not mistaken her previous interrogating look. Nor was it his only disturbing query; he was conscious of the same disappointment now that he could examine her face more attentively, as in his first cursory glance. She was certainly handsome; if there was no longer the freshness of youth, there was still the indefinable charm of the woman of thirty, and with it the delicate curves of matured muliebrity and repose. There were lines, particularly around the mouth and fringed eyelids, that were deepened as by pain; and the chin, even in its rounded fullness, had the angle of determination. From what was visible, below the brown linen duster that she wore, she

appeared to be tastefully although not richly
dressed.

As the coach at last drove away from the
station, a grizzled, farmer-looking man seated
beside her uttered a sigh of relief, so palpable as to attract the general attention.
Turning to his fair neighbor with a smile
of uncouth but good-humored apology, he
said in explanation : —

"You 'll excuse me, miss ! I don't know
ezactly how *you 're* feelin', — for judging
from your looks and gin'ral gait, you 're a
stranger in these parts, — but ez for *me,* I
don't mind sayin' that I never feel ezactly
safe from these yer road agents and stage
robbers ontil arter we pass Skinner's station.
All along thet Galloper's Ridge it 's jest
tech and go like; the woods is swarmin'
with 'em. But once past Skinner's, you 're
all right. They never dare go below that.
So ef you don't mind, miss, for it 's bein'
in your presence, I 'll jest pull off my butes
and ease my feet for a spell."

Neither the inconsequence of this singular request, nor the smile it evoked on the
faces of the other passengers, seemed to disturb the lady's abstraction. Scarcely lifting

her eyes from her book, she bowed a grave
assent.

"You see, miss," he continued, "and
you gents," he added, taking the whole
coach into his confidence, "I've got over
forty ounces of clean gold dust in them
butes, between the upper and lower sole, —
and it's mighty tight packing for my feet.
Ye kin heft it," he said, as he removed one
boot and held it up before them. "I put
the dust there for safety — kalkilatin' that
while these road gentry allus goes for a
man's pockets and his body belt, they never
thinks of his butes, or haven't time to go
through 'em." He looked around him with
a smile of self-satisfaction.

The murmur of admiring comment was,
however, broken by a burly-bearded miner
who sat in the middle seat. "Thet's pretty
fair, as far as it goes," he said smilingly,
"but I reckon it wouldn't go far ef you
started to run. I've got a simpler game
than that, gentlemen, and ez we're all
friends here, and the danger's over, I don't
mind tellin' ye. The first thing these yer
road agents do, after they've covered the
driver with their shot guns, is to make the

passengers get out and hold up their hands.
That, ma'am," — explanatorily to the lady,
who betrayed only a languid interest, — " is
to keep 'em from drawing their revolvers.
A revolver is the last thing a road agent
wants, either in a man's hand or in his
holster. So I sez to myself, ' Ef a six-
shooter ain't of no account, wot 's the use
of carryin' it?' So I just put my shooting-
iron in my valise when I travel, and fill
my holster with my gold dust, so! It 's a
deuced sight heavier than a revolver, but
they don't feel its weight, and don't keer to
come nigh it. And I 've been 'held up'
twice on t' other side of the Divide this
year, and I passed free every time ! "

The applause that followed this revelation
and the exhibition of the holster not only
threw the farmer's exploits into the shade,
but seemed to excite an emulation among
the passengers. Other methods of securing
their property were freely discussed ; but
the excitement culminated in the leaning
forward of a passenger who had, up to that
moment, maintained a reserve almost equal
to the fair unknown. His dress and general appearance were those of a professional

man; his voice and manner corroborated the presumption.

"I don't think, gentlemen," he began with a pleasant smile, " that any man of us here would like to be called a coward; but in fighting with an enemy who never attacks, or even appears, except with a deliberately prepared advantage on his side, it is my opinion that a man is not only justified in avoiding an unequal encounter with him, but in circumventing by every means the object of his attack. You have all been frank in telling your methods. I will be equally so in telling mine, even if I have perhaps to confess to a little more than you have; for I have not only availed myself of a well-known rule of the robbers who infest these mountains, to exempt all women and children from their spoliation, — a rule which, of course, they perfectly understand gives them a sentimental consideration with all Californians, — but I have, I confess, also availed myself of the innocent kindness of one of that charming and justly exempted sex." He paused and bowed courteously to the fair unknown. "When I entered this coach I had with me a bulky parcel which was manifestly too large for my pockets, yet as evidently too small and too valuable to be intrusted to the ordinary luggage. Seeing my difficulty, our charming companion opposite, out of the very kindness and innocence of her heart, offered to make a place for it in her satchel, which was not full. I accepted the offer joyfully. When I state to you, gentlemen, that that package contained valuable government bonds to a considerable amount, I do so, not to claim your praise for any originality of my own, but to make this public avowal to our fair fellow passenger for securing to me this most perfect security and immunity from the road agent that has been yet recorded."

With his eyes riveted on the lady's face, Key saw a faint color rise to her otherwise impassive face, which might have been called out by the enthusiastic praise that followed the lawyer's confession. But he was painfully conscious of what now seemed to him a monstrous situation! Here was, he believed, the actual accomplice of the road agents calmly receiving the complacent and puerile confessions of the men who were seeking to outwit them. Could he, in

ordinary justice to them, to himself, or the
mission he conceived he was pursuing, re-
frain from exposing her, or warning them
privately? But was he certain? Was a
vague remembrance of a profile momentarily seen — and, as he must even now admit,
inconsistent with the full face he was gazing at — sufficient for such an accusation?
More than that, was the protection she had
apparently afforded the lawyer consistent
with the function of an accomplice!

" Then if the danger 's over," said the
lady gently, reaching down to draw her
satchel from under the seat, " I suppose I
may return it to you."

" By no means! Don't trouble yourself!
Pray allow me to still remain your debtor, —
at least as far as the next station," said the
lawyer gallantly.

The lady uttered a languid sigh, sank
back in her seat, and calmly settled herself
to the perusal of her book. Key felt his
cheeks beginning to burn with the embarrassment and shame of his evident miscon-
ception. And here he was on his way to
Marysville, to follow a woman for whom
he felt he no longer cared, and for whose

pursuit he had no longer the excuse of justice.

" Then I understand that you have twice seen these road agents," said the professional man, turning to the miner. " Of course, you could be able to identify them ? "

" Nary a man! You see they 're all masked, and only one of 'em ever speaks."

" The leader or chief ? "

" No, the orator."

" The orator ? " repeated the professional man in amazement.

" Well, you see, *I* call him the orator, for he 's mighty glib with his tongue, and reels off all he has to say like as if he had it by heart. He 's mighty rough on you, too, sometimes, for all his high-toned style. Ef he thinks a man is hidin' anything he jest scalps him with his tongue, and blamed if I don't think he likes the chance of doin' it. He 's got a regular set speech, and he 's bound to go through it all, even if he makes everything wait, and runs the risk of capture. Yet he ain't the chief, — and even I 've heard folks say ain't got any responsibility if he is took, for he don't tech anybody or anybody's money, and could n't be prosecuted. I reckon he's some sort of a broken-down lawyer — d'ye see?"

"Not much of a lawyer, I imagine," said the professional man, smiling, "for he'll find himself quite mistaken as to his share of responsibility. But it's a rather clever way of concealing the identity of the real leader."

"It's the smartest gang that was ever started in the Sierras. They fooled the sheriff of Sierra the other day. They gave him a sort of idea that they had a kind of hidin'-place in the woods whar they met and kept their booty, and, by jinks! he goes down thar with his hull posse, — just spilin' for a fight, — and only lights upon a gang of innocent greenhorns, who were boring for silver on the very spot where he allowed the robbers had their den! He ain't held up his head since."

Key cast a quick glance at the lady to see the effect of this revelation. But her face — if the same profile he had seen at the window — betrayed neither concern nor curiosity. He let his eyes drop to the smart boot that peeped from below her gown, and the thought of his trying to identify it with

the slipper he had picked up seemed to him
as ridiculous as his other misconceptions.
He sank back gloomily in his seat; by
degrees the fatigue and excitement of the
day began to mercifully benumb his senses;
twilight had fallen and the talk had ceased.
The lady had allowed her book to drop in
her lap as the darkness gathered, and had
closed her eyes; he closed his own, and
slipped away presently into a dream, in which
he saw the profile again as he had seen it in
the darkness of the hollow, only that this
time it changed to a full face, unlike the
lady's or any one he had ever seen. Then
the window seemed to open with a rattle, and
he again felt the cool odors of the forest; but
he awoke to find that the lady had only
opened her window for a breath of fresh air.
It was nearly eight o' clock; it would be an
hour yet before the coach stopped at the
next station for supper; the passengers were
drowsily nodding; he closed his eyes and
fell into a deeper sleep, from which he awoke
with a start.

The coach had stopped!

CHAPTER IV.

"IT can't be Three Pines yet," said a passenger's voice, in which the laziness of sleep still lingered, "or else we've snoozed over five mile. I don't see no lights; wot are we stoppin' for?" The other passengers struggled to an upright position. One nearest the window opened it; its place was instantly occupied by the double muzzle of a shot-gun! No one moved. In the awe-stricken silence the voice of the driver rose in drawling protestation.

"It ain't no business o' mine, but it sorter strikes me that you chaps are a-playin' it just a little too fine this time! It ain't three miles from Three Pine Station and forty men   Of course, that's your lookout, — not mine!"

The audacity of the thing had evidently struck even the usually taciturn and phlegmatic driver into his first expostulation on record.

"Your thoughtful consideration does you great credit," said a voice from the darkness, "and shall be properly presented to our manager; but at the same time we wish it understood that we do not hesitate to take any risks in strict attention to our business and our clients. In the mean time you will expedite matters, and give your passengers a chance to get an early tea at Three Pines, by handing down that treasure-box and mail-pouch. Be careful in handling that blunderbuss you keep beside it; the last time it unfortunately went off, and I regret to say slightly wounded one of your passengers. Accidents of this kind, interfering, as they do, with the harmony and pleasure of our chance meetings, cannot be too highly deplored."

"By gosh!" ejaculated an outside passenger in an audible whisper.

"Thank you, sir," said the voice quietly; "but as I overlooked you, I will trouble you now to descend with the others."

The voice moved nearer; and, by the light of a flaming bull's-eye cast upon the coach, it could be seen to come from a stout, medium-sized man with a black mask, which, however, showed half of a smooth, beardless face, and an affable yet satirical mouth. The speaker cleared his throat with the slight preparatory cough of the practiced orator, and, approaching the window, to Key's intense surprise, actually began in the identical professional and rhetorical style previously indicated by the miner.

" Circumstances over which we have no control, gentlemen, compel us to oblige you to alight, stand in a row on one side, and hold up your hands. You will find the attitude not unpleasant after your cramped position in the coach, while the change from its confined air to the wholesome night-breeze of the Sierras cannot but prove salutary and refreshing. It will also enable us to relieve you of such so-called valuables and treasures in the way of gold dust and coin, which I regret to say too often are misapplied in careless hands, and which the teachings of the highest morality distinctly denominate as the root of all evil! I need not inform you, gentlemen, as business men, that promptitude and celerity of compliance will insure dispatch, and shorten an interview which has been sometimes needlessly, and, I regret to say, painfully protracted."

He drew back deliberately with the same monotonous precision of habit, and disclosed the muzzles of his confederates' weapons still leveled at the passengers. In spite of their astonishment, indignation, and discomfiture, his practiced effrontery and deliberate display appeared in some way to touch their humorous sense, and one or two smiled hysterically, as they rose and hesitatingly filed out of the vehicle. It is possible, however, that the leveled shot-guns contributed more or less directly to this result.

Two masks began to search the passengers under the combined focus of the bull's-eyes, the shining gun-barrels, and a running but still carefully prepared commentary from the spokesman. " It is to be regretted that business men, instead of intrusting their property to the custody of the regularly constituted express agent, still continue to secrete it on their persons; a custom that, without enhancing its security, is not only an injustice to the express company, but a great detriment to dispatch. We also wish to point out that while we do not as a rule interfere with the possession of articles of ordinary personal use or adornment, such as simple jewelry or watches, we reserve our right to restrict by confiscation the vulgarity and unmanliness of diamonds and enormous fob.chains."

The act of spoliation was apparently complete, yet it was evident that the orator was restraining himself for a more effective climax. Clearing his throat again and stepping before the impatient but still mystified file of passengers, he reviewed them gravely. Then in a perfectly pitched tone of mingled pain and apology, he said slowly : —

" It would seem that, from no wish of our own, we are obliged on this present occasion to suspend one or two of our usual rules. We are not in the habit of interfering with the wearing apparel of our esteemed clients ; but in the interests of ordinary humanity we are obliged to remove the boots of the gentleman on the extreme left, which evidently give him great pain and impede his locomotion. We also seldom deviate from our rule of obliging our clients to hold up their hands during this examination ; but we gladly make an exception in favor of the gentleman next to him, and permit him to hand us the altogether too heavily weighted holster which presses upon his hip. Gentlemen," said the orator, slightly raising his voice, with a deprecating gesture, "you need not be alarmed! The indignant movement of our friend, just now, was not to draw his revolver, — for it is n't there!" He paused while his companions speedily removed the farmer's boots and the miner's holster, and with a still more apologetic air approached the coach, where only the lady remained erect and rigid in her corner. "And now," he said with simulated hesitation, "we come to the last and to us the most painful suspension of our rules. On these very rare occasions, when we have been honored with the presence of the fair sex, it has been our invariable custom not only to leave them in the undisturbed possession of their property, but even of their privacy as well. It is with deep regret that on this occasion we are obliged to make an exception. For in the present instance, the lady, out of the gentleness of her heart and the politeness of her sex, has burdened herself not only with the weight but the responsibility of a package forced upon her by one of the passengers. We feel, and we believe, gentlemen, that most of you will agree with us, that so scandalous and unmanly an attempt to evade our rules and violate the sanctity of the lady's immunity will never be permitted. For your own sake, madam, we are compelled to ask you for the satchel under your seat. It will be returned to you when the package is removed."

"One moment," said the professional man indignantly, "there is a man here whom you have spared, — a man who lately joined us. Is that man," pointing to the astonished Key, "one of your confederates?"

"That man," returned the spokesman with a laugh, "is the owner of the Sylvan Hollow Mine. We have spared him because we owe him some consideration for having been turned out of his house at the dead of night while the sheriff of Sierra was seeking us." He stopped, and then in an entirely different voice, and in a totally changed manner, said roughly, "Tumble in there, all of you, quick! And you, sir" (to Key), — "I'd advise you to ride outside. Now, driver, raise so much as a rein or a whiplash until you hear the signal — and by God! you'll know what next." He stepped back, and seemed to be instantly swallowed up in the darkness; but the light of a solitary bull's-eye — the holder himself invisible — still showed the muzzles of the guns covering the driver. There was a momentary stir of voices within the closed coach, but an angry roar of "Silence!" from the darkness hushed it.

The moments crept slowly by; all now were breathless. Then a clear whistle rang from the distance, the light suddenly was extinguished, the leveled muzzles vanished with it, the driver's lash fell simultaneously on the backs of his horses, and the coach leaped forward.

The jolt nearly threw Key from the top, but a moment later it was still more difficult to keep his seat in the headlong fury of their progress. Again and again the lash descended upon the maddened horses, until the whole coach seemed to leap, bound, and swerve with every stroke. Cries of protest and even distress began to come from the interior, but the driver heeded it not. A window was suddenly let down; the voice of the professional man saying, "What's the matter? We're not followed. You are imperiling our lives by this speed," was answered only by, " Will some of ye throttle that d—d fool?" from the driver, and the renewed fall of the lash. The wayside trees appeared a solid plateau before them, opened, danced at their side, closed up again behind them,— but still they sped along. Rushing down grades with the speed of an avalanche, they ascended again without drawing rein, and as if by sheer momentum; for the heavy vehicle now seemed to have a diabolical energy of its own. It ground scattered rocks to powder with its crushing wheels, it swayed heavily on ticklish corners, recovering itself with the resistless forward propulsion of the straining teams, until the lights of Three Pine Station began to glitter through the trees. Then a succession of yells broke from the driver, so strong and dominant that they seemed to outstrip even the speed of the unabated cattle. Lesser lights were presently seen running to and fro, and on the outermost fringe of the settlement the stage pulled up before a crowd of wondering faces, and the driver spoke.

" We've been held up on the open road, by G—d, not *three miles* from whar ye

early evening. Here a number of his despoiled companions were obliged to wait, to
communicate with their friends. Happily,
the exemption that had made them indignant
enabled him to continue his journey with
a full purse. But he was content with a
modest surveillance of the lady from the top
of the coach.

On arriving at Stockton this surveillance
became less easy. It was the terminus of
the stage-route, and the divergence of others
by boat and rail. If he were lucky enough
to discover which one the lady took, his presence now would be more marked, and might
excite her suspicion. But here a circumstance, which he also believed to be providential, determined him. As the luggage
was being removed from the top of the coach,
he overheard the agent tell the expressman
to check the "lady's" trunk to San Luis.
Key was seized with an idea which seemed to
solve the difficulty, although it involved a
risk of losing the clue entirely. There were
two routes to San Luis, one was by stage, and
direct, though slower; the other by steamboat and rail, via San Francisco. If he
took the boat, there was less danger of her

discovering him, even if she chose the same
conveyance; if she took the direct stage, —
and he trusted to a woman's avoidance of the
hurry of change and transshipment for that
choice, — he would still arrive at San Luis,
via San Francisco, an hour before her. He
resolved to take the boat; a careful scrutiny
from a stateroom window of the arriving
passengers on the gangplank satisfied him
that she had preferred the stage. There
was still the chance that in losing sight of
her she might escape him, but the risk
seemed small. And a trifling circumstance
had almost unconsciously influenced him —
after his romantic and superstitious fashion
— as to this final step.

He had been singularly moved when he
heard that San Luis was the lady's probable
destination. It did not seem to bear any
relation to the mountain wilderness and the
wild life she had just quitted; it was apparently the most antipathic, incongruous,
and inconsistent refuge she could have
taken. It offered no opportunity for the
disposal of booty, or for communication with
the gang. It was less secure than a crowded
town. An old Spanish mission and monas-

tery college in a sleepy pastoral plain, — it had even retained its old-world flavor amidst American improvements and social revolution. He knew it well. From the quaint college cloisters, where the only reposeful years of his adventurous youth had been spent, to the long Alameda, or double avenues of ancient trees, which connected it with the convent of Santa Luisa, and some of his youthful "devotions," — it had been the nursery of his romance. He was amused at what seemed to be the irony of fate, in now linking it with this folly of his maturer manhood; and yet he was uneasily conscious of being more seriously affected by it. And it was with a greater anxiety than this adventure had ever yet cost him that he at last arrived at the San José hotel, and from a balcony corner awaited the coming of the coach. His heart beat rapidly as it approached. She was there! But at her side, as she descended from the coach, was the mysterious horseman of the Sierra road. Key could not mistake the well-built figure, whatever doubt there had been about the features, which had been so carefully concealed. With the astonishment of this rediscovery, there flashed across him again the fatefulness of the inspiration which had decided him not to go in the coach. His presence there would have no doubt warned the stranger, and so estopped this convincing dénouement. It was quite possible that her companion, by relays of horses and the advantage of bridle cut-offs, could have easily followed the Three Pine coach and joined her at Stockton. But for what purpose? The lady's trunk, which had not been disturbed during the first part of the journey, and had been forwarded at Stockton untouched before Key's eyes, could not have contained booty to be disposed of in this forgotten old town.

The register of the hotel bore simply the name of " Mrs. Barker," of Stockton, but no record of her companion, who seemed to have disappeared as mysteriously as he came. That she occupied a sitting-room on the same floor as his own — in which she was apparently secluded during the rest of the day — was all he knew. Nobody else seemed to know her. Key felt an odd hesitation, that might have been the result of some vague fear of implicating her prematurely,

in making any marked inquiry, or imperiling his secret by the bribed espionage
of servants. Once when he was passing
her door he heard the sounds of laughter,
— albeit innocent and heart-free, — which
seemed so inconsistent with the gravity of
the situation and his own thoughts that he
was strangely shocked. But he was still
more disturbed by a later occurrence. In
his watchfulness of the movements of his
neighbor he had been equally careful of his
own, and had not only refrained from regis-
tering his name, but had enjoined secrecy
upon the landlord, whom he knew. Yet the
next morning after his arrival, the porter
not answering his bell promptly enough, he
so far forgot himself as to walk to the staircase, which was near the lady's room, and
call to the employee over the balustrade. As
he was still leaning over the railing, the
faint creak of a door, and a singular magnetic consciousness of being overlooked,
caused him to turn slowly, but only in time
to hear the rustle of a withdrawing skirt as
the door was quickly closed. In an instant
he felt the full force of his foolish heedless-
ness, but it was too late. Had the mys-

terious fugitive recognized him ? Perhaps
not ; their eyes had not met, and his face
had been turned away.

He varied his espionage by subterfuges,
which his knowledge of the old town made
easy. He watched the door of the hotel,
himself unseen, from the windows of a bil-
liard saloon opposite, which he had frequented in former days. Yet he was surprised the same afternoon to see her, from
his coigne of vantage, reëntering the hotel,
where he was sure he had left her a few moments ago. Had she gone out by some other
exit, — or had she been disguised ? But on
entering his room that evening he was confounded by an incident that seemed to him
as convincing of her identity as it was audacious. Lying on his pillow were a few dead
leaves of an odorous mountain fern, known
only to the Sierras. They were tied together by a narrow blue ribbon, and had evidently been intended to attract his attention.
As he took them in his hand, the distinguishing subtle aroma of the little sylvan
hollow in the hills came to him like a memory and a revelation ! He summoned the
chambermaid ; she knew nothing of them,

or indeed of any one who had entered his
room. He walked cautiously into the hall;
the lady's sitting-room door was open, the
room was empty. "The occupant," said the
chambermaid, "had left that afternoon."
He held the proof of her identity in his
hand, but she herself had vanished! That
she had recognized him there was now no
doubt: had she divined the real object of
his quest, or had she accepted it as a mere
sentimental gallantry at the moment when
she knew it was hopeless, and she herself
was perfectly safe from pursuit? In either
event he had been duped. He did not know
whether to be piqued, angry, — or relieved of
his irresolute quest.

Nevertheless, he spent the rest of the twilight and the early evening in fruitlessly
wandering through the one long thoroughfare of the town, until it merged into the
bosky Alameda, or spacious grove, that connected it with Santa Luisa. By degrees his
chagrin and disappointment were forgotten
in the memories of the past, evoked by the
familiar pathway. The moon was slowly
riding overhead, and silvering the carriage-
way between the straight ebony lines of

trees, while the footpaths were diapered with
black and white checkers. The faint tinkling of a tram-car bell in the distance ap-
prised him of one of the few innovations of
the past. The car was approaching him,
overtook him, and was passing, with its
faintly illuminated windows, when, glancing
carelessly up, he beheld at one of them the
profile of the face which he had just thought
he had lost forever!

He stopped for an instant, not in indecision this time, but in a grim resolution
to let no chance escape him now. The car
was going slowly; it was easy to board it
now, but again the tinkle of the bell indicated that it was stopping at the corner of
a road beyond. He checked his pace, — a
lady alighted, — it was she! She turned
into the cross - street, darkened with the
shadows of some low suburban tenement
houses, and he boldly followed. He was
fully determined to find out her secret, and
even, if necessary, to accost her for that purpose. He was perfectly aware what he was
doing, and all its risks and penalties; he
knew the audacity of such an introduction,
but he felt in his left-hand pocket for the

sprig of fern which was an excuse for it;
he knew the danger of following a possible
confidante of desperadoes, but he felt in his
right-hand pocket for the derringer that was
equal to it. They were both there; he was
ready.

He was nearing the convent and the oldest and most ruinous part of the town. He
did not disguise from himself the gloomy
significance of this; even in the old days the
crumbling adobe buildings that abutted on
the old garden wall of the convent were the
haunts of lawless Mexicans and vagabond
peons. As the roadway began to be rough
and uneven, and the gaunt outlines of the
sagging roofs of tiles stood out against the
sky above the lurking shadows of ruined
doorways, he was prepared for the worst.
As the crumbling but still massive walls of
the convent garden loomed ahead, the tall,
graceful, black - gowned figure he was following presently turned into the shadow
of the wall itself. He quickened his pace,
lest it should again escape him. Suddenly it stopped, and remained motionless.
He stopped, too. At the same moment
it vanished!

He ran quickly forward to where it had stood, and found himself before a large iron gate, with a smaller one in the centre, that had just clanged to on its rusty hinges. He rubbed his eyes ! — the place, the gate, the wall, were all strangely familiar ! Then he stepped back into the roadway, and looked at it again. He was not mistaken.

He was standing before the porter's lodge of the Convent of the Sacred Heart.

CHAPTER V.

THE day following the great stagecoach
robbery found the patient proprietor of
Collinson's Mill calm and untroubled in his
usual seclusion. The news that had thrilled
the length and breadth of Galloper's Ridge
had not touched the leafy banks of the
dried-up river; the hue and cry had followed the stage-road, and no courier had
deemed it worth his while to diverge as far
as the rocky ridge which formed the only
pathway to the mill. That day Collinson's
solitude had been unbroken even by the
haggard emigrant from the valley, with his
old monotonous story of hardship and pri-
vation. The birds had flown nearer to the
old mill, as if emboldened by the unwonted
quiet. That morning there had been the
half human imprint of a bear's foot in the
ooze beside the mill - wheel; and coming
home with his scant stock from the woodland pasture, he had found a golden squirrel

— a beautiful, airy embodiment of the brown woods itself — calmly seated on his bar-counter, with a biscuit between its baby hands. He was full of his characteristic reveries and abstractions that afternoon; falling into them even at his wood - pile, leaning on his axe — so still that an emerald-throated lizard, who had slid upon the log, went to sleep under the forgotten stroke.

But at nightfall the wind arose, — at first as a distant murmur along the hillside, that died away before it reached the rocky ledge; then it rocked the tops of the tall redwoods behind the mill, but left the mill and the dried leaves that lay in the river-bed undisturbed. Then the murmur was prolonged, until it became the continuous trouble of some far-off sea, and at last the wind possessed the ledge itself; driving the smoke down the stumpy chimney of the mill, rattling the sun-warped shingles on the roof, stirring the inside rafters with cool breaths, and singing over the rough projections of the outside eaves. At nine o'clock he rolled himself up in his blankets before the fire, as was his wont, and fell asleep.

It was past midnight when he was awakened by the familiar clatter of boulders down the grade, the usual simulation of a wild rush from without that encompassed the whole mill, even to that heavy impact against the door, which he had heard once before. In this he recognized merely the ordinary phenomena of his experience, and only turned over to sleep again. But this time the door rudely fell in upon him, and a figure strode over his prostrate body, with a gun leveled at his head.

He sprang sideways for his own weapon, which stood by the hearth. In another second that action would have been his last, and the solitude of Seth Collinson might have remained henceforward unbroken by any mortal. But the gun of the first figure was knocked sharply upward by a second man, and the one and only shot fired that night sped harmlessly to the roof. With the report he felt his arms gripped tightly behind him; through the smoke he saw dimly that the room was filled with masked and armed men, and in another moment he was pinioned and thrust into his empty armchair. At a signal three of the men left the room, and he could hear them

exploring the other rooms and outhouses.
Then the two men who had been standing
beside him fell back with a certain disci-
plined precision, as a smooth-chinned man
advanced from the open door. Going to
the bar, he poured out a glass of whiskey,
tossed it off deliberately, and, standing in
front of Collinson, with his shoulder against
the chimney and his hand resting lightly on
his hip, cleared his throat. Had Collinson
been an observant man, he would have noticed that the two men dropped their eyes
and moved their feet with a half impatient,
perfunctory air of waiting. Had he witnessed the stage-robbery, he would have recognized in the smooth-faced man the presence
of " the orator." But he only gazed at him
with his dull, imperturbable patience.

" We regret exceedingly to have to use
force to a gentleman in his own house,"
began the orator blandly ; " but we feel it
our duty to prevent a repetition of the unhappy incident which occurred as we entered. We desire that you should answer
a few questions, and are deeply grateful
that you are still able to do so, — which
seemed extremely improbable a moment or

two ago." He paused, coughed, and leaned back against the chimney. "How many men have you here besides yourself?"

"Nary one," said Collinson.

The interrogator glanced at the other men, who had reëntered. They nodded significantly.

"Good!" he resumed. "You have told the truth — an excellent habit, and one that expedites business. Now, is there a room in this house with a door that locks? Your front door *does n't.*"

"No."

"No cellar nor outhouse?"

"No."

"We regret that; for it will compel us, much against our wishes, to keep you bound as you are for the present. The matter is simply this: circumstances of a very pressing nature oblige us to occupy this house for a few days, — possibly for an indefinite period. We respect the sacred rites of hospitality too much to turn you out of it; indeed, nothing could be more distasteful to our feelings than to have you, in your own person, spread such a disgraceful report through the chivalrous Sierras. We must therefore keep you a close prisoner, — open, however, to an offer. It is this: we propose to give you five hundred dollars for this property as it stands, provided that you leave it, and accompany a pack-train which will start to-morrow morning for the lower valley as far as Thompson's Pass, binding yourself to quit the State for three months and keep this matter a secret. Three of these gentlemen will go with you. They will point out to you your duty; their shot-guns will apprise you of any dereliction from it. What do you say?"

" Who yer talking to?" said Collinson in a dull voice.

" You remind us," said the orator suavely, "that we have not yet the pleasure of knowing."

" My name's Seth Collinson."

There was a dead silence in the room, and every eye was fixed upon the two men. The orator's smile slightly stiffened.

" Where from?" he continued blandly.

" Mizzouri."

" A very good place to go back to, — through Thompson's Pass. But you have n't answered our proposal."

" I reckon I don't intend to sell this house, or leave it," said Collinson simply.

" I trust you will not make us regret the fortunate termination of your little accident, Mr. Collinson," said the orator with a singular smile. " May I ask why you object to selling out? Is it the figure?"

"The house is n't mine," said Collinson deliberately. " I built this yer house for my wife wot I left in Mizzouri. It 's hers. I kalkilate to keep it, and live in it ontil she comes fur it! And when I tell ye that she is dead, ye kin reckon just what chance ye have of ever gettin' it."

There was an unmistakable start of sensation in the room, followed by a silence so profound that the moaning of the wind on the mountain-side was distinctly heard. A well-built man, with a mask that scarcely concealed his heavy mustachios, who had been standing with his back to the orator in half contemptuous patience, faced around suddenly and made a step forward as if to come between the questioner and questioned. A voice from the corner ejaculated, " By G—d!"

" Silence," said the orator sharply. Then

still more harshly he turned to the others:
" Pick him up, and stand him outside with
a guard ; and then clear out, all of you ! "

The prisoner was lifted up and carried
out ; the room was instantly cleared ; only
the orator and the man who had stepped
forward remained. Simultaneously they
drew the masks from their faces, and stood
looking at each other. The orator's face
was smooth and corrupt; the full, sensual
lips wrinkled at the corners with a sardonic
humor ; the man who confronted him appeared to be physically and even morally
his superior, albeit gloomy and discon-
tented in expression. He cast a rapid
glance around the room, to assure himself
that they were alone ; and then, straighten-
ing his eyebrows as he backed against the
chimney, said : —

" D—d if I like this, Chivers ! It's
your affair ; but it's mighty low-down work
for a man ! "

" You might have made it easier if you
had n't knocked up Bryce's gun. That
would have settled it, though no one guessed
that the cur was her husband," said Chivers
hotly.

"If you want it settled *that way*, there's still time," returned the other with a slight sneer. "You've only to tell him that you're the man that ran away with his wife, and you'll have it out together, right on the ledge at twelve paces. The boys will see you through. In fact," he added, his sneer deepening, "I rather think it's what they're expecting."

"Thank you, Mr. Jack Riggs," said Chivers sardonically. "I dare say it would be more convenient to some people, just before our booty is divided, if I were drilled through by a blundering shot from that hayseed; or it would seem right to your high-toned chivalry if a dead-shot as I am knocked over a man who may have never fired a revolver before; but I don't exactly see it in that light, either as a man or as your equal partner. I don't think you quite understand me, my dear Jack. If you don't value the only man who is identified in all California as the leader of this gang (the man whose style and address has made it popular — yes, *popular*, by G—d! — to every man, woman, and child who has heard of him; whose sayings and

doings are quoted by the newspapers; whom
people run risks to see; who has got the
sympathy of the crowd, so that judges hesitate to issue warrants and constables to
serve them), — if *you* don't see the use of
such a man, *I* do. Why, there's a column
and a half in the 'Sacramento Union' about
our last job, calling me the 'Claude Duval'
of the Sierras, and speaking of my courtesy
to a lady! A *lady!* — *his* wife, by G—d!
our confederate! My dear Jack, you not
only don't know business values, but, 'pon
my soul, you don't seem to understand humor! Ha, ha!'"

For all his cynical levity, for all his affected exaggeration, there was the ring of
an unmistakable and even pitiable vanity in
his voice, and a self-consciousness that suffused his broad cheeks and writhed his full
mouth, but seemed to deepen the frown on
Riggs's face.

"You know the woman hates it, and
would bolt if she could, — even from you,"
said Riggs gloomily. "Think what she
might do if she knew her husband were
here. I tell you she holds our lives in the
hollow of her hand."

"That's your fault, Mr. Jack Riggs; you would bring your sister with her infernal convent innocence and simplicity into our hut in the hollow. She was meek enough before that. But this is sheer nonsense. I have no fear of her. The woman don't live who would go back on Godfrey Chivers — for a husband! Besides, she went off to see your sister at the convent at Santa Clara as soon as she passed those bonds off on Charley to get rid of! Think of her traveling with that d—d fool lawyer all the way to Stockton, and his bonds (which we had put back in her bag) alongside of them all the time, and he telling her he was going to stop their payment, and giving her the letter to mail for him! — eh? Well, we'll have time to get rid of her husband before she gets back. If he don't go easy — well " —

"None of that, Chivers, you understand, once for all!" interrupted Riggs peremptorily. "If you cannot see that your making away with that woman's husband would damn that boasted reputation you make so much of and set every man's hand against us, *I* do, and I won't permit it. It's a

rotten business enough, — our coming on
him as we have ; and if this was n't the only
God-forsaken place where we could divide
our stuff without danger and get it away off
the highroads, I 'd pull up stakes at once."

"Let her stay at the convent, then, and
be d—d to her," said Chivers roughly.
" She 'll be glad enough to be with your
sister again ; and there 's no fear of her
being touched there."

"But I want to put an end to that, too,"
returned Riggs sharply. " I do not choose
to have my sister any longer implicated
with *our* confederate or *your* mistress. No
more of that — you understand me ? "

The two men had been standing side by
side, leaning against the chimney. Chivers
now faced his companion, his full lips
wreathed into an evil smile.

" I think I understand you, Mr. Jack
Riggs, or — I beg your pardon — Rivers,
or whatever your real name may be," he
began slowly. " Sadie Collinson, the mistress of Judge Godfrey Chivers, formerly of
Kentucky, was good enough company for
you the day you dropped down upon us in
our little house in the hollow of Galloper's

Ridge. We were living quite an idyllic, pastoral life there, weren't we? — she and me; hidden from the censorious eye of society and — Collinson, obeying only the voice of Nature and the little birds. It was a happy time," he went on with a grimly affected sigh, disregarding his companion's impatient gesture. " You were young then, waging *your* fight against society, and fresh — uncommonly fresh, I may say — from your first exploit. And a very stupid, clumsy, awkward exploit, too, Mr. Riggs, if you will pardon my freedom. You wanted money, and you had an ugly temper, and you had lost both to a gambler; so you stopped the coach to rob him, and had to kill two men to get back your paltry thousand dollars, after frightening a whole coach-load of passengers, and letting Wells, Fargo, and Co.'s treasure-box with fifty thousand dollars in it slide. It was a stupid, a blundering, a *cruel* act, Mr. Riggs, and I think I told you so at the time. It was a waste of energy and material, and made you, not a hero, but a stupid outcast! I think I proved this to you, and showed you how it might have been done."

" Dry up on that," interrupted Riggs impatiently. " You offered to become my partner, and you did."

" Pardon me. Observe, my impetuous friend, that my contention is that you — *you* — poisoned our blameless Eden in the hollow; that *you* were our serpent, and that this Sadie Collinson, over whom you have become so fastidious, whom you knew as my mistress, was obliged to become our confederate. You did not object to her when we formed our gang, and her house became our hiding-place and refuge. You took advantage of her woman's wit and fine address in disposing of our booty; you availed yourself, with the rest, of the secrets she gathered as *my* mistress, just as you were willing to profit by the superior address of her paramour — your humble servant — when your own face was known to the sheriff, and your old methods pronounced brutal and vulgar. Excuse me, but I must insist upon *this*, and that you dropped down upon me and Sadie Collinson exactly as you have dropped down here upon her husband."

" Enough of this!" said Riggs angrily. " I admit the woman is part and parcel of the gang, and gets her share, — or you get it for her," he added sneeringly; "but that does n't permit her to mix herself with my family affairs."

"Pardon me again," interrupted Chivers softly. "Your memory, my dear Riggs, is absurdly defective. We knew that you had a young sister in the mountains, from whom you discreetly wished to conceal your real position. We respected, and I trust shall always respect, your noble reticence. But do you remember the night you were taking her to school at Santa Clara, — two nights before the fire, — when you were recognized on the road near Skinner's, and had to fly with her for your life, and brought her to us, — your two dear old friends, ' Mr. and Mrs. Barker of Chicago,' who had a pastoral home in the forest? You remember how we took her in, — yes, doubly took her in, — and kept your secret from her? And do you remember how this woman (this mistress of *mine* and *our* confederate), while we were away, saved her from the fire on our only horse, caught the stage-coach, and brought her to the convent?"

Riggs walked towards the window, turned,

and coming back, held out his hand. " Yes, she did it; and I thanked her, as I thank you." He stopped and hesitated, as the other took his hand. " But, blank it all, Chivers, don't you see that Alice is a young girl, and this woman is — you know what I mean. Somebody might recognize *her*, and that would be worse for Alice than even if it were known what Alice's *brother* was. G—d! if these two things were put together, the girl would be ruined forever."

" Jack," said Chivers suddenly, " you want this woman out of the way. Well — dash it all! — she nearly separated us, and I 'll be frank with you as between man and man. I 'll give her up! There are women enough in the world, and hang it, we 're partners, after all! "

" Then you abandon her ? " said Riggs slowly, his eyes fixed on his companion.

" Yes. She 's getting a little too maundering lately. It will be a ticklish job to manage, for she knows too much ; but it will be done. There 's my hand on it."

Riggs not only took no notice of the proffered hand, but his former look of discontent came back with an ill-concealed addition of loathing and contempt.

" We 'll drop that now," he said shortly;
" we 've talked here alone long enough
already. The men are waiting for us." He
turned on his heel into the inner room.
Chivers remained standing by the chimney
until his stiffened smile gave way under the
working of his writhing lips; then he
turned to the bar, poured out and swallowed
another glass of whiskey at a single gulp,
and followed his partner with half-closed
lids that scarcely veiled his ominous eyes.

The men, with the exception of the sentinels stationed on the rocky ledge and the
one who was guarding the unfortunate Collinson, were drinking and gambling away
their perspective gains around a small pile
of portmanteaus and saddle-bags, heaped in
the centre of the room. They contained the
results of their last successes, but one pair
of saddle-bags bore the mildewed appearance
of having been *cached*, or buried, some time
before. Most of their treasure was in pack-
ages of gold dust; and from the conversation
that ensued, it appeared that, owing to the
difficulties of disposing of it in the mountain towns, the plan was to convey it by
ordinary pack mule to the unfrequented

valley, and thence by an emigrant wagon, on the old emigrant trail, to the southern counties, where it could be no longer traced. Since the recent robberies, the local express companies and bankers had refused to receive it, except the owners were known and identified. There had been but one box of coin, which had already been speedily divided up among the band. Drafts, bills, bonds, and valuable papers had been usually intrusted to one "Charley," who acted as a flying messenger to a corrupt broker in Sacramento, who played the rôle of the band's "fence." It had been the duty of Chivers to control this delicate business, even as it had been his peculiar function to open all the letters and documents. This he had always lightened by characteristic levity and sarcastic comments on the private revelations of the contents. The rough, ill-spelt letter of the miner to his wife, inclosing a draft, or the more sentimental effusion of an emigrant swain to his sweetheart, with the gift of a "specimen," had always received due attention at the hands of this elegant humorist. But the operation was conducted to-night with business severity and silence. The two leaders sat opposite to each other, in what might have appeared to the rest of the band a scarcely veiled surveillance of each other's actions. When the examination was concluded, and the more valuable inclosures put aside, the despoiled letters were carried to the fire and heaped upon the coals. Presently the chimney added its roar to the moaning of the distant hillside, a few sparks leaped up and died out in the midnight air, as if the pathos and sentiment of the unconscious correspondents had exhaled with them.

"That's a d—d foolish thing to do," growled French Pete over his cards.

"Why?" demanded Chivers sharply.

"Why? — why, it makes a flare in the sky that any scout can see, and a scent for him to follow."

"We're four miles from any traveled road," returned Chivers contemptuously, "and the man who could see that glare and smell that smoke would be on his way here already."

"That reminds me that that chap you've tied up — that Collinson — allows he wants to see you," continued French Pete.

" To see *me!* " repeated Chivers. " You mean the Captain? "

" I reckon he means *you*," returned French Pete ; " he said the man who talked so purty."

The men looked at each other with a smile of anticipation, and put down their cards. Chivers walked towards the door ; one or two rose to their feet as if to follow, but Riggs stopped them peremptorily. " Sit down," he said roughly ; then, as Chivers passed him, he added to him in a lower tone, " Remember."

Slightly squaring his shoulders and opening his coat, to permit a rhetorical freedom, which did not, however, prevent him from keeping touch with the butt of his revolver, Chivers stepped into the open air. Collinson had been moved to the shelter of an overhang of the roof, probably more for the comfort of the guard, who sat cross-legged on the ground near him, than for his own. Dismissing the man with a gesture, Chivers straightened himself before his captive.

" We deeply regret that your unfortunate determination, my dear sir, has been the means of depriving *us* of the pleasure of

your company, and *you* of your absolute
freedom; but may we cherish the hope that
your desire to see me may indicate some
change in your opinion?"

By the light of the sentry's lantern left
upon the ground, Chivers could see that Collinson's face wore a slightly troubled and
even apologetic expression.

"I 've bin thinkin'," said Collinson, raising his eyes to his captor with a singularly
new and shy admiration in them, "mebbee
not so much of *wot* you said, ez *how* you said
it, and it 's kinder bothered me, sittin' here,
that I ain't bin actin' to you boys quite on
the square. I 've said to myself, 'Collinson,
thar ain't another house betwixt Bald Top
and Skinner's whar them fellows kin get a
bite or a drink to help themselves, and you
ain't offered 'em neither. It ain't no matter
who they are or how they came: whether
they came crawling along the road from the
valley, or dropped down upon you like them
rocks from the grade; yere they are, and
it 's your duty, ez long ez you keep this yer
house for your wife in trust, so to speak, for
wanderers.' And I ain't forgettin' yer
ginerel soft style and easy gait with me when

you kem here. It ain't every man as could
walk into another man's house arter the
owner of it had grabbed a gun, ez soft-speak-
in', ez overlookin', and ez perlite ez you.
I 've acted mighty rough and low-down, and
I know it. And I sent for you to say that
you and your folks kin use this house and
all that 's in it ez long ez you 're in trouble.
I 've told you why I could n't sell the house
to ye, and why I could n't leave it. But ye
kin use it, and while ye 're here, and when
you go, Collinson don't tell nobody. I don't
know what ye mean by ' binding myself ' to
keep your secret; when Collinson says a
thing he sticks to it, and when he passes his
word with a man, or a man passes his word
with him, it don't need no bit of paper."

There was no doubt of its truth. In the
grave, upraised eyes of his prisoner, Chivers
saw the certainty that he could trust him.
even far more than he could trust any one
within the house he had just quitted. But
this very certainty, for all its assurance of
safety to himself, filled him, not with remorse, which might have been an evanescent emotion, but with a sudden alarming
and terrible consciousness of being in the

presence of a hitherto unknown and immeasurable power ! He had no pity for the man who trusted him ; he had no sense of shame in taking advantage of it ; he even felt an intellectual superiority in this want of sagacity in his dupe ; but he still felt in some way defeated, insulted, shocked, and frightened. At first, like all scoundrels, he had measured the man by himself ; was suspicious and prepared for rivalry ; but the grave truthfulness of Collinson's eyes left him helpless. He was terrified by this unknown factor. The right that contends and fights often stimulates its adversary ; the right that yields leaves the victor vanquished. Chivers could even have killed Collinson in his vague discomfiture, but he had a terrible consciousness that there was something behind him that he could not make way with. That was why this accomplished rascal felt his flaccid cheeks grow purple and his glib tongue trip before his captive.

But Collinson, more occupied with his own shortcomings, took no note of this, and Chivers quickly recovered his wits, if not his former artificiality. " All right," he said quickly, with a hurried glance at the door behind him. "Now that you think better of it, I'll be frank with you, and tell you I'm your friend. You understand, — your friend. Don't talk much to those men — don't give yourself away to them;" he laughed this time in absolute natural embarrassment. "Don't talk about your wife, and this house, but just say you've made the thing up with me, — with *me*, you know, and I'll see you through." An idea, as yet vague, that he could turn Collinson's unexpected docility to his own purposes, possessed him even in his embarrassment, and he was still more strangely conscious of his inordinate vanity gathering a fearful joy from Collinson's evident admiration. It was heightened by his captive's next words.

"Ef I was n't tied I'd shake hands with ye on that. You're the kind o' man, Mr. Chivers, that I cottoned to from the first. Ef this house was n't *hers*, I'd a' bin tempted to cotton to yer offer, too, and mebbee made yer one myself, for it seems to me your style and mine would sorter jibe together. But I see you *sabe* what's in my mind, and make allowance. *We* don't want no bit o' paper to shake hands on that. Your secret

and your folk's secret is mine, and I don't
blab that any more than I'd blab to them
wot you've just told me."

Under a sudden impulse, Chivers leaned
forward, and, albeit with somewhat unsteady
hands and an embarrassed will, untied the
cords that held Collinson in his chair. As
the freed man stretched himself to his full
height, he looked gravely down into the
bleared eyes of his captor, and held out his
strong right hand. Chivers took it. Whether
there was some occult power in Collinson's
honest grasp, I know not; but there sprang
up in Chivers's agile mind the idea that a
good way to get rid of Mrs. Collinson was to
put her in the way of her husband's finding
her, and for an instant, in the contemplation
of that idea, this supreme rascal absolutely
felt an embarrassing glow of virtue.

CHAPTER VI.

THE astonishment of Preble Key on recognizing the gateway into which the mysterious lady had vanished was so great that
he was at first inclined to believe her entry
there a mere trick of his fancy. That the
confederate of a gang of robbers should be
admitted to the austere recesses of the convent, with a celerity that bespoke familiarity, was incredible. He again glanced up
and down the length of the shadowed but
still visible wall. There was no one there.
The wall itself contained no break or recess
in which one could hide, and this was the
only gateway. The opposite side of the
street in the full moonlight stared emptily.
No! Unless she were an illusion herself
and his whole chase a dream, she *must* have
entered here.

But the chase was not hopeless. He had
at least tracked her to a place where she
could be identified. It was not a hotel,
which she could leave at any moment un-

observed. Though he could not follow her
and penetrate its seclusion now, he could
later — thanks to his old associations with
the padres of the contiguous college — gain
an introduction to the Lady Superior on
some pretext. She was safe there that
night. He turned away with a feeling of
relief. The incongruity of her retreat assumed a more favorable aspect to his hopes.
He looked at the hallowed walls and the
slumbering peacefulness of the gnarled old
trees that hid the convent, and a gentle
reminiscence of his youth stole over him.
It was not the first time that he had gazed
wistfully upon that chaste refuge where,
perhaps, the bright eyes that he had followed in the quaint school procession under
the leafy Alameda in the afternoon, were
at last closed in gentle slumber. There
was the very grille through which the
wicked Conchita — or, was it Dolores? —
had shot her Parthian glance at the lingering student. And the man of thirty-five,
prematurely gray and settled in fortune,
smiled as he turned away, and forgot the
adventuress of thirty who had brought him
there.

The next morning he was up betimes and at the college of San José. Father Cipriano, a trifle more snuffy and aged, remembered with delight his old pupil. Ah! it was true, then, that he had become a mining president, and that was why his hair was gray; but he trusted that Don Preble had not forgot that this was not all of life, and that fortune brought great responsibilities and cares. But what was this, then? He *had* thought of bringing out some of his relations from the States, and placing a niece in the convent. That was good and wise. Ah, yes. For education in this new country, one must turn to the church. And he would see the Lady Superior? Ah! that was but the twist of one's finger and the lifting of a latch to a grave superintendent and a gray head like that. Of course, he had not forgotten the convent and the young señoritas, nor the discipline and the suspended holidays. Ah! it was a special grace of our Lady that he, Father Cipriano, had not been worried into his grave by those foolish *muchachos*. Yet, when he had extinguished a snuffy chuckle in his red bandana handkerchief, Key knew that he would accompany him to the convent that noon.

It was with a slight stirring of shame over his elaborate pretext that he passed the gate of the Sacred Heart with the good father. But it is to be feared that he speedily forgot that in the unexpected information that it elicited. The Lady Superior was gracious, and even enthusiastic. Ah, yes, it was a growing custom of the American caballeros — who had no homes, nor yet time to create any — to bring their sisters, wards, and nieces here, and — with a dove-like side-glance towards Key — even the young señoritas they wished to fit for their Christian brides! Unlike the caballero, there were many business men so immersed in their affairs that they could not find time for a personal examination of the convent, — which was to be regretted, — but who, trusting to the reputation of the Sacred Heart and its good friends, simply sent the young lady there by some trusted female companion. Notably this was the case of the Señor Rivers, — did Don Preble ever know him? — a great capitalist in the Sierras, whose sweet young sister, a naïve,

ingenuous creature, was the pride of the
convent. Of course, it was better that it
was so. Discipline and seclusion had to be
maintained. The young girl should look
upon this as her home. The rules for visitors were necessarily severe. It was rare
indeed — except in a case of urgency, such
as happened last night — that even a lady,
unless the parent of a scholar, was admitted
to the hospitality of the convent. And this
lady was only the friend of that same sister
of the American capitalist, although she was
the one who had brought her there. No,
she was not a relation. Perhaps Don Preble
had heard of a Mrs. Barker, — the friend of
Rivers of the Sierras. It was a queer combination of names. But what will you?
The names of Americanos mean nothing.
And Don Preble knows them not. Ah!
possibly? — good! The lady would be
remembered, being tall, dark, and of fine
presence, though sad. A few hours earlier
and Don Preble could have judged for himself, for, as it were, she might have passed
through this visitors' room. But she was
gone — departed by the coach. It was
from a telegram — those heathen contri-

vances that blurt out things to you, with
never an excuse, nor a smile, nor a kiss of
the hand! For her part, she never let her
scholars receive them, but opened them
herself, and translated them in a Christian
spirit, after due preparation, at her leisure.
And it was this telegram that made the
Señora Barker go, or, without doubt, she
would have of herself told to the Don
Preble, her compatriot of the Sierras, how
good the convent was for his niece.

Stung by the thought that this woman
had again evaded him, and disconcerted
and confused by the scarcely intelligible
information he had acquired, Key could
with difficulty maintain his composure.
" The caballero is tired of his long *pasear*,"
said the Lady Superior gently. " We will
have a glass of wine in the lodge waiting-
room." She led the way from the reception
room to the outer door, but stopped at the
sound of approaching footsteps and rustling
muslin along the gravel walk. " The second
class are going out," she said, as a gentle
procession of white frocks, led by two nuns,
filed before the gateway. " We will wait
until they have passed. But the señor can
see that my children do not look unhappy."

They certainly looked very cheerful, although they had halted before the gateway
with a little of the demureness of young
people who know they are overlooked by
authority, and had bumped against each
other with affected gravity. Somewhat
ashamed of his useless deception, and the
guileless simplicity of the good Lady Superior, Key hesitated and began : " I am afraid
that I am really giving you too much
trouble," and suddenly stopped.

For as his voice broke the demure silence,
one of the nearest — a young girl of apparently seventeen — turned towards him with
a quick and an apparently irresistible impulse, and as quickly turned away again.
But in that instant Key caught a glimpse of
a face that might not only have thrilled him
in its beauty, its freshness, but in some
vague suggestiveness. Yet it was not that
which set his pulses beating ; it was the look
of joyous recognition set in the parted lips
and sparkling eyes, the glow of childlike
innocent pleasure that mantled the sweet
young face, the frank confusion of suddenly realized expectancy and longing. A
great truth gripped his throbbing heart, and

held it still. It was the face that he had
seen in the hollow!

The movement of the young girl was too
marked to escape the eye of the Lady Superior, though she had translated it differently. "You must not believe our young
ladies are all so rude, Don Preble," she
said dryly; "though our dear child has
still some of the mountain freedom. And
this is the Señor Rivers's sister. But possibly — who knows?" she said gently, yet
with a sudden sharpness in her clear eyes,
— "perhaps she recognized in your voice a
companion of her brother."

Luckily for Key, the shock had been so
sudden and overpowering that he showed
none of the lesser symptoms of agitation or
embarrassment. In this revelation of a
secret, that he now instinctively felt was
bound up with his own future happiness, he
exhibited none of the signs of a discovered
intriguer or unmasked Lothario. He said
quietly and coldly: "I am afraid I have
not the pleasure of knowing the young lady,
and certainly have never before addressed
her." Yet he scarcely heard his companion's voice, and answered mechanically, see-

ing only before him the vision of the girl's
bewitching face, in its still more bewitching consciousness of his presence. With all
that he now knew, or thought he knew,
came a strange delicacy of asking further
questions, a vague fear of compromising *her*,
a quick impatience of his present deception;
even his whole quest of her seemed now to
be a profanation, for which he must ask
her forgiveness. He longed to be alone to
recover himself. Even the temptation to
linger on some pretext, and wait for her
return and another glance from her joyous
eyes, was not as strong as his conviction of
the necessity of cooler thought and action.
He had met his fate that morning, for good
or ill; that was all he knew. As soon as
he could decently retire, he thanked the
Lady Superior, promised to communicate
with her later, and taking leave of Father Cipriano, found himself again in the
street.

Who was she, what was she, and what
meant her joyous recognition of him? It
is to be feared that it was the last question
that affected him most, now that he felt that
he must have really loved her from the first.

Had she really seen him before, and had
been as mysteriously impressed as he was?
It was not the reflection of a conceited man,
for Key had not that kind of vanity, and
he had already touched the humility that is
at the base of any genuine passion. But
he would not think of that now. He had
established the identity of the other woman,
as being her companion in the house in the
hollow on that eventful night; but it was
her profile that he had seen at the window.
The mysterious brother Rivers might have
been one of the robbers, — perhaps the one
who accompanied Mrs. Barker to San José.
But it was plain that the young girl had
no complicity with the actions of the gang,
whatever might have been her companion's
confederation. In the prescience of a true
lover, he knew that she must have been
deceived and kept in utter ignorance of it.
There was no look of it in her lovely, guileless eyes; her very impulsiveness and in-
genuousness would have long since betrayed
the secret. Was it left for him, at this very
outset of his passion, to be the one to tell
her? Could he bear to see those frank,
beautiful eyes dimmed with shame and sor-

row? His own grew moist. Another idea
began to haunt him. Would it not be wiser,
even more manly, for him — a man over
twice her years — to leave her alone with
her secret, and so pass out of her innocent
young life as chancefully as he had entered
it? But was it altogether chanceful? Was
there not in her innocent happiness in him
a recognition of something in him better
than he had dared to think himself? It
was the last conceit of the humility of love.

He reached his hotel at last, unresolved,
perplexed, yet singularly happy. The clerk
handed him, in passing, a business-looking
letter, formally addressed. Without opening it, he took it to his room, and throwing
himself listlessly on a chair by the window
again tried to think. But the atmosphere
of his room only recalled to him the mysterious gift he had found the day before on
his pillow. He felt now with a thrill that
it must have been from *her.* How did she
convey it there? She would not have intrusted it to Mrs. Barker. The idea struck
him now as distastefully as it seemed improbable. Perhaps she had been here herself with her companion — the convent some-

times made that concession to a relative or well-known friend. He recalled the fact that he had seen Mrs. Barker enter the hotel alone, after the incident of the opening door, while he was leaning over the balustrade. It was *she* who was alone *then*, and had recognized his voice; and he had not known it. She was out again to-day with the procession. A sudden idea struck him. He glanced quickly at the letter in his hand, and hurriedly opened it. It contained only three lines, in a large formal hand, but they sent the swift blood to his cheeks.

"I heard your voice to-day for the third time. I want to hear it again. I will come at dusk. Do not go out until then."

He sat stupefied. Was it madness, audacity, or a trick? He summoned the waiter. The letter had been left by a boy from the confectioner's shop in the next block. He remembered it of old, — a resort for the young ladies of the convent. Nothing was easier than conveying a letter in that way. He remembered with a shock of disillusion and disgust that it was a common device of silly but innocent assignation.

Was he to be the ridiculous accomplice of a
schoolgirl's extravagant escapade, or the de-
luded victim of some infamous plot of her
infamous companion? He could not believe
either; yet he could not check a certain revulsion of feeling towards her, which only a
moment ago he would have believed impossible.

Yet whatever was her purpose, he must
prevent her coming there at any hazard.
Her visit would be the culmination of her
folly, or the success of any plot. Even
while he was fully conscious of the material
effect of any scandal and exposure to her,
even while he was incensed and disillusion-
ized at her unexpected audacity, he was un-
usually stirred with the conviction that she
was wronging herself, and that more than
ever she demanded his help and his consideration. Still she must not come. But
how was he to prevent her? It wanted but
an hour of dusk. Even if he could again
penetrate the convent on some pretext at
that inaccessible hour for visitors, — twilight, — how could he communicate with
her? He might intercept her on the way,
and persuade her to return; but she must
be kept from entering the hotel.

He seized his hat and rushed downstairs.
But here another difficulty beset him. It
was easy enough to take the ordinary road
to the convent, but would *she* follow that
public one in what must be a surreptitious
escape? And might she not have eluded
the procession that morning, and even now
be concealed somewhere, waiting for the
darkness to make her visit. He concluded
to patrol the block next to the hotel, yet
near enough to intercept her before she
reached it, until the hour came. The time
passed slowly. He loitered before shop windows, or entered and made purchases, with
his eye on the street. The figure of a pretty
girl, — and there were many, — the fluttering ribbons on a distant hat, or the flashing
of a cambric skirt around the corner sent a
nervous thrill through him. The reflection
of his grave, abstracted face against a shop
window, or the announcement of the work-
ings of his own mine on a bulletin board, in
its incongruity with his present occupation,
gave him an hysterical impulse to laugh.
The shadows were already gathering, when
he saw a slender, graceful figure disappear
in the confectioner's shop on the block

below. In his elaborate precautions, he had
overlooked that common trysting spot. He
hurried thither, and entered. The object of
his search was not there, and he was compelled to make a shamefaced, awkward survey of the tables in an inner refreshment
saloon to satisfy himself. Any one of the
pretty girls seated there might have been
the one who had just entered, but none was
the one he sought. He hurried into the
street again, — he had wasted a precious
moment, — and resumed his watch. The
sun had sunk, the Angelus had rung out of
a chapel belfry, and shadows were darken-
ing the vista of the Alameda. She had not
come. Perhaps she had thought better of
it ; perhaps she had been prevented ; perhaps the whole appointment had been only a
trick of some day-scholars, who were laughing at him behind some window. In proportion as he became convinced that she
was not coming, he was conscious of a keen
despair growing in his heart, and a sicken-
ing remorse that he had ever thought of
preventing her. And when he at last re-
luctantly reëntered the hotel, he was as
miserable over the conviction that she was

not coming as he had been at her expected
arrival. The porter met him hurriedly in
the hall.

"Sister Seraphina of the Sacred Heart
has been here, in a hurry to see you on a
matter of importance," he said, eyeing Key
somewhat curiously. "She would not wait
in the public parlor, as she said her business
was confidential, so I have put her in a private sitting-room on your floor."

Key felt the blood leave his cheeks. The
secret was out for all his precaution. The
Lady Superior had discovered the girl's
flight, — or her attempt. One of the gov-
erning sisterhood was here to arraign him
for it, or at least prevent an open scandal.
Yet he was resolved; and seizing this last
straw, he hurriedly mounted the stairs, determined to do battle at any risk for the
girl's safety, and to perjure himself to any
extent.

She was standing in the room by the window. The light fell upon the coarse serge
dress with its white facings, on the single
girdle that scarcely defined the formless
waist, on the huge crucifix that dangled un-
gracefully almost to her knees, on the

hideous, white-winged coif that, with the
coarse but dense white veil, was itself a renunciation of all human vanity. It was a
figure he remembered well as a boy, and
even in his excitement and half resentment
touched him now, as when a boy, with a
sense of its pathetic isolation. His head
bowed with boyish deference as she approached gently, passed him a slight salutation, and closed the door that he had forgotten to shut behind him.

Then, with a rapid movement, so quick
that he could scarcely follow it, the coif, veil,
rosary, and crucifix were swept off, and the
young pupil of the convent stood before
him.

For all the sombre suggestiveness of her
disguise and its ungraceful contour, there
was no mistaking the adorable little head,
tumbled all over with silky tendrils of hair
from the hasty withdrawal of her coif, or
the blue eyes that sparkled with frank delight beneath them. Key thought her more
beautiful than ever. Yet the very effect of
her frankness and beauty was to recall him
to all the danger and incongruity of her
position.

" This is madness, " he said quickly. " You may be followed here and discovered in this costume at any moment ! " Nevertheless, he caught the two little hands that had been extended to him, and held them tightly, and with a frank familiarity that he would have wondered at an instant before.

" But I won't, " she said simply. " You see I 'm doing a 'half-retreat' ; and I stay with Sister Seraphina in her room ; and she always sleeps two hours after the Angelus ; and I got out without anybody knowing me, in her clothes. I see what it is," she said, suddenly bending a reproachful glance upon him, " you don't like me in them. I know they 're just horrid ; but it was the only way I could get out."

" You don't understand me, " he said eagerly. " I don't like you to run these dreadful risks and dangers for " — He would have said " for me, " but added with sudden humility — " for nothing. Had I dreamed that you cared to see me, I would have arranged it easily without this indiscretion, which might make others misjudge you. Every instant that you remain here — worse, every moment that you are away from the

convent in that disguise, is fraught with
danger. I know you never thought of it."

" But I did," she said quietly ; " I thought
of it, and thought that if Sister Seraphina
woke up, and they sent for me, you would
take me away with you to that dear little
hollow in the hills, where I first heard your
voice. You remember it, don't you? You
were lost, I think, in the darkness, and I
used to say to myself afterwards that *I* found
you. That was the first time. Then the
second time I heard you, was here in the hall.
I was alone in the other room, for Mrs. Barker
had gone out. I did not know you were here,
but I knew your voice. And the third time
was before the convent gate, and then I knew
you knew me. And after that I did n't think
of anything but coming to you ; for I knew
that if I was found out, you would take me
back with you, and perhaps send word to my
brother where we were, and then " — She
stopped suddenly, with her eyes fixed on
Key's blank face. Her own grew blank, the
joy faded out of her clear eyes, she gently
withdrew her hand from his, and without a
word began to resume her disguise.

" Listen to me," said Key passionately.

"I am thinking only of *you*. I want to, and *will*, save you from any blame, — blame you do not understand even now. There is still time. I will go back to the convent with you at once. You shall tell me everything; I will tell you everything on the way."

She had already completely resumed her austere garb, and drew the veil across her face. With the putting on her coif she seemed to have extinguished all the joyous youthfulness of her spirit, and moved with the deliberateness of renunciation towards the door. They descended the staircase without a word. Those who saw them pass made way for them with formal respect.

When they were in the street, she said quietly, "Don't give me your arm — Sisters don't take it." When they had reached the street corner, she turned it, saying, "This is the shortest way."

It was Key who was now restrained, awkward, and embarrassed. The fire of his spirit, the passion he had felt a moment before, had gone out of him, as if she were really the character she had assumed. He said at last desperately : —

"How long did you live in the hollow ?"

"Only two days. My brother was bringing me here to school, but in the stage coach there was some one with whom he had quarreled, and he did n't want to meet him with me. So we got out at Skinner's, and came to the hollow, where his old friends, Mr. and Mrs. Barker, lived."

There was no hesitation nor affectation in her voice. Again he felt that he would as soon have doubted the words of the Sister she represented as her own.

"And your brother — did you live with him?"

"No. I was at school at Marysville until he took me away. I saw little of him for the past two years, for he had business in the mountains — very rough business, where he could n't take me, for it kept him away from the settlements for weeks. I think it had something to do with cattle, for he was always having a new horse. I was all alone before that, too ; I had no other relations ; I had no friends. We had always been moving about so much, my brother and I. I never saw any one that I liked, except you, and until yesterday I had only *heard* you."

Her perfect naïveté alternately thrilled

him with pain and doubt. In his awkward-
ness and uneasiness he was brutal.

"Yes, but you must have met somebody
— other men — here even, when you were
out with your schoolfellows, or perhaps on
an adventure like this."

Her white coif turned towards him
quickly. "I never wanted to know anybody else. I never cared to see anybody
else. I never would have gone out in this
way but for you," she said hurriedly.
After a pause she added in a frightened
tone: "That did n't sound like your voice
then. It did n't sound like it a moment ago
either."

"But you are sure that you know my
voice," he said, with affected gayety. "There
were two others in the hollow with me that
night."

"I know that, too. But I know even
what you said. You reproved them for
throwing a lighted match in the dry grass.
You were thinking of *us* then. I know it."

"Of *us?*" said Key quickly.

"Of Mrs. Barker and myself. We were
alone in the house, for my brother and her
husband were both away. What you said

seemed to forewarn me, and I told her. So we were prepared when the fire came nearer, and we both escaped on the same horse."

"And you dropped your shoes in your flight," said Key laughingly, "and I picked them up the next day, when I came to search for you. I have kept them still."

"They were *her* shoes," said the girl quickly. "I couldn't find mine in our hurry, and hers were too large for me, and dropped off." She stopped, and with a faint return of her old gladness said, "Then you *did* come back? I *knew* you would."

"I should have stayed *then*, but we got no reply when we shouted. Why was that?" he demanded suddenly.

"Oh, we were warned against speaking to any stranger, or even being seen by any one while we were alone," returned the girl simply.

"But why?" persisted Key.

"Oh, because there were so many high-waymen and horse-stealers in the woods. Why, they had stopped the coach only a few weeks before, and only a day or two ago, when Mrs. Barker came down. *She* saw them!"

Key with difficulty suppressed a groan. They walked on in silence for some moments, he scarcely daring to lift his eyes to the decorous little figure hastening by his side. Alternately touched by mistrust and pain, at last an infinite pity, not unmingled with a desperate resolution, took possession of him.

" I must make a confession to you, Miss Rivers," he began with the bashful haste of a very boy, " that is " — he stammered with a half hysteric laugh, — " that is — a confession as if you were really a sister or a priest, you know — a sort of confidence to you — to your dress. I *have* seen you, or *thought* I saw you before. It was that which brought me here, that which made me follow Mrs. Barker — my only clue to you — to the door of that convent. That night, in the hollow, I saw a profile at the lighted window, which I thought was yours."

" *I* never was near the window," said the young girl quickly. " It must have been Mrs. Barker."

" I know that now," returned Key. " But remember, it was my only clue to you. I mean," he added awkwardly, " it was the means of my finding you."

"I don't see how it made you think of me, whom you never saw, to see another woman's profile," she retorted, with the faintest touch of asperity in her childlike voice. "But," she added, more gently and with a relapse into her adorable naïveté, "most people's profiles look alike."

"It was not that," protested Key, still awkwardly, "it was only that I realized something — only a dream, perhaps."

She did not reply, and they continued on in silence. The gray wall of the convent was already in sight. Key felt he had achieved nothing. Except for information that was hopeless, he had come to no nearer understanding of the beautiful girl beside him, and his future appeared as vague as before; and, above all, he was conscious of an inferiority of character and purpose to this simple creature, who had obeyed him so submissively. Had he acted wisely? Would it not have been better if he had followed her own frankness, and —

"Then it was Mrs. Barker's profile that brought you here?" resumed the voice beneath the coif. "You know she has gone back. I suppose you will follow?"

" You will not understand me," said Key desperately. " But," he added in a lower voice, " I shall remain here until you do."

He drew a little closer to her side.

" Then you must not begin by walking so close to me," she said, moving slightly away ; " they may see you from the gate. And you must not go with me beyond that corner. If I have been missed already they will suspect you."

" But how shall I know ? " he said, attempting to take her hand. " Let me walk past the gate. I cannot leave you in this uncertainty."

" You will know soon enough," she said gravely, evading his hand. " You must not go further now. Good-night."

She had stopped at the corner of the wall. He again held out his hand. Her little fingers slid coldly between his.

" Good-night, Miss Rivers."

" Stop ! " she said suddenly, withdrawing her veil and lifting her clear eyes to his in the moonlight. " You must not say *that* — it is n't the truth. I can't bear to hear it from *your* lips, in *your* voice. My name is *not* Rivers ! "

"Not Rivers — why?" said Key, astounded.

"Oh, I don't know why," she said half despairingly; "only my brother did n't want me to use my name and his here, and I promised. My name is 'Riggs' — there! It's a secret — you must n't tell it; but I could not bear to hear *you* say a lie."

"Good-night, Miss Riggs," said Key sadly.

"No, nor that either," she said softly. "Say Alice."

"Good-night, Alice."

She moved on before him. She reached the gate. For a moment her figure, in its austere, formless garments, seemed to him to even stoop and bend forward in the humility of age and self-renunciation, and she vanished within as into a living tomb.

Forgetting all precaution, he pressed eagerly forward, and stopped before the gate. There was no sound from within; there had evidently been no challenge nor interruption. She was safe.

CHAPTER VII.

THE reappearance of Chivers in the mill with Collinson, and the brief announcement that the prisoner had consented to a satisfactory compromise, were received at first with a half contemptuous smile by the party; but for the commands of their leaders, and possibly a conviction that Collinson's fatuous coöperation with Chivers would be safer than his wrath, which might not expend itself only on Chivers, but imperil the safety of all, it is probable that they would have informed the unfortunate prisoner of his real relations to his captor. In these circumstances, Chivers's half satirical suggestion that Collinson should be added to the sentries outside, and guard his own property, was surlily assented to by Riggs, and complacently accepted by the others. Chivers offered to post him himself, — not without an interchange of meaning glances with Riggs, — Collinson's own gun was returned to him, and the strangely assorted pair left the mill amicably together.

But however humanly confident Chivers was in his companion's faithfulness, he was not without a rascal's precaution, and determined to select a position for Collinson where he could do the least damage in any aberration of trust. At the top of the grade, above the mill, was the only trail by which a party in force could approach it. This was to Chivers obviously too strategic a position to intrust to his prisoner, and the sentry who guarded its approach, five hundred yards away, was left unchanged. But there was another " blind " trail, or cut-off, to the left, through the thickest undergrowth of the woods, known only to his party. To place Collinson there was to insure him perfect immunity from the approach of an enemy, as well as from any confidential advances of his fellow sentry. This done, he drew a cigar from his pocket, and handing it to Collinson, lighted another for himself, and leaning back comfortably against a large boulder, glanced complacently at his companion.

" You may smoke until I go, Mr. Collin-

son, and even afterwards, if you keep the
bowl of your pipe behind a rock, so as to be
out of sight of your fellow sentry, whose advances, by the way, if I were you, I should
not encourage. Your position here, you see,
is a rather peculiar one. You were saying,
I think, that a lingering affection for your
wife impelled you to keep this place for her,
although you were convinced of her death?"

Collinson's unaffected delight in Chivers's
kindliness had made his eyes shine in the
moonlight with a doglike wistfulness. "I
reckon I did say that, Mr. Chivers," he said
apologetically, "though it ain't goin' to interfere with you usin' the shanty jest now."

"I was n't alluding to that, Collinson,"
returned Chivers, with a large rhetorical
wave of the hand, and an equal enjoyment
in his companion's evident admiration of
him, "but it struck me that your remark,
nevertheless, implied some doubt of your
wife's death, and I don't know but that your
doubts are right."

"Wot's that?" said Collinson, with a
dull glow in his face.

Chivers blew the smoke of his cigar lazily
in the still air. "Listen," he said. "Since

your miraculous conversion a few moments ago, I have made some friendly inquiries about you, and I find that you lost all trace of your wife in Texas in '52, where a number of her fellow emigrants died of yellow fever. Is that so?"

"Yes," said Collinson quickly.

"Well, it so happens that a friend of mine," continued Chivers slowly, "was in a train which followed that one, and picked up and brought on some of the survivors."

"That was the train wot brought the news," said Collinson, relapsing into his old patience. "That's how I knowed she had n't come."

"Did you ever hear the names of any of its passengers?" said Chivers, with a keen glance at his companion.

"Nary one! I only got to know it was a small train of only two wagons, and it sorter melted into Californy through a southern pass, and kinder petered out, and no one ever heard of it agin, and that was all."

"That was *not* all, Collinson," said Chivers lazily. "*I* saw the train arrive at South Pass. I was awaiting a friend and

his wife. There was a lady with them, one
of the survivors. I did n't hear her name,
but I think my friend's wife called her
'Sadie.' I remember her as a rather pretty
woman — tall, fair, with a straight nose and
a full chin, and small slim feet. I saw her
only a moment, for she was on her way to
Los Angeles, and was, I believe, going to
join her husband somewhere in the Sierras."

The rascal had been enjoying with intense
satisfaction the return of the dull glow in
Collinson's face, that even seemed to animate
the whole length of his angular frame as it
turned eagerly towards him. So he went on,
experiencing a devilish zest in this description of his mistress to her husband, apart
from the pleasure of noting the slow awak-
ening of this apathetic giant, with a sensation akin to having warmed him into life.
Yet his triumph was of short duration. The
fire dropped suddenly out of Collinson's
eyes, the glow from his face, and the dull
look of unwearied patience returned.

"That's all very kind and purty of yer,
Mr. Chivers," he said gravely; "you 've
got all my wife's pints thar to a dot, and it
seems to fit her jest like a shoe I picked up

t' other day. But it was n't my Sadie, for
ef she 's living or had lived, she 'd bin just
yere ! "

The same fear and recognition of some
unknown reserve in this trustful man came
over Chivers as before. In his angry resentment of it he would have liked to blurt
out the infidelity of the wife before her husband, but he knew Collinson would not believe him, and he had another purpose now.
His full lips twisted into a suave smile.

" While I would not give you false hopes,
Mr. Collinson," he said, with a bland smile,
" my interest in you compels me to say that
you may be over confident and wrong.
There are a thousand things that may have
prevented your wife from coming to you, —
illness, possibly the result of her exposure,
poverty, misapprehension of your place of
meeting, and, above all, perhaps some false
report of your own death. Has it ever
occurred to you that it is as possible for her
to have been deceived in that way as for
you ? "

" Wot yer say ? " said Collinson, with a
vague suspicion.

" What I mean. You think yourself jus-

tified in believing your wife dead, because
she did not seek you here ; may she not feel
herself equally justified in believing the same
of you, because you had not sought her elsewhere ? ''

" But it was writ that she was comin' yere,
and — I boarded every train that come in
that fall, " said Collinson, with a new irritation, unlike his usual calm.

" Except one, my dear Collinson, — except one," returned Chivers, holding up a
fat forefinger smilingly. " And that may
be the clue. Now, listen ! There is still a
chance of following it, if you will. The name
of my friends were Mr. and Mrs. Barker.
I regret, " he added, with a perfunctory
cough, " that poor Barker is dead. He was
not such an exemplary husband as you are,
my dear Collinson, and I fear was not all
that Mrs. Barker could have wished ; enough
that he succumbed from various excesses, and
did not leave me Mrs. Barker's present address. But she has a young friend, a ward,
living at the convent of Santa Luisa, whose
name is Miss Rivers, who can put you in
communication with her. Now, one thing
more : I can understand your feelings, and

that you would wish at once to satisfy your mind. It is not, perhaps, to my interest nor the interest of my party to advise you, but," he continued, glancing around him, " you have an admirably secluded position here, on the edge of the trail, and if you are missing from your post to-morrow morning, I shall respect your feelings, trust to your honor to keep this secret, and—consider it useless to pursue you! "

There was neither shame nor pity in his heart, as the deceived man turned towards him with tremulous eagerness, and grasped his hand in silent gratitude. But the old rage and fear returned, as Collinson said gravely : —

"You kinder put a new life inter me, Mr. Chivers, and I wish I had yer gift o' speech to tell ye so. But I 've passed my word to the Capting thar and to the rest o' you folks that I 'd stand guard out yere, and I don't go back o' my word. I mout, and I mout n't find my Sadie ; but she would n't think the less o' me, arter these years o' waitin', ef I stayed here another night, to guard the house I keep in trust for her, and the strangers I 've took in on her account."

" As you like, then, " said Chivers, contracting his lips, " but keep your own counsel to-night. There may be those who would like to deter you from your search. And now I will leave you alone in this delightful moonlight. I quite envy you your unrestricted communion with Nature. *Adios, amigo, adios!* "

He leaped lightly on a large rock that overhung the edge of the grade, and waved his hand.

" I would n't do that, Mr. Chivers," said Collinson, with a concerned face ; " them rocks are mighty ticklish, and that one in partiklar. A tech sometimes sends 'em scooting."

Mr. Chivers leaped quickly to the ground, turned, waved his hand again, and disappeared down the grade.

But Collinson was no longer alone. Hitherto his characteristic reveries had been of the past, — reminiscences in which there was only recollection, no imagination, and very little hope. Under the spell of Chivers's words his fancy seemed to expand; he began to think of his wife as she might be now, — perhaps ill, despairing, wandering hopelessly,

even ragged and footsore, or — believing *him*
dead — relapsing into the resigned patience
that had been his own; but always a new
Sadie, whom he had never seen or known before. A faint dread, the lightest of misgiv-
ings (perhaps coming from his very ignorance), for the first time touched his steadfast
heart, and sent a chill through it. He shoul-
dered his weapon, and walked briskly towards
the edge of the thick-set woods. There were
the fragrant essences of the laurel and
spruce—baked in the long-day sunshine that
had encompassed their recesses—still coming
warm to his face ; there were the strange
shiftings of temperature throughout the
openings, that alternately warmed and chilled
him as he walked. It seemed so odd that
he should now have to seek her instead
of her coming to him ; it would never be
the same meeting to him, away from
the house that he had built for her ! He
strolled back, and looked down upon it, nestling on the ledge. The white moonlight
that lay upon it dulled the glitter of lights in
its windows, but the sounds of laughter and
singing came to even his unfastidious ears with
a sense of vague discord. He walked back

again, and began to pace before the thick-set
wood. Suddenly he stopped and listened.

To any other ears but those accustomed
to mountain solitude it would have seemed
nothing. But, familiar as he was with all
the infinite disturbances of the woodland,
and even the simulation of intrusion caused
by a falling branch or lapsing pine-cone, he
was arrested now by a recurring sound, unlike any other. It was an occasional muffled
beat — interrupted at uncertain intervals,
but always returning in regular rhythm,
whenever it was audible. He knew it was
made by a cantering horse; that the intervals were due to the patches of dead leaves
in its course, and that the varying movement was the effect of its progress through
obstacles and underbrush. It was therefore coming through some " blind " cut-off
in the thick-set wood. The shifting of the
sound also showed that the rider was unfamiliar with the locality, and sometimes wandered from the direct course; but the unfail-
ing and accelerating persistency of the sound,
in spite of these difficulties, indicated haste
and determination.

He swung his gun from his shoulder,

and examined its caps. As the sound came nearer, he drew up beside a young spruce at the entrance of the thicket. There was no necessity to alarm the house, or call the other sentry. It was a single horse and rider, and he was equal to that. He waited quietly, and with his usual fateful patience. Even then his thoughts still reverted to his wife; and it was with a singular feeling that he, at last, saw the thick underbrush give way before a woman, mounted on a sweating but still spirited horse, who swept out into the open. Nevertheless, he stopped in front of her, and called : —

"Hold up thar!"

The horse recoiled, nearly unseating her. Collinson caught the reins. She lifted her whip mechanically, yet remained holding it in the air, trembling, until she slipped, half struggling, half helplessly, from the saddle to the ground. Here she would have again fallen, but Collinson caught her sharply by the waist. At his touch she started and uttered a frightened "No!" At her voice Collinson started.

"Sadie!" he gasped.

"Seth!" she half whispered.

They stood looking at each other. But Collinson was already himself again. The man of simple directness and no imagination saw only his wife before him — a little breathless, a little flurried, a little disheveled from rapid riding, as he had sometimes seen her before, but otherwise unchanged. Nor had *he* changed; he took her up where he had left her years ago. His grave face only broadened into a smile, as he held both her hands in his.

" Yes, it 's me — Lordy ! Why, I was comin' only to-morrow to find ye, Sade ! "

She glanced hurriedly around her. " To — to find me," she said incredulously.

" Sartain ! That ez, I was goin' to ask about ye, — goin' to ask about ye at the convent."

" At the convent ? " she echoed with a frightened amazement.

" Yes, why, Lordy ! Sade — don't you see ? You thought I was dead, and I thought you was dead, — that 's what 's the matter. But I never reckoned that you 'd think me dead until Chivers allowed that it must be so."

Her face whitened in the moonlight. " Chivers ? " she said blankly.

" In course; but nat'rally you don't know him, honey. He only saw you onc't. But it was along o' that, Sade, that he told me he reckoned you wasn't dead, and told me how to find you. He was mighty kind and consarned about it, and he even allowed I'd better slip off to you this very night."

" Chivers," she repeated, gazing at her husband with bloodless lips.

" Yes, an awful purty-spoken man. Ye'll have to get to know him, Sade. He's here with some of his folks az hez got inter trouble — I'm forgettin' to tell ye. You see" —

" Yes, yes, yes ! " she interrupted hysterically; " and this is the Mill ? "

" Yes, lovey, the Mill — my mill — *your* mill — the house I built for you, dear. I'd show it to you now, but you see, Sade, I'm out here standin' guard."

" Are *you* one of them ? " she said, clutching his hand desperately.

" No, dear," he said soothingly, — " no ; only, you see, I giv' my word to 'em as I giv' my house to-night, and I'm bound to protect them and see 'em through. Why, Lordy ! Sade, you'd have done the same — for Chivers."

"Yes, yes," she said, beating her hands together strangely, "of course. He was so kind to bring me back to you. And you might have never found me but for him."

She burst into an hysterical laugh, which the simple-minded man might have over-looked but for the tears that coursed down her bloodless face.

"What 's gone o' ye, Sadie," he said in a sudden fear, grasping her hands; "that laugh ain't your'n — that voice ain't your'n. You 're the old Sadie, ain't ye?" He stopped. For a moment his face blanched as he glanced towards the mill, from which the faint sound of bacchanalian voices came to his quick ear. "Sadie, dear, ye ain't thinkin' anything agin' me? Ye ain't al-lowin' I 'm keeping anythin' back from ye?"

Her face stiffened into rigidity; she dashed the tears from her eyes. "No," she said quickly. Then after a moment she added, with a faint laugh, "You see we have n't seen each other for so long — it 's all so sudden — so unexpected."

"But you kem here, just now, calkilatin' to find me?" said Collinson gravely.

"Yes, yes," she said quickly, still grasping both his hands, but with her head slightly turned in the direction of the mill.

"But who told ye where to find the mill?" he said, with gentle patience.

"A friend," she said hurriedly. "Perhaps," she added, with a singular smile, "a friend of the friend who told you."

"I see," said Collinson, with a relieved face and a broadening smile, "it's a sort of fairy story. I'll bet, now, it was that old Barker woman that Chivers knows."

Her teeth gleamed rigidly together in the moonlight, like a death's-head. "Yes," she said dryly, "it was that old Barker woman. Say, Seth," she continued, moistening her lips slowly, "you're guarding this place alone?"

"Thar's another feller up the trail, — a sentry, — but don't you be afeard, he can't hear us, Sade."

"On this side of the mill?"

"Yes! Why, Lord love ye, Sadie! t' other side o' the mill it drops down straight to the valley; nobody comes yer that way but poor low-down emigrants. And it's miles round to come by the valley from the summit."

and sick. Listen. Your hoss is just over thar feedin'. I 'll put you back on him, run in and tell 'em I 'm off, and be with ye in a jiffy, and take ye back to Skinner's."

" Wait, " she said softly. " Wait."

" Or to the Silver Hollow — it 's not so far."

She had caught his hands again, her rigid face close to his. " What hollow ? — speak ! " she said breathlessly.

" The hollow whar a friend o' mine struck silver. He 'll take yur in."

Her head sank against his shoulder. " Let me stay here," she answered, " and wait."

He supported her tenderly, feeling the gentle brushing of her hair against his cheek as in the old days. He was content to wait, holding her thus. They were very silent ; her eyes half closed, as if in exhaustion, yet with the strange suggestion of listening in the vacant pupils.

" Ye ain't hearin' anythin', deary ? " he said, with a troubled face.

" No ; but everything is so deathly still," she said in a frightened whisper.

It certainly was very still. A singular hush

seemed to have slid over the landscape ; there was no longer any sound from the mill ; there was an ominous rest in the woodland, so perfect that the tiny rustle of an uneasy wing in the tree above them had made them start ; even the moonlight seemed to hang suspended in the air.

" It 's like the lull before the storm," she said with her strange laugh.

But the non-imaginative Collinson was more practical. " It 's mighty like that earthquake weather before the big shake thet dried up the river and stopped the mill. That was just the time I got the news o' your bein' dead with yellow fever. Lord ! honey, I allus allowed to myself thet suthin' was happenin' to ye then."

She did not reply ; but he, holding her figure closer to him, felt it trembling with a nervous expectation. Suddenly she threw him off, and rose to her feet with a cry. " There ! " she screamed frantically, " they 've come ! they 've come ! "

A rabbit had run out into the moonlight before them, a gray fox had dashed from the thicket into the wood, but nothing else.

" Who 's come ? " said Collinson, staring at her.

"The sheriff and his posse! They're surrounding them now. Don't you hear?" she gasped.

There was a strange rattling in the direction of the mill, a dull rumble, with wild shouts and outcries, and the trampling of feet on its wooden platform. Collinson staggered to his feet; but at the same moment he was thrown violently against his wife, and they both clung helplessly to the tree, with their eyes turned toward the ledge. There was a dense cloud of dust and haze hanging over it.

She uttered another cry, and ran swiftly towards the rocky grade. Collinson ran quickly after her, but as she reached the grade he suddenly shouted, with an awful revelation in his voice, "Come back! Stop, Sadie, for God's sake!" But it was too late. She had already disappeared; and as he reached the rock on which Chivers had leaped, he felt it give way beneath him.

But there was no sound, only a rush of wind from the valley below. Everything lapsed again into its awful stillness. As the cloud lifted from where the mill had stood, the moon shone only upon empty space.

There was a singular murmuring and whispering from the woods beyond that increased in sound, and an hour later the dry bed of the old mill-stream was filled with a rushing river.

CHAPTER VIII.

PREBLE KEY returned to his hotel from the convent, it is to be feared, with very little of that righteous satisfaction which is supposed to follow the performance of a good deed, He was by no means certain that what he had done was best for the young girl. He had only shown himself to her as a worldly monitor of dangers, of which her innocence was providentially unconscious. In his feverish haste to avert a scandal, he had no chance to explain his real feelings ; he had, perhaps, even exposed her thwarted impulses to equally naïve but more dangerous expression, which he might not have the opportunity to check. He tossed wakefully that night upon his pillow, tormented with alternate visions of her adorable presence at the hotel, and her bowed, renunciating figure as she reëntered the convent gate. He waited expectantly the next day for the message she had promised,

and which he believed she would find some
way to send. But no message was forth-
coming. The day passed, and he became
alarmed. The fear that her escapade had
been discovered again seized him. If she
were in close restraint, she could neither send
to him, nor could he convey to her the solicitude and sympathy that filled his heart.
In her childish frankness she might have
confessed the whole truth, and this would
not only shut the doors of the convent
against him, under his former pretext, but
compromise her still more if he boldly
called. He waylaid the afternoon procession ; she was not among them. Utterly
despairing, the wildest plans for seeing her
passed through his brain, — plans that recalled his hot-headed youth, and a few
moments later made him smile at his extravagance, even while it half frightened him
at the reality of his passion. He reached
the hotel heart-sick and desperate. The
porter met him on the steps. It was with a
thrill that sent the blood leaping to his
cheeks that he heard the man say : —

" Sister Seraphina is waiting for you in
the sitting-room."

There was no thought of discovery or scandal in Preble Key's mind now ; no doubt or hesitation as to what he would do, as he sprang up the staircase. He only knew that he had found her again, and was happy! He burst into the room, but this time remembered to shut the door behind him. He looked eagerly towards the window where she had stood the day before, but now she rose quickly from the sofa in the corner, where she had been seated, and the missal she had been reading rolled from her lap to the floor. He ran towards her to pick it up. Her name — the name she had told him to call her — was passionately trembling on his lips, when she slowly put her veil aside, and displayed a pale, kindly, middle-aged face, slightly marked by old scars of smallpox. It was not Alice ; it was the real Sister Seraphina who stood before him.

His first revulsion of bitter disappointment was so quickly followed by a realization that all had been discovered, and his sacrifice of yesterday had gone for naught, that he stood before her, stammering, but without the power to say a word. Luckily

for him, his utter embarrassment seemed to
reassure her, and to calm that timidity
which his brusque man-like irruption might
well produce in the inexperienced, contemplative mind of the recluse. Her voice was
very sweet, albeit sad, as she said gently : —

"I am afraid I have taken you by surprise ; but there was no time to arrange for
a meeting, and the Lady Superior thought
that I, who knew all the facts, had better
see you confidentially. Father Cipriano
gave us your address."

Amazed and wondering, Key bowed her
to a seat.

"You will remember," she went on softly,
"that the Lady Superior failed to get any
information from you regarding the brother
of one of our dear children, whom he com-
mitted to our charge through a — a companion or acquaintance — a Mrs. Barker.
As she was armed with his authority by
letter, we accepted the dear child through
her, permitted her as his representative to
have free access to his sister, and even
allowed her, as an unattended woman, to
pass the night at the convent. We were
therefore surprised this morning to receive a

letter from him, absolutely forbidding any further intercourse, correspondence, or association of his sister with this companion, Mrs. Barker. It was necessary to inform the dear child of this at once, as she was on the point of writing to this woman; but we were pained and shocked at her reception of her brother's wishes. I ought to say, in justice to the dear child, that while she is usually docile, intelligent, and tractable to discipline, and a *dévote* in her religious feelings, she is singularly impulsive. But we were not prepared for the rash and sudden step she has taken. At noon to-day she escaped from the convent!"

Key, who had been following her with relief, sprang to his feet at this unexpected culmination.

"Escaped!" he said. "Impossible! I mean," he added, hurriedly recalling himself, "your rules, your discipline, your attendants are so perfect."

"The poor impulsive creature has added sacrilege to her madness — a sacrilege we are willing to believe she did not understand, for she escaped in a religious habit — my own."

" But this would sufficiently identify her,"
he said, controlling himself with an effort.

" Alas, not so! There are many of us
who go abroad on our missions in these garments, and they are made all alike, so as to
divert rather than attract attention to any
individuality. We have sent private mes-
sengers in all directions, and sought her
everywhere, but without success. You will
understand that we wish to avoid scandal,
which a more public inquiry would create."

" And you come to me," said Key, with a
return of his first suspicion, in spite of his
eagerness to cut short the interview and be
free to act, — "to me, almost a stranger?"

" Not a stranger, Mr. Key," returned the
religieuse gently, " but to a well-known
man — a man of affairs in the country where
this unhappy child's brother lives — a friend
who seems to be sent by Heaven to find out
this brother for us, and speed this news to
him. We come to the old pupil of Father
Cipriano, a friend of the Holy Church; to
the kindly gentleman who knows what it is
to have dear relations of his own, and who
only yesterday was seeking the convent
to " —

" Enough ! " interrupted Key hurriedly,
with a slight color. " I will go at once. I
do not know this man, but I will do my best
to find him. And this — this — young girl?
You say you have no trace of her ? May she
not still be here ? I should have some clue
by which to seek her — I mean that I could
give to her brother."

" Alas ! we fear she is already far away
from here. If she went at once to San Luis,
she could have easily taken a train to San
Francisco before we discovered her flight.
We believe that it was the poor child's intent to join her brother, so as to intercede
for her friend — or, perhaps, alas ! to seek
her."

" And this friend left yesterday morning ? " he said quickly, yet concealing a feeling of relief. " Well, you may depend on
me ! And now, as there is no time to be
lost, I will make my arrangements to take
the next train." He held out his hand,
paused, and said in almost boyish embarrassment : " Bid me God speed, Sister Seraphina ! "

" May the Holy Virgin aid you," she
said gently. Yet, as she passed out of the

door, with a grateful smile, a characteristic
reaction came over Key. His romantic belief in the interposition of Providence was
not without a tendency to apply the ordinary
rules of human evidence to such phenomena.
Sister Seraphina's application to him seemed
little short of miraculous interference; but
what if it were only a trick to get rid of
him, while the girl, whose escapade had
been discovered, was either under restraint
in the convent, or hiding in Santa Luisa?
Yet this did not prevent him from mechanically continuing his arrangements for departure. When they were completed, and he
had barely time to get to the station at San
Luis, he again lingered in vague expectation
of some determining event.

The appearance of a servant with a tele-
graphic message at this moment seemed to
be an answer to this instinctive feeling. He
tore it open hastily. But it was only a
single line from his foreman at the mine,
which had been repeated to him from the
company's office in San Francisco. It read,
" Come at once — important."

Disappointed as it left him, it determined
his action; and as the train steamed out of

San Luis, it for a while diverted his attention from the object of his pursuit. In any
event, his destination would have been Skinner's or the Hollow, as the point from which
to begin his search. He believed with Sister
Seraphina that the young girl would make
her direct appeal to her brother ; but even
if she sought Mrs. Barker, it would still be
at some of the haunts of the gang. The letter to the Lady Superior had been post-
marked from "Bald Top," which Key knew
to be an obscure settlement less frequented
than Skinner's. Even then it was hardly
possible that the chief of the road agents
would present himself at the post-office, and
it had probably been left by some less known
of the gang. A vague idea, that was
hardly a suspicion, that the girl might have
a secret address of her brother's, without
understanding the reasons for its secrecy,
came into his mind. A still more vague
hope, that he might meet her before she
found her brother, upheld him. It would be
an accidental meeting on her part, for he no
longer dared to hope that she would seek or
trust him again. And it was with very little
of his old sanguine quality that, travel-worn

and weary, he at last alighted at Skinner's.
But his half careless inquiry if any lady
passengers had lately arrived there, to his
embarrassment produced a broad smile on
the face of Skinner.

"You're the second man that asked that
question, Mr. Key," he said.

"The second man?" ejaculated Key nervously.

"Yes; the first was the sheriff of Sierra.
He wanted to find a tall, good-looking
woman, about thirty, with black eyes. I
hope that ain't the kind o' girl you're looking arter — is it? for I reckon she's gin
you both the slip."

Key protested with a forced laugh that it
was not, yet suddenly hesitated to describe
Alice; for he instantly recognized the
portrait of her friend, the assumed Mrs.
Barker. Skinner continued in lazy confidence: —

"Ye see they say that the sheriff had
sorter got the dead wood on that gang o'
road agents, and had hemmed 'em in somewhar betwixt Bald Top and Collinson's. But
that woman was one o' their spies, and spotted his little game, and managed to give 'em

the tip, so they got clean away. Anyhow, they ain't bin heard from since. But the big shake has made scoutin' along the ledges rather stiff work for the sheriff. They say the valley near Long Cañon's chock full o' rock and slumgullion that's slipped down."

"What do you mean by the big shake?" asked Key in surprise.

"Great Scott! you didn't hear of it? Didn't hear of the 'arthquake that shook us up all along Galloper's the other night? Well," he added disgustedly, "that's jist the conceit of them folks in the bay, that can't allow that *anythin'* happens in the mountains!"

The urgent telegrams of his foreman now flashed across Key's preoccupied mind. Possibly Skinner saw his concern. "I reckon your mine is all right, Mr. Key. One of your men was over yere last night, and didn't say nothin'."

But this did not satisfy Key; and in a few minutes he had mounted his horse and was speeding towards the Hollow, with a remorseful consciousness of having neglected his colleagues' interests. For himself, in

the utter prepossession of his passion for
Alice, he cared nothing. As he dashed
down the slope to the Hollow, he thought
only of the two momentous days that she
had passed there, and the fate that had
brought them so nearly together. There
was nothing to recall its sylvan beauty in
the hideous works that now possessed it, or
the substantial dwelling-house that had taken
the place of the old cabin. A few hurried
questions to the foreman satisfied him of the
integrity of the property. There had been
some alarm in the shaft, but there was no
subsidence of the " seam," nor any difficulty
in the working. " What I telegraphed you
for, Mr. Key, was about something that has
cropped up way back o' the earthquake.
We were served here the other day with a
legal notice of a claim to the mine, on account of previous work done on the ledge
by the last occupant."

" But the cabin was built by a gang of
thieves, who used it as a hoard for their
booty," returned Key hotly, " and every one
of them are outlaws, and have no standing
before the law." He stopped with a pang
as he thought of Alice. And the blood

rushed to his cheeks as the foreman quietly
continued : —

"But the claim ain't in any o' their
names. It's allowed to be the gift of their
leader to his young sister, afore the out-
lawry, and it's in *her* name — Alice Riggs
or something."

Of the half-dozen tumultuous thoughts
that passed through Key's mind, only one
remained. It was purely an act of the brother's to secure some possible future benefit
for his sister. And of this she was perfectly
ignorant! He recovered himself quickly,
and said with a smile : —

"But *I* discovered the ledge and its au-
riferous character myself. There was no
trace or sign of previous discovery or mining
occupation."

"So I jedged, and so I said, and thet puts
ye all right. But I thought I'd tell ye; for
mining laws is mining laws, and it's the one
thing ye can't get over, " he added, with the
peculiar superstitious reverence of the Californian miner for that vested authority.

But Key scarcely listened. All that he
had heard seemed only to link him more fate-
fully and indissolubly with the young girl.

He was already impatient of even this slight
delay in his quest. In his perplexity his
thoughts had reverted to Collinson's: the
mill was a good point to begin his search
from; its good-natured, stupid proprietor
might be his guide, his ally, and even his
confidant.

When his horse was baited, he was again
in the saddle. "If yer going Collinson's
way, yer might ask him if he's lost a horse,"
said the foreman. "The morning after the
shake, some of the boys picked up a mustang,
with a make-up lady's saddle on." Key
started! While it was impossible that it
could have been ridden by Alice, it might
have been by the woman who had preceded
her.

"Did you make any search?" he in-
quired eagerly; "there may have been an
accident."

"I reckon it wasn't no accident," returned
the foreman coolly, "for the riata was loose
and trailing, as if it had been staked out, and
broken away."

Without another word, Key put spurs to
his horse and galloped away, leaving his companion staring after him. Here was a clue:

the horse could not have strayed far; the broken tether indicated a camp; the gang had been gathered somewhere in the vicinity where Mrs. Barker had warned them, — perhaps in the wood beyond Collinson's. He would penetrate it alone. He knew his danger; but as a *single* unarmed man he might be admitted to the presence of the leader, and the alleged claim was a sufficient excuse. What he would say or do afterwards depended upon chance. It was a wild scheme — but he was reckless. Yet he would go to Collinson's first.

At the end of two hours he reached the thick-set wood that gave upon the shelf at the top of the grade which descended to the mill. As he emerged from the wood into the bursting sunlight of the valley below, he sharply reined in his horse and stopped. Another bound would have been his last. For the shelf, the rocky grade itself, the ledge below, and the mill upon it, were all gone! The crumbling outer wall of the rocky grade had slipped away into immeasurable depths below, leaving only the sharp edge of a cliff, which incurved towards the woods that had once stood behind the mill, but

which now bristled on the very edge of a
precipice. A mist was hanging over its
brink and rising from the valley; it was a
full-fed stream that was coursing through the
former dry bed of the river and falling down
the face of the bluff. He rubbed his eyes,
dismounted, crept along the edge of the precipice, and looked below : whatever had sub-
sided and melted down into its thousand feet
of depth, there was no trace left upon its
smooth face. Scarcely an angle of drift or
débris marred the perpendicular ; the burial
of all ruin was deep and compact ; the era-
sure had been swift and sure — the obliteration complete. It might have been the pre-
cipitation of ages, and not of a single night.
At that remote distance it even seemed as if
grass were already growing over this enormous sepulchre, but it was only the tops of
the buried pines. The absolute silence, the
utter absence of any mark of convulsive
struggle, even the lulling whimper of falling waters, gave the scene a pastoral repose.

So profound was the impression upon Key
and his human passion that it at first seemed
an ironical and eternal ending of his quest.

It was with difficulty that he reasoned that the catastrophe occurred before Alice's flight, and that even Collinson might have had time to escape. He slowly skirted the edge of the chasm, and made his way back through the empty woods behind the old mill-site towards the place where he had dismounted. His horse seemed to have strayed into the shadows of this covert; but as he approached him, he was amazed to see that it was not his own, and that a woman's scarf was lying over its side-saddle. A wild idea seized him, and found expression in an impulsive cry : —

"Alice!"

The woods echoed it; there was an interval of silence, and then a faint response. But it was *her* voice. He ran eagerly forward in that direction, and called again; the response was nearer this time, and then the tall ferns parted, and her lithe, graceful figure came running, stumbling, and limping towards him like a wounded fawn. Her face was pale and agitated, the tendrils of her light hair were straying over her shoulder, and one of the sleeves of her school-gown was stained with blood and dust. He caught

the white and trembling hands that were
thrust out to him eagerly.

" It is *you!* " she gasped. " I prayed for
some one to come, but I did not dream it
would be *you.* And then I heard *your*
voice — and I thought it could be only a
dream until you called a second time."

" But you are hurt," he exclaimed passionately. " You have met with some accident ! "

" No, no ! " she said eagerly. " Not *I*
— but a poor, poor man I found lying on
the edge of the cliff. I could not help him
much, I did not care to leave him. No one
would come ! I have been with him alone,
all the morning ! Come quick, he may be
dying."

He passed his arm around her waist
unconsciously ; she permitted it as unconsciously, as he half supported her figure
while they hurried forward.

" He had been crushed by something, and
was just hanging over the ledge, and could
not move nor speak," she went on quickly.
" I dragged him away to a tree, — it took
me hours to move him, he was so heavy, —
and I got him some water from the stream

and bathed his face, and blooded all my sleeve."

" But what were you doing here?" he asked quickly.

A faint blush crossed the pallor of her delicate cheek. She looked away quickly. " I — was going to find my brother at Bald Top," she replied at last hurriedly. " But don't ask me now — only come quick, do."

" Is the wounded man conscious? Did you speak with him? Does he know who you are?" asked Key uneasily.

" No! he only moaned a little and opened his eyes when I dragged him. I don't think he even knew what had happened."

They hurried on again. The wood lightened suddenly. " Here!" she said in a half whisper, and stepped timidly into the open light. Only a few feet from the fatal ledge, against the roots of a buckeye, with *her* shawl thrown over him, lay the wounded man.

Key started back. It was Collinson!

His head and shoulders seemed uninjured; but as Key lifted the shawl, he saw that the long, lank figure appeared to melt away

below the waist into a mass of shapeless
and dirty rags. Key hurriedly replaced the
shawl, and, bending over him, listened to
his hurried respiration and the beating of
his heart. Then he pressed a drinking-flask
to his lips. The spirit seemed to revive
him ; he slowly opened his eyes. They fell
upon Key with quick recognition. But the
look changed ; one could see that he was
trying to rise, but that no movement of the
limbs accompanied that effort of will, and
his old patient, resigned look returned. Key
shuddered. There was some injury to the
spine. The man was paralyzed.

" I can't get up, Mr. Key," he said in a
faint but untroubled voice, " nor seem to
move my arms, but you 'll just allow that
I 've shook hands with ye — all the same."

" How did this happen?" said Key
anxiously.

" Thet 's wot gets me ! Sometimes I
reckon I know, and sometimes I don't.
Lyin' thar on thet ledge all last night, and
only jest able to look down into the old valley, sometimes it seemed to me ez if I fell
over and got caught in the rocks trying to
save my wife ; but then when I kem to

think sensible, and know my wife was n't there at all, I get mystified. Sometimes I think I got ter thinkin' of my wife only when this yer young gal thet 's bin like an angel to me kem here and dragged me off the ledge, for you see she don't belong here, and hez dropped on to me like a sperrit."

" Then you were not in the house when the shock came ? " said Key.

" No. You see the mill was filled with them fellers as the sheriff was arter, and it went over with 'em — and I " —

" Alice," said Key, with a white face, " would you mind going to my horse, which you will find somewhere near yours, and bringing me a medicine case from my saddle-bags ? "

The innocent girl glanced quickly at her companion, saw the change in his face, and, attributing it to the imminent danger of the injured man, at once glided away. When she was out of hearing, Key leaned gravely over him : —

" Collinson, I must trust you with a secret. I am afraid that this poor girl who helped you is the sister of the leader of that gang the sheriff was in pursuit of. She has been kept in perfect ignorance of her brother's crimes. She must *never* know them — nor even know his fate! If he perished utterly in this catastrophe, as it would seem — it was God's will to spare her that knowledge. I tell you this, to warn you in anything you say before her. She *must* believe, as I shall try to make her believe, that he has gone back to the States — where she will perhaps, hereafter, believe that he died. Better that she should know nothing — and keep her thought of him unchanged."

" I see — I see — I see, Mr. Key," murmured the injured man. " Thet 's wot I 've been sayin' to myself lyin' here all night. Thet 's wot I bin sayin' o' my wife Sadie, — her that I actooally got to think kem back to me last night. You see I 'd heerd from one o' those fellars that a woman like unto her had been picked up in Texas and brought on yere, and that mebbe she was somewhar in Californy. I was that foolish — and that ontrue to her, all the while knowin', as I once told you, Mr. Key, that ef she 'd been alive she 'd bin yere — that I

believed it true for a minit! And that was
why, afore this happened, I had a dream,
right out yer, and dreamed she kem to me,
all white and troubled, through the woods.
At first I thought it war my Sadie; but
when I see she warn't like her old self, and
her voice was strange and her laugh was
strange — then I knowed it was n't her, and
I was dreamin'. You 're right, Mr. Key,
in wot you got off just now — wot was it?
Better to know nothin' — and keep the old
thoughts unchanged."

"Have you any pain?" asked Key after
a pause.

"No; I kinder feel easier now."

Key looked at his changing face. "Tell
me," he said gently, "if it does not tax
your strength, all that has happened here,
all you know. It is for *her* sake."

Thus adjured, with his eyes fixed on Key,
Collinson narrated his story from the irruption of the outlaws to the final catastrophe.
Even then he palliated their outrage with
his characteristic patience, keeping still his
strange fascination for Chivers, and his
blind belief in his miserable wife. The
story was at times broken by lapses of faint-

ness, by a singular return of his old abstraction and forgetfulness in the midst of a sentence, and at last by a fit of coughing, that left a few crimson bubbles on the corners of his mouth. Key lifted his eyes anxiously; there was some grave internal injury, which the dying man's resolute patience had suppressed. Yet, at the sound of Alice's returning step, Collinson's eyes brightened, apparently as much at her coming as from the effect of the powerful stimulant Key had taken from his medicine case.

"I thank ye, Mr. Key," he said faintly; "for I 've got an idea I ain't got no great time before me, and I 've got suthin' to say to you, afore witnesses " — his eyes sought Alice's in half apology — " afore witnesses, you understand. Would you mind standin' out thar, afore me, in the light, so I kin see you both, and you, miss, rememberin', ez a witness, suthin' I got to tell to him? You might take his hand, miss, to make it more regular and lawlike."

The two did as he bade them, standing side by side, painfully humoring what seemed to them to be wanderings of a dying man.

"Thar was a young fellow," said Collinson in a steady voice, "ez kem to my shanty a night ago on his way to the — the — valley. He was a sprightly young fellow, gay and chipper-like, and he sez to me, confidential-like, 'Collinson,' sez he, 'I 'm off to the States this very night on business of importance; mebbe I 'll be away a long time — for years! You know,' sez he, 'Mr. Key, in the Hollow! Go to him,' sez he, 'and tell him ez how I had n't time to get to see him; tell him,' sez he, 'that *Rivers* ' — you 've got the name, Mr. Key? — you 've got the name, miss? — 'that *Rivers* wants him to say this to his little sister from her lovin' brother. And tell him,' sez he, this yer *Rivers*, 'to look arter her, being alone.' You remember that, Mr. Key? you remember it, miss? You see, I remembered it, too, being, so to speak, alone myself " — he paused, and added in a faint whisper — " till now."

Then he was silent. That innocent lie was the first and last upon his honest lips; for as they stood there, hand in hand, they saw his plain, hard face take upon itself, at first, the gray, ashen hues of the rocks around him, and then and thereafter something of the infinite tranquillity and peace of that wilderness in which he had lived and died, and of which he was a part.

Contemporaneous history was less kindly. The " Bald Top Sentinel " congratulated its readers that the late seismic disturbance was accompanied with very little loss of life, if any. " It is reported that the proprietor of a low shebeen for emigrants in an obscure hollow had succumbed from injuries ; but," added the editor, with a fine touch of Western humor, " whether this was the result of his being forcibly mixed up with his own tanglefoot whiskey or not, we are unable to determine from the evidence before us." For all that, a small stone shaft was added later to the rocks near the site of the old mill, inscribed to the memory of this obscure " proprietor," with the singular legend : " Have ye faith like to him ? " And those who knew only of the material catastrophe, looking around upon the scene of desolation it commemorated, thought grimly that it must be faith indeed, and — were wiser than they knew.

"You smiled, Don Preble," said the Lady Superior to Key a few weeks later, "when I told to you that many caballeros thought it most discreet to intrust their future brides to the maternal guardianship and training of the Holy Church; yet, of a truth, I meant not *you*. And yet — eh! well, we shall see."